THE
WISH
FOR
KINGS

Also by Lewis H. Lapham

FORTUNE'S CHILD
MONEY AND CLASS IN AMERICA
IMPERIAL MASQUERADE

THE
WISH
FOR
KINGS

Democracy

at Bay

LEWIS H. LAPHAM

GROVE PRESS
NEW YORK

PUBLISHED BY GROVE PRESS
A DIVISION OF GROVE PRESS, INC.
841 BROADWAY
NEW YORK, NY 10003-4793

PUBLISHED IN CANADA BY GENERAL PUBLISHING COMPANY, LTD.

LIBRARY OF CONGRESS CATALOGING-IN-PUBLICATION DATA

LAPHAM, LEWIS H.
THE WISH FOR KINGS : DEMOCRACY AT BAY / LEWIS H. LAPHAM.—1ST ED.
P.   CM.
ISBN 0-8021-1446-6 (ALK. PAPER)
1. ELITE (SOCIAL SCIENCES)—UNITED STATES.   2. INCOME
DISTRIBUTION—UNITED STATES.   3. DEMOCRACY—UNITED STATES.
4. POLITICAL CULTURE—UNITED STATES.   I. TITLE.
HN90.E4L36   1993
305.5′2—DC20   92-27255
CIP

MANUFACTURED IN THE UNITED STATES OF AMERICA

PRINTED ON ACID-FREE PAPER

DESIGNED BY KATHY KIKKERT

FIRST EDITION 1993

10   9   8   7   6   5   4   3   2   1

To John R. MacArthur
who is wary of merchants,
let alone kings

Acknowledgments

Numerous individuals supported the writing of this book with their generous advice and patient corrections, but I'm especially indebted to my assistant, Ann Gollin, and my editor, Emily Heckman.

Contents

THE
WISH
FOR
KINGS

1

Democracy at Bay

AMERICA REMAINS DEMOCRATIC, NOT IN

THE LITERAL SENSE OF BEING A DEMOC-

RACY, BUT IN THE MORAL SENSE OF CON-

SISTING OF DEMOCRATS.

—G. K. Chesterton

During the months immediately following the collapse of the Berlin Wall in December 1989, no American politician of any distinction or rank missed a chance to congratulate one of the lesser nations of the earth on its imitation of the American democracy. The senator or the governor or the county supervisor presented himself as the smiling host welcoming into the clean and well-lighted rooms of "the American way of life" the ragged and less fortunate guests, who—sadly and through no fault of their

3

own—had been forced to wander for so many years in ideological darkness. The tone of the compliment was invariably complacent, the orator invariably well supplied with edifying texts and photo opportunities. First the German crowds dancing in the streets; then the apprentice democrats triumphant in Budapest and Warsaw and Prague; lastly and most gloriously, the Russian disavowal of communism and the dissolution of the Soviet Empire into the fragments of a fledgling free market. And always the Americans, saying, in effect, "You see, we were right all along; we were right, and you were wrong, and if you know what's good for you, you will go forth and prosper in a brave new world under the light of an American moon."

But by the winter of 1992 the comforting certainties of the cold war were sorely missed. Lacking the dark backcloth of Communist menace against which they were accustomed to projecting the bright images of American virtue, most of the country's politicians no longer were sure what was meant by the word *democracy*, and in the midst of a bleak economic recession they were hard pressed to find the proofs of prosperity even in the broad light of the American day. Their confusion found expression in the year's presidential campaigns. Everybody knew that something important had happened, but nobody knew exactly what, and during the nine months between President George Bush's State of the Union Address in January and Governor Bill Clinton's election in November, one or another of the candidates—if not Jerry Brown or Pat Buchanan, then Vice President Dan Quayle or H. Ross Perot—called into question most of the prior assumptions about the national state of political grace. Who and what was American? How was it possible to sustain the promise of democracy without the revenue to pay for all the degrees of subsidy and entitlement? If the federal bureaucracy in Washington was incompetent as well as corrupt, was it because the constitutional machinery had broken down, or was it because the ruling and possessing classes had decided that the practice of democratic government was both a risk and a luxury that they were no longer willing to finance? What was the use of free

expression to people so frightened of the future that they preferred the reassurance of the authoritative lie? Why insist on the
guarantee of so many superfluous civil liberties when everybody
already had enough trouble with unemployment and foreign
cars, with too much crime in the streets, too many aliens crossing
the border and never enough money to pay the bills?

None of the questions offered easy answers, and as early as
January the candidates in the Democratic primaries auditioning
their laments and promises in the woods of New Hampshire
discovered that the voters were sullen and resentful. Many of
them were out of work, and their mistrust of politics and politicians was as plain as the snow on the trees. Not knowing what
else to say, the candidates talked about money and appealed to the
emotions of self-pity. Democratic politics trades in only two
markets: the market in expectation and the market in blame. The
collapse in the former engenders a boom in the latter, and the
failures in the nation's economy bid up the prices for supernatural
villains. The public opinion polls suddenly acquired the aspects
of a funeral march, and the mathematical proofs of pessimism
began to show up in the newspapers as often as the obituary
notices. The once-triumphant American middle class—the vic-
tors of the cold war and the saviors of Kuwait—was transformed
into a citizenry betrayed. Victims all—seduced and abandoned,
tricked by circumstance, delivered into bondage by vicious confidence men selling cheap imitations of the American Dream.

By the third week of January I understood that the phrase "the
forgotten middle class" was a term of art, a euphemism for the
modestly affluent and well-to-do, the not-poor and the nonblack.
Like the Republicans before them, the Democrats had learned to
divide the country into only two classes: the middle class (both
remembered and forgotten) and the underclass, which was invisible. The candidates were interested only in the first of these
classes, in the prospective voters among whom they could recognize the presence of both money and resentment.

As I watched the gentlemen on C-Span, debating one another or
making their financial presentations in high school gymnasiums, I

understood that I was looking at a troop of mutual fund salesmen, trying to drum up business among a crowd of nervous investors. With the exception of Jerry Brown, they had come to sell the suckers a choice of what Wall Street calls financial products—tax and investment credits, depreciation allowances, insurance policies, rebates and exemptions, etc., etc.—and they canvassed the state, promising to perform one or more of the hoped-for miracles of economic deliverance. Were too many people out of work? Elect Tsongas or Kerrey or Clinton or Harkin, and within a matter of months (if not weeks or days or hours), lo and behold, out of the ground or over the hills from Vermont, jobs would arrive by the regiment or battalion. Did too many people lack health insurance? Were too many people unable to buy houses or send their children to decent schools? Were too many people worried about the departure of the American Dream? Elect Tsongas or Kerrey or Clinton or Harkin, and within a matter of months (if not weeks or days or hours), lo and behold, out of the sky or from lands far away . . .

None of which, of course, was new to the Republicans. On January 28 President Bush made of his State of the Union Address the political equivalent of an automobile dealer's pitch for a Labor Day sale. He offered a complete portfolio of financial goods and services, but he improved the Democratic deal with cash back from this year's withholding tax and with an accelerated rate of depreciation for companies that bought expensive equipment (mainframe computers, corporate aircraft, etc.) between February 1, 1992, and January 1, 1993. The budget director, Richard Darman, explained the small print to the Senate Finance Committee, and as I watched him flip cheerfully through the supporting charts, I wondered why he didn't sing a variation on one of those television car commercials in which the pretty girl tells everybody to buy now and save.

What was so dispiriting about the early presentations in both New Hampshire and Washington was the contempt with which the salesmen regarded their customers. They had come to buy votes, and they assumed that their audiences were as cynical as themselves. A vote was a commodity; so was a tax break, and so was medical insurance; and it wasn't going to do anybody any good to lose sight of the bottom line. The election was about what was in it for me—me the candidate, me the voter, me the purveyor of public opinion polls. Avoiding the difficult questions about either the nature or purpose of the American enterprise, the candidates were careful never to utter a word or a phrase that might be confused with a principled conviction. All present complacently assumed that America had long ago attained a state of moral perfection and that what was wrong with the country could be corrected by a judicious rearrangement of the bond portfolio.

But the voters weren't as dumb or as cynical as the politicians liked to think, and when, alone among the candidates, former Governor Jerry Brown refused to define the election as a matter of narrow interests and short-term profits, his idealism invoked loud cheering and long applause. Under the rubric of "we the people" taking the government back from parasitical bureaucrats in Washington, Brown proposed nothing less than a thorough revision of the American political system. But he couldn't divorce himself from his prior association with the system that he so eloquently maligned (i.e., the reckless Governor Moonbeam, known to every crooked politician in California), and it was left to H. Ross Perot, the Texas billionaire adopting the unlikely pose of a rural populist, to seize the role of the man on the white horse come to rid the capital of the spendthrift fools squandering the nation's treasure on idle luxuries and useless toys.

Perot entered the national political theater through the green-room of "Larry King Live," announcing his willingness to serve as president of the United States in an apparently offhand remark to the effect that he would pay the cost of the campaign with $100 million of his own money if the American people placed his name on the ballot in each of the fifty states. Had he been a poor man, or even a merely rich real estate developer blessed with a net worth of $100 million, his offer might have been seen as satire or farce. But Perot commanded assets in excess of $2.5 billion, and the miracle of his fortune preserved him from ridicule. Much of what he said about the wreckage of the national economy was both obvious and true. His audiences conferred on Perot the benefit of the American belief that the rich man is not only wise but also unencumbered with reasons to steal, and his proposition aroused enthusiasm everywhere in the country. The rising of Perot's name in the public opinion polls magnified the popular interpretation of the government in Washington as a synonym for waste, mismanagement, and fraud. The suspicion was confirmed by the news of the check-cashing scandal in the House of Representatives that showed so many of the esteemed members (332 of the possible 512) so carelessly indifferent to the laws of common necessity. While a good many ordinary citizens were losing their jobs, the gentry in both the House and the Senate apparently were paying for their private pleasures with public money. Among citizens less fortunate, many of them suffering the effects of prolonged recession, the news wasn't well received. The blatant inequalities expressed in adjoining headlines further inflamed the feelings of popular resentment, and by the third week in March the political grandees in Washington were renouncing their privileges—limousines, prescription drugs, stationery, meals, flowers, barbers, aerobic instructors, paintings on loan from the National Gallery, etc.—as hastily as escaping burglars emptying their pockets of evidence. At least fifty members of Congress waived their incumbent's right to stand for reelection, and functionaries in all denominations, elected and unelected, stopped using military aircraft for reasons of their own convenience and imposed charges on services that they had been accustomed to accepting as gifts from a grateful people. Even President Bush pretended that he knew what was meant by the terrible word *change* and cast himself as a noble "outsider" ranged against the wicked "insiders" (i.e., the Democratic majority in Congress) obstructing justice and feeding like swine on the pork rinds of the federal fisc.

The panic communicated itself to the established news media, and by late April the readers of the country's more respectable newspapers could have been forgiven for thinking that the American public had been transformed into a pack of rabid dogs. The editorial apologists for the status quo took note of the early election returns—the palpable disgust for Governor Bill Clinton and President George Bush, the protest votes cast for Patrick Buchanan and Jerry Brown, the enthusiasm for Perot—and they inflated the signs of disenchantment into the fear of mass revolt. Anthony Lewis in *The New York Times* saw portents of irresponsible "nihilism." David Broder in *The Washington Post* decried "the limited benefits of direct democracy" and wished that the business of nominating a presidential candidate could be conducted by the people who knew better—the professional politicians and the important providers of campaign funds. Roger Ailes, a Republican political strategist, looked through the window of the public opinion polls and said, "Something weird is going on out there—fear, anger, ugliness."

The American people were doing nothing more unusual than expressing their opinion of their elected government, but the news media, faithfully reflecting the interests of the government in question, heard their modest complaint as both an insult and an outrage. During the two weeks that Jerry Brown was campaigning in the New York primary election both *The Wall Street Journal* and *The New York Times* portrayed him as a vicious radical. Various defenders of the moral beauty of the status quo (among them William Safire and Sidney Blumenthal as well as Mr. Lewis) condemned Brown as a demagogue, a hypocrite, a "spoiler," an enemy of meaningful political reform, a "false Messiah," an opportunist blighted with a "paranoia like Oliver Stone's." When Governor Brown's campaign collapsed for want of coherence, the established news media shifted their hysteria to Perot. For six consecutive days in late May *The New York Times* published detailed accounts of Perot's record as a duplicitous charlatan: Perot seen as a friend of Richard Nixon; Perot's fortune understood as a gift of government subsidy; Perot losing sixty million dollars in Wall Street in the recession of 1973; Perot as autocrat; Perot as conspiracy theorist. None of the discoveries and revelations diminished the noncandidate's standing in the polls, and the worried guardians of the nation's property and conscience began to search the history books for precedents of deliverance. Writing in *The New York Times Magazine*, Kevin Phillips, columnist and privy councillor to the conservative factions of the Republican party, reminded his readers that twice before in its history— in the 1890s and the 1930s—the United States had managed to diffuse what he called "the politics of frustration." But his tone was both worried and urgent, and he thought that his friends in Washington would be well advised to hurry up with their fabrication of a plausible "set of policies capable of attracting angry voters and welding them into a new centrist governing coalition"—i.e., for God's sake, quiet the rabble with a decent sum of ransom money.

The tone of the editorial alarm was so shrill that I was reminded of the Tory pamphleteers in Boston in the 1760s, despising the unruly American colonists (among them James Otis, Samuel Adams, and anybody else who objected to the writs of assistance or the Stamp Act) as a multitude of "foreign seamen, servants, Negroes and other persons of mean and vile condition." No mob had smashed the glass in the windows of the Rayburn Building; nobody had clubbed a tax collector or hung the effigy of Chief Justice William Rehnquist from a tree in front of Faneuil Hall, but *The Wall Street Journal*'s editorial page echoed the sentiments of the young Gouverneur Morris, who, on passing through New York soon after the American Revolution, was appalled by the sight of the beggars in the street: "The mob begin to think and reason, poor reptiles! . . . [T]hey bask in the sun, and 'ere noon they will bite, depend upon it. The gentry begin to fear this."

The ritual denunciation of Washington is as traditional to a presidential election year as the band music and airport press conference, but in the spring of 1992 the storm of words was blowing more strongly than usual, and the senior statesmen of the news media spoke on behalf of a ruling establishment that had good reason to be nervous. What had become apparent during the early months of the primary campaigns was that the United States, accurately described, is an oligarchy, a govern-

ment of the rich, by the rich and for the rich. Owing in large part
to the diligence of the Reagan administration, the United States
by 1990 had so arranged its financial affairs that 10 percent of the
population held at least 70 percent of the nation's wealth, and 5
percent of the population owned all of the nation's capital assets.
Different authorities stressed different sets of statistics, but all the
numbers told the same dismal and undemocratic story: The income received by the richest 1 percent of American families
improved by 49.8 percent in the years between 1977 and 1988;
simultaneously, and by no means as a matter of chance, the
income earned by families in the poorest 1 percent of the population declined by 14.8 percent. By 1985, for the first time in the
country's history, the money that the American people earned
from capital (i.e., from rents, dividends, and interest) equaled the
amounts earned in wages. By 1991 it was no longer possible to
pretend that everybody was as equal as everybody else. It was
equally clear that the Reagan administration's several revisions of
the tax laws sustained, often in great luxury, the American equivalent of a *rentier* class.

Measured as a percentage of the population, the presiding
oligarchy is small—probably no more than between 2 percent
and 5 percent—but measured as an absolute number of ambitious and well-connected individuals, the oligarchy is large—
possibly as many as four million people united in their devotion
to the systems in place and the wisdom in office. By and large
they are the people who manage the government, own the media
and the banks, operate the universities, print the money, and
write the laws. I don't know why so many people fail to take the
point. Among the current advertisements for America the beautiful and America the good, none seems to me more ludicrous than
the one that presents the United States as a classless society. I
would have thought the image easily dispelled by an afternoon's
shopping on Rodeo Drive or by a brief visit—subject to the
approval of the security guards—to one of the country's heavily
defended suburbs.

The columnists who worried that the American people might

learn to hold their political and financial overlords in contempt were careful to say nothing about the contempt in which those same overlords hold the American people. The proof of this latter disregard presents itself in every city street—in the lists of the unemployed and the legion of dead fish in the nation's rivers, in the prisons crowded to capacity, and in the number of children who don't know how to read. The debasement of the citizenry, like the despoliation of the landscape, doesn't happen by accident. The labor of plundering a subject people isn't a freak of nature or the work of trolls or the fault of the Japanese. Specific individuals with specific purposes in mind break open the doors and steal the silver.[1]

Democracy announces its presence by a few fundamental traits of character, among them a reasonably honest discussion of public issues, the accountability of the governors to the governed, and equal protection under the law. None of these characteristics have distinguished the governments in Washington for the last twenty years, and in last year's presidential campaign the American people expressed a demand for some sort of meaningful change. The oligarchy, of course, doesn't welcome change (not unless it can be pressed into the service of a profit or constrained by a bureaucratic acronym), and so the problem of the campaign was one of recognition. Which of the three candidates offered the best hope of restoring belief in the possibility of democratic government? The proposition took many forms, most of them specious. Instead of trying to answer the question, Who and what is American?, the candidates talked about cultural elitism and family values, about theoretical tax rates and imaginary budgets. Rather than attempt to define the traits of character and temperament that bind the society together, they found it easier to describe the divisions of interest that drive it apart. None of them had any trouble herding the voters into categories (rich against poor, black against white, male against female, young against old) to whom they could sell the fear of the month or the slogan of the week. If on November 3 the answers to the important questions were as ambiguous as the results in Oregon, where the citizenry voted overwhelmingly for congressional term limits but at the same time reelected all five of their incumbent representatives in the Senate and the House, the campaign at least indicated the degree at which the American system of government presently stands at odds with its constitutional hopes and purposes. It isn't the practice of democracy that is at fault but that the habits of liberty have fallen into disuse, and the promise of democracy no longer inspires or exalts a majority of the people lucky enough to have been born under its star.

Certainly President Bush made no secret of his loyalty to the cause of oligarchy, and the violent feeling of disgust that he aroused among so many of his fellow citizens had as much to do with his voice and manner as it did with his politics. He was too closely identified with the premises of the cold war, and his congenital failure to find the right words was in keeping with his temperament and the nature of his experience as a child of fortune and America's most gracious guest. Members in good standing at the nation's better country clubs find it difficult to take seriously the desires of people unlike themselves, and they constantly ask the peevish questions, Who are all those other people out there, and what in heaven's name do they want? It was impossible to listen to President Bush speak without being reminded of the all but complete estrangement of the American *rentier* class from the discomforts of a less privileged existence. The president's ignorance of what most people would understand as the law of common necessity was apparent in all his campaign speeches, but it was most embarrassingly evident during the week after rioting and fire had laid waste to roughly twenty-five square miles of South-Central Los Angeles. Appearing briefly among the ruins to offer his condolences, President Bush arrived at dawn on Thursday, riding in a heavily armored limousine flying a White House flag under the protective escort of the Secret Service, the Los Angeles Police Department, and the National Guard. His advisers allowed him to remain in the vicinity of Vermont and Western avenues for no longer than three hours in the early morning, before too many people were out in the streets.

C-Span's television cameras followed him on his courtier's progress through the ashes of an urban slum, and he said what he was supposed to say about healing the wounds of racial injustice and rebuilding America's destiny. Walking in streets still sour with the smell of smoke, the president was obviously disturbed by what he saw of the wreckage, and his impromptu remarks sometimes veered off in the direction of unfamiliar emotion. Addressing a small congregation in a Baptist church, he said: "We are embarrassed by interracial violence and prejudice. We are ashamed. We should take nothing but sorrow out of all that and do our level best to see that it's eliminated from the American dream."

Clearly the president was disturbed by the sorrow and resentment of the few people to whom he spoke, but his words were somehow tentative and contingent. His palpable uneasiness admirably represented the attitude of a social and political class that would rather have been talking about something else. As I watched him keep to his schedule of polite concern, I understood that it was a small drawing-room story about George Bush (his conduct and deportment under trying circumstances), not a large and tragic story about a society that could inflict upon itself the despairing ruin of South-Central Los Angeles.

By Friday morning the president had recovered his optimism and his sense of political proportion. He announced a gift of nineteen million dollars (for clinics and schools and the harrying of drug dealers), and he went to a hospital to visit a fireman severely wounded by gunfire on the first night of the rioting. Partly paralyzed and unable to speak, the fireman lay on his bed watching Mr. Bush sign autographs and hand out tiepins. The president was cheerful but nervous, and in a moment of awkward silence he said to the fireman's wife, "This is fantastic. We're glad to be here. Absolutely."

A similar insouciance had characterized the president's State of the Union Address to the Congress in the winter of 1991. The war in Iraq was then in progress, and although Mr. Bush clearly wished to make as much as possible of his pose as military hero, he also had a chance to say a few words about the recession in progress in the United States. He spoke on January 29, and January had been an especially grim month along the whole line of the economic front. The Bank of New England failed on January 6, at a cost to the government of $2.3 billion; on January 7 the Defense Department canceled a $52 billion weapons contract, obliging two defense contractors (McDonnell Douglas and General Dynamics) to lay off ten thousand workers in St. Louis and Fort Worth; over the course of the next two weeks the unemployment rate reached 6 percent; Eastern Airlines collapsed, and Pan American World Airways filed for protection under the bankruptcy laws; numerous major corporations, among them Occidental Petroleum and the Manufacturers Hanover Bank, halved the dividend paid to stockholders; the governors of twenty-eight states declared what one of them called "financial martial law" and preached what another of them called "the gospels of austerity" (i.e., more taxes and fewer public services); the big automobile companies reported heavy losses; and the consumer confidence index receded to its lowest ebb since the Great Depression.

Together with the news of general and institutional failure, the media supplied a fund of grim anecdotes that measured the winter's defeats in the specific instances of individual suffering and panic: people losing jobs, houses, their definitions of self; a woman in Iowa too frightened to go into a store because she couldn't afford to buy anything; a former owner of a marketing company in California glad of the chance to clean toilets; two high school students in North Carolina who had given up the hope of college; and a woman in Massachusetts saying, "It's scary; it's like unemployed people are coming out of the sky, there are so many of them."

The casualty reports failed to make much of an impression on President Bush. Buoyed by the applause of a jubilant Congress, the president talked mostly about his beloved war in Iraq and his exciting collection of planes and boats in the Persian Gulf. He took up the question of the nation's troubled economic affairs with an air of faint distaste, as if any extended discussion about money were somehow beneath the dignity of a gentleman. About a third of the way into his speech he descended to the topic by means of a transition from the patriotic heights of sententious moralism.

"We are resolute and resourceful," he said. "If we can selflessly confront evil for the sake of good in a land so far away, then surely we can make this land all that it should be."

For the next fifteen minutes Mr. Bush read through the list of catchwords that his speech writers deemed appropriate to the occasion: "hard work of freedom," "shining purpose," "thousand points of light," "next American century," "economic expansion temporarily interrupted," "what America is all about," etc., etc. He dutifully performed the ritual of polite phrases, and at one point he even went so far as to try to express a feeling of heartfelt concern. Blinking earnestly in the light, his voice reaching for the note of tremulous sincerity, he said: "I know, tonight, in some regions of our country, people are in genuine economic distress. And I hear them."

The effect was embarrassing. It was obvious that Mr. Bush didn't hear anybody who wasn't talking to him about the sport of war in "a land so far away." His attempt at genuine emotion proved as unctuous and vacant as the sentiment sent to an unknown nephew on a Hallmark card. His failure was one of the imagination, what his handlers in the 1988 election campaign recognized as his difficulty with "the vision thing." His words were empty because he couldn't see through the veil of abstraction (deficit, interest rate, percentage of unemployed, loans defaulted, etc.) to the scenes of human suffering implicit in the numbers. He didn't know—quite literally—what he was talking about.

Listening to him speak, I remembered that among the members of the oligarchy money has no discernible reality in the hands of lesser mortals because lesser mortals have no decent use for it. The philosophers of the reactionary right dress up this congenital selfishness with the argument that although money is good for the rich, it is bad for the poor.[2]

If George Bush clearly represented the interests of a selfish oligarchy, the promise expressed in the figure of H. Ross Perot was grounded in contradiction. The exit polls collected during the California primary elections in early June showed Perot enjoying extraordinary popular support when measured against both President Bush and Governor Bill Clinton, and all the instruments of the media took up the theme of a mysterious descent by a god in a machine. How could such things be? Who could explain Perot's astonishing entrance onto the stage of the presidential campaign? Both in print and on television, every columnist and political analyst of any weight or consequence ran through the entire repertoire of solemn speculation: general disgust with the status quo, Bush's weakness, Clinton's irrelevance, end of the cold war, wages of recession, collapse of a two-party system, hatred of Washington, triumph of television, era of new politics, democracy lost, democracy regained. But nobody remarked upon the exalted place of money in the American imagination, and the unanimous silence on the metaphysics of Perot's money—i.e., its divine radiance—answered most of the questions about Perot's political triumph.

The commentators understood the non sequitur implicit in the term *populist billionaire*, but they discussed Perot's wealth only in its secular aspects—as the means with which to hire expensive political strategists and buy unlimited quantities of television time. What they neglected to mention was the spiritual meaning that Americans impart to the texts of money. By embodying the dream of unlimited wealth, Perot embodied the dream of perfect independence. Here at last was a man free to say what he meant, whose every statement wasn't prepared by a speech writer or geared to an opinion poll, and Perot's lack of hesitation between the thought and the word supported the belief that he could speak on behalf of the common good.

The aura of myth and dream preserved Perot not only from ridicule but also from the standard assaults of the suspicious media. No matter how often the newspapers depicted him as a paranoid fantast or a would-be tyrant, Perot's image continued to float as blithely as a campaign balloon over the heads of mortal politicians doomed to answer the questions. Allegations deemed awkward or inconvenient Perot either flatly denied or dismissed as the impiety of the godless eastern media. He disarmed his critics with his homespun humor, referring to the directors of General Motors, with whom he once had unpleasant dealings, as "pet rocks" and saying of that company's standard of incompetence, "I never could understand why it takes six years to build a car when it only took four years to win World War II." Pressed to explain the discrepancy between his theory of law and order and the spirit of the Constitution, he said, "We can amend that dang Constitution if we have to," and on the question of the environmental summit meeting in Rio de Janeiro, he said, with similar insouciance, "I don't know a thing about it." With surprisingly few exceptions, all of Perot's associates—former, current, commercial, and political—testified to the authoritarian temper of his mind. One was either with him or against him; he lacked the patience for compromise; anybody who disagreed with him was either a fool or a knave. As president of Electronic Data Systems, the computer services company on which he founded his fortune, he imposed on the hired help codes of dress and deportment. When a Texas newspaper printed a story that Perot thought unflattering, he berated the publisher with the threat of blackmail. His temperament was apparently that of a vindictive prig, a man who delighted in his sobriquet of "the billionaire scoutmaster" and who clearly would prefer to conduct the affairs of government as if he were the chairman of a transnational corporation engaged in the manufacture of justice instead of barbed wire or soap.

None of the contradictions in Perot's character—the avowed autocrat championing the cause of populist revolt, the humble and plainspoken servant of the people asking, in effect, to be elected king—dissuaded his admirers from the hope that he represented the country's only chance at democratic change, and by the end of June the story of H. Ross Perot was the story of the 1992 election. Neither President Bush nor Governor Clinton could as easily command the headlines, and by comparison with Perot's caustic and offhand wit their speeches seemed empty and boring and long. Had Perot not retired on July 16 from his still-undeclared presidential campaign, he might have received at least as many votes as were awarded in the November election to President Bush. Implicit in that possibility was the spirit of genuine rebellion. If over the course of only eight brief months an all-but-unknown computer salesman could nearly achieve par value with the president of the United States who only a year earlier had enjoyed a measure of public approval in the vicinity of 80 percent, then clearly a great many people, maybe as many as the twenty million who voted for Perot in November as well as the forty-five million who didn't bother to go to the polls, believed themselves excluded from the business of government. It was also clear that the traditional American political narrative had lost both its force and its coherence.

Perot's absence from the campaign during most of the summer shifted the hope of substantive change or improvement in the nation's political condition to Governor Bill Clinton. Prior to the entrances and exits of Jerry Brown, Pat Buchanan, and H. Ross Perot, the hope would have seemed farfetched. The objections had less to do with Clinton's character (his liaison with Gennifer Flowers, his avoidance of the military draft during the Vietnam War, his brother's drug dealing, and his wife's ambition) than with his indebtedness to the New York banks and the adoring welcome bestowed on his candidacy by the Washington news media. Accepting the Democratic presidential nomination at Madison Square Garden in New York, Clinton did his best to present himself as a Republican in mufti, a candidate who shunned the word *liberal*, and who was proud to declare his faith in "entrepreneurial government" and "the noble endeavor" of American business. But he was careful to avoid any close association with those factions of the Democratic party (liberals, blacks, the poor) likely to remind people that he was not a Republican.

Like President Bush, he avoided any meaningful discussion of the deficit, the insolvency of the banking system, or the rigging of the credit markets in a way that favors public over private borrowing. He adjusted his campaign promises to reflect the findings of a poll or focus group, and his opinions were those that his audiences wished to hear. Over the course of the campaign he described himself as "probusiness and prolabor," "for economic growth and for protecting the environment," "for affirmative action but against quotas," "for legal abortions but also for making abortion as rare as possible." He made little or no mention of crime, and when he was asked how he would have voted in Congress on the question of going to war with Iraq in the winter of 1991, he said that he would have voted with the majority but sympathized with the minority. When Perot summoned representatives from both the Democratic and Republican campaigns to Dallas in September to explain why they deserved his political blessing, Clinton groveled as fawningly as Bush at the feet of the newly minted prince. During the three debates in October he was careful to say nothing that might offend Perot, and never once did he permit himself the use of the word *justice*, presumably on the ground that it might be mistaken, like the word *liberty*, as a criticism of his corporate sponsors. When he was asked about the miserable quality of the education and health care inflicted on most people in the country, he spoke only about the loss of "competitiveness," never about human suffering. Like the evangelist or faith healer, he was careful to deliver the good news in a language empty of historical or existential context. Politics was never about who has the power to do what to whom, but always, as he said on the night of his election on the steps of the State Capitol in Little Rock, about the clash of giant abstractions, about "the fight between hope and fear, the fight between division and unity, the fight between blame and taking responsibility . . . and may God bless America."

If the last irony of the 1992 campaign cast Governor Clinton as the enemy of privilege and the tribune of the people, the citizens who turned up at the polls on November 3 in unusually large numbers brought with them the sense that maybe for once in their lives their votes might mean something. Their presence measured the extent to which the democratic idea is still vividly at large in the public imagination. It wasn't that the voters were particularly fond of Clinton or expected him to make good on his promises. Even among those who voted for him, 49 percent of the respondents questioned at the exit polls were convinced that he was a liar. But at least he wasn't Bush, who offered no hope of change, and he wasn't Perot, who maybe presaged too much change.

The task of restoring belief in the democratic idea—as opposed to promoting the ritual fictions of a sham democracy made of Fourth of July speeches and editorials in USA Today—presupposes the collaboration of an oligarchy that sees some advantage in the enterprise. If the odds at the moment don't favor the work of experiment and renewal, it is because among the American ruling and possessing classes (i.e., the people who pay for the hiring of presidents) the distrust of democracy is as traditional as Yankee Doodle Dandy. At the Constitutional Convention in Philadelphia in the summer of 1787, most of the delegates feared what they called "the turbulent passions" of the common man. Anticipating the ethos of the Reagan and Bush administrations, John Jay observed that "the people who own the country ought to govern it." John Adams thought that the "great functions of state" should be reserved for "the rich, the well-born and the able." James Madison worried about reckless agitation for "an abolition of debts, or an equal division of property and other wicked projects." The delegates wished to confine the popular spirit of rebellion let dangerously loose in the streets by the excitements of the revolutionary war, and it was with grudging reluctance that they granted the common people a voice in the government. They did so not for reasons of high-minded principle, but because they recognized in one another the rapaciousness of wolves and feared the despotism of which they knew they were entirely capable. They expected the rich to plunder the poor and the poor to prey upon the rich.

Throughout the history of American business and politics the

cause of oligarchy always has been a popular one, lavishly fi-
nanced and loudly promoted, appealing not only to the propertied classes but also to the expectant capitalists hoping to become
as rich and as insolent as their landlords. In the late twentieth
century, as in the early nineteenth, a clear majority of American
businessmen has shown a profound aversion for anything that
remotely resembles a free market or a genuine risk. At their
annual conventions they sometimes make brave speeches about
the joys of "risk taking" and the wonders of "entrepreneurship,"
but what they know and trust is the rigged price, the safe monopoly, and the sure percentage. By and large, and certainly in its
primary and steadier movements, the national economy depends
not only on systematic price-fixing and noncompetitive bidding
but also on the guarantee of government intervention. The theory of the free market works at the margins of the economy—
among cabdrivers and the owners of pizza parlors who make the
mistake of borrowing $20,000 instead of $20 million—but the
central pillars of the American enterprise rest so firmly on the
foundation stones of federal subsidy that in the spring of 1992,
almost two years after the cold war had come to an end, the
Congress couldn't bring itself to harm the military budget. The
concern for employment in the defense industries persuaded the
politicians to subtract only $1 billion from the prior year's appro-
priation of $292 billion. [3]

Like most chambers of commerce and the editors of *Forbes*
magazine, the American oligarchy doesn't like to admit to a state
of economic affairs that could be so easily confused with social-
ism, and throughout the hectic decade of the 1980s a chorus of
self-styled entrepreneurs—"men of vision," "men in search of
excellence," etc.—complained of the thousand and one ways in
which the coils of government regulation strangled their initiative
and bound the arm of honest labor. The complaint was as preposterous as their bragging about their individualism and self-
reliance. No class of businessmen in the history of the known
world had been so cosseted by the servants of government as the
one that enjoyed the patronage of the Reagan administration, but

never once did I hear any of the gentlemen in the grillroom acknowledge their abject dependence on the gifts from Washington: the mortgage deductions on residential real estate, myriad investment credits and tax exemptions, preferential interest rates, Social Security payments, subsidies to entire industries (defense, real estate, agriculture, highway construction, etc.), tariffs, the bankruptcy laws, the licenses granted to television stations, the banking laws, the concessions given to the savings and loan associations. Of all the federal money distributed as transfer payments to individual Americans during the decade of the 1980s, only a relatively small percentage found its way into the hands of the poor.

The federal treasury at the moment supplies 45 percent of the nation's income. The politicians dress up the deals in the language of law or policy, but they're in the business of brokering the tax revenue, and what keeps them in office is not their talent for oratory but their skill at redistributing the national income in a way that rewards their clients, patrons, friends, and campaign contributors. They trade in every known commodity—school lunches, tax exemptions, water and mineral rights, aluminum siding, dairy subsidies, pension benefits, highway contracts, prison uniforms—and they work the levers of government like gamblers pulling at slot machines. As with the subsidizing of the farms and the defense industry, so also with paying off the bad debt acquired by savings and loan associations. Except for the taxpayers (who, as always, didn't know what was being promised in their name), none of the ladies and gentlemen privy to the workings of the swindle took the slightest risk. Always and whenever possible, the participants zealously adhered to the traditional American principles of "no money down" and "something for nothing."

The same economic maxims governed the settling of the old American frontier and the amassing of the gaudier fortunes synonymous with the decade of the Reagan prosperity. Sometimes it was the leveraged buy-out deal; sometimes it was the Wall Street practice of insider trading; sometimes it was a revision of the tax law or a contract bestowed by the Department of Housing and Urban Development. At HUD the resident shills didn't even bother to pretend that they were playing with anything other than a marked deck. If the real estate developer knew the right people in the administration, then he received the contract. If not, not. Explaining the procedure to a congressional committee investigating the extent of the fraud, DuBois L. Gilliam, formerly a deputy assistant secretary at HUD and now one of the few government officials serving a term in prison, described his public offices as "the best political machine I've ever seen. We dealt strictly in politics."

Other oligarchies at other moments in the nation's history have conducted similar raids on the public treasury, but mostly they had the wit not to give press interviews and the good luck not to wreck the economy that provided them with their new fortunes. The recent generation of America's guests—both Democrat and Republican, in the political as well as the commercial orders—made the mistake of confusing fraud with ideological doctrine. Being vain as well as greedy, they advertised their rapaciousness under the rubrics of noble economic theory (the Laffer curve, the leveraged buy-out, the junk bond), and they posed for their portraits in the business magazines among the trophies of their success (houses in Palm Springs, corporate aircraft, paintings by Rauschenberg, monogrammed golf balls), grinning like amateur sportsmen among the deer antlers and the ornamental trout.

Given the dependence of the economy on the grace and favor of Washington, the apologists for the American oligarchy who preach the official sermons on the sacred text of the "free market" must make up in patriotic fervor what they lack in evidence. During the summer of 1991, at the same time that the Bush administration was steadfastly denying the possibility of recession, a declaration of the orthodox faith showed up in the spring issue of *Policy Review*, a quarterly journal published by the Heritage Foundation that embodies the greater wisdom of the Republican party, the larger corporations, and the Wall Street banks.

Under the title "The Vision Thing: Conservatism for the Nineties," the editors presented brief essays by no fewer than thirty-nine well-known voices of the conservative conscience, among them Russell Kirk, Senator Jesse Helms, Fred Barnes, Phyllis Schlafly, Fred C. Iklé, Ken Tomlinson, former Governor Pete du Pont, William E. Simon, and Pat Robertson.

They recited the national economic creed in the sweet soprano voices of a choir of castrati, and on reading their improving lessons, I was struck by the collective tone of inane complacence. It was as if I had been invited to an ideological variant of the Mad Hatter's tea party staged at an expensive conference center in Aspen or Palm Springs. I could imagine the guests dressed for croquet or golf, seated in white wicker chairs, admiring the postcard views of the sea or the mountains, busily arranging and rearranging their briefing papers, exchanging idiotic solemnities with the aplomb of a club steward handing around the potted shrimp. Many of them had furnished the specious economic theory that justified the raids on the federal treasury during the heyday of the Reagan administration, but none of them seemed to have noticed the corollary damage done to the rest of society's hope for the future. Nobody said a word about the debt, about the HUD or savings and loan swindles, about the numerous public officials indicted for theft or fraud, about the mismanagement of the military budget, about the squalor of the nation's cities and the wreckage of the nation's schools.

Everybody talked instead about the triumph of new money, which proved what one of their number described as the "moral superiority of the free economy over statism." Although the participants occasionally differed among themselves on what they regarded as minor points of doctrine (most notably with regard to the still-troubling and unsettled questions of crime, race, health, education, and the environment), all present expressed their calm and beatific agreement on the principal articles of capitalist faith ("the free market," "economic liberty," "the commonwealth of freedom").

I read the anthology of self-congratulation with a feeling of embarrassment, as if I were reading a parody. So many of the remarks were so far removed from the realms of common experience that I began to wonder if any of the ladies and gentlemen in the lawn chairs had ever met an automobile worker, bought a dress in a shopping mall, traveled to Hoboken, seen a slum, or read an insurance claim. Every now and then one of their company admitted to having heard—at a less refined conference—a really awful rumor (about illiteracy or sexually transmitted diseases), but if the rumors were true (as probably they were not), then undoubtedly it was the fault of the "imperial Congress" or the "spiritual decay" said to be rotting the moral tissue of the nation. Nor did many of the guests of the symposium seem to have the least idea of what it might mean to sell their labor in a competitive market. Of the thirty-nine seers in residence, all but four owed their livings to some sort of subsidy or dole, either as politicians drawing an allowance of public money or as ministers of philanthropic foundations relying on the charity of the tax laws.

The tables of organization of the modern American oligarchy were founded on the premises of the national security state and the bureaucratic imperatives of the cold war. The victories of the Second World War promoted the belief among the American ruling classes that they had been armed with the mandate of heaven. Twice during the first half of the twentieth century, the European powers had all but annihilated themselves, and in 1945 what was left of Western civilization seemed to have passed into the American account. Japan was in ruins, and so was Germany; China was in the midst of civil war; France had disintegrated, both as a nation and as the embodiment of an idea; and the British were so exhausted with the effort of imperial ambition that they voted Churchill out of office within two months of the German surrender. If in 1941 the American presence outside the Western hemisphere consisted only of a few islands in the Pacific, by 1945 the United States bestrode the narrow world like a colossus, presiding over an arc of territories and client states that extended from the Bismarck Archipelago to the North Sea. Largely by invitation and default, the Americans had acquired the semblance of empire, and the new proconsuls, most of whom had expected to become Wall Street lawyers or bond salesmen, found it easy enough to imagine that they were the heirs not only of the Greek and Christian past but also of the earth and all its creation. Within a decade the presumptions of entitlement had become as commonplace among the sons of immigrant peddlers as among the daughters of the *haute bourgeoisie*, among the intellectual as among the merchant classes. The feeling of amplitude was sustained by the miracle of the reawakened consumer markets, and the habits of extravagance, once plausible only in the children of the rich, were embraced by people eager to believe that the nation's military prowess was a proof of its virtue and grace.

In the name of making the world safe for democracy, the United States revised its own democratic traditions and constitutional principles. By presidential fiat and Defense Department decree, the newly appointed guarantors of the world's peace suppressed the turbulent and newly un-American habits of free speech. The evil presence of the Soviet menace justified the proliferation of an always larger ruling class and the demand for always larger sums of money, and for forty years the patriotic hymn in Washington was scored for trumpets and muffled drums—more weapons, more power, more secrecy, more marble, more wiretaps, more grandeur. As the American government increasingly became a secret government, conducted behind closed doors in the presence of court favorites, a succession of American presidents took it into their heads to play at the great game of the cold war as if they were the progeny of Bismarck or the Duke of Wellington. The loud and raucous task of democratic government gave way to the more decorous notion of attending stately summit conferences, ordering covert operations, and moving flags on maps.

Troubled officials sometimes referred to what they called "the paradox" implicit in the waging of secret war under the covenants of a free, open, and democratic society. Their embarrassment didn't prevent the gradual substitution of palace intrigue for candid debate and the preference, at least in official circles, for the virtue of loyalty as opposed to the spirit of liberty. The government learned to define freedom as freedom for the state, not for the citizens. The national interest became the parochial interest of the ruling class, not the multifarious interests of the individuals subsumed under the rubric of "the American people." The question was one of how a government by the judicious few could best control and improve the instincts of the foolish many. Like Hillary Clinton's law professors and the delegates to the Constitutional Convention, the custodians of the American state in the aftermath of the Second World War mostly represented the propertied classes, and they believed themselves morally and intellectually superior to the democratic rabble, which, in the opinion of Averell Harriman, wanted nothing better than to "go to the movies and drink Coke."

Dean Acheson, secretary of state in the Truman administration, understood that if the government wished to do as it pleased, then it would be necessary to come up with a phrase, a slogan, or an article of faith that could serve as a pretext for arbitrary decision. Knowing that the American people might balk at the adventure of the cold war if they thought that the subject was open to discussion, he informed his confederates in the State Department in the spring of 1947 that a militant American foreign policy had to be presented as a "nonpartisan issue," that any and all domestic political quarreling about the country's purposes "stopped at the water's edge."

"If we can make them believe that," Acheson said, "we're off to the races."

Among the promoters of the national security state the theory of nonpartisanship was accorded the weight of biblical revelation, and for the next two generations it proved invaluable to a succession of presidents bent on waging declared and undeclared wars in Korea, Vietnam, Guatemala, Grenada, Panama, Cambodia, Lebanon, Nicaragua, and the Persian Gulf. President John F. Kennedy elaborated the theory into a doctrine not unlike the divine right of kings. At a press conference in May 1962 Kennedy dressed up the arrogance of his thought in bland abstraction:

> Most of us are conditioned for many years to have a political viewpoint—Republican or Democratic, liberal, conservative, or moderate. The fact of the matter is that most of the problems . . . that we now face are technical problems, are administrative problems. They are very sophisticated judgments, which do not lend themselves to the great sort of passionate movements which have stirred this country so often in the past. [They] deal with questions which are now beyond the comprehension of most men.

To President Bush the word *nonpartisan* was the alpha and omega of government by administrative decree: a word for all seasons; a word that avoided the embarrassment of forthright political argument; a word with which to send the troops to Saudi Arabia, postpone decisions on the budget, diffuse the blame for the savings and loan swindle. The White House staff took pride in the techniques of what its operatives referred to as "conflict avoidance." Speaking to a writer for *The New Republic* in August 1990, one of Bush's senior press agents said, "We don't do [political] fighting in this administration. We do bipartisan compromising."

But in a true democracy everything is partisan. Democratic politics is about nothing else except being partisan, and the American dialectic assumes argument not only as the normal but also as the necessary condition of existence. If democracy means anything at all—if it isn't what Gore Vidal called "the great American nonsense word" or what H. L. Mencken regarded a "fancy abstraction for the collective fear and prejudice of an ignorant mob"—it means the freedom of mind and the perpetual expansion of the discovery that the world is not oneself. A democracy is about individuals who trust their own judgments, rely on the strength of their own thoughts, and speak in their own voices. Citizens, not courtiers. People who live for others and not for the opinion of others, who believe that they can forge their energy and their intelligence into the shape of their own destiny and their own future. People who recognize in other people the worth of their variant theories, tastes, customs, and opinions, who know, as did Justice Learned Hand, that the spirit of liberty is the spirit which is not too sure that it is right.

With reference to domestic political arguments, the word *consensus* serves the same purpose as does the word *nonpartisan* in the realm of foreign affairs. It is another sleight of hand that makes possible the perpetual avoidance of any question that might excite the democratic passions of a free people bent on governing themselves. The trick is to say as little as possible in a language so bland that the speaker no longer can be accused of harboring an unpleasant opinion. The mere mention of the word *politics* brings with it the odor of something low and rotten and mean. Adhere firmly to the safe cause, talk about the flag or drugs or the deficit (never about race or class or justice), and follow the yellow brick road to the wonderful land of "consensus." In place of honest argument among consenting adults the politicians substitute a lullaby for frightened children, the pretense that conflict doesn't really exist, that we have achieved the blessed state, a state which (because we all are American and therefore content) sustains the corollary illusion that we no longer need politics.

For two centuries the American dialectic defined itself as the argument between the haves and the have-nots, between what Jefferson called "the party of the restless many and the party of the privileged few," and the American experiment prospered to the extent that enough people possessed enough courage to sustain the quarrel between capital and labor, government and governed, city and town, matter and mind. It is precisely these arguments (i.e., the very stuff and marrow of democracy) that the words *consensus* and *nonpartisan* seek to annul. The monied interest always favored the party of the few (whether it was described as Federalist or Whig or Republican), but the faction on the other side of the aisle (variously denominated as Democratic or Populist or Liberal) usually managed to muster enough of a dissent to maintain the balance of an argument.

The balance no longer holds, and although the passing of the democratic spirit can be plotted on the chart of American politics across a span of half a century, the course of that passage was made explicit under the last twelve years of Republican rule. It was the exemplary cynicism of the Reagan administration that proved even more destructive of the democratic idea than the ruin of the economy. During the early years of the administration, in what was known as "Morning in America," even people who recognized the shoddiness of Reagan's bombast thought that the country could stand a little encouragement—some gaudy tinsel and loud advertising, a lot of parades, a few safe and well-publicized military exploits, and a steady supply of easy profits. The country had heard enough of Jimmy Carter's sermons, and it was sick of listening to prophecies of the American future that could be so easily confused with a coroner's report. In return for the illusion that the United States was still first in the world's rankings, the country indulged Reagan in his claptrap economic and geopolitical theories. For a few years it didn't seem to matter that the Laffer curve and the Strategic Defense Initiative had been imported from the land of Oz. What difference did it make as long as the Japanese were willing to lend money and Rambo was victorious in the movies? Reagan taught the country that it wasn't necessary for a president to know anything about law, or foreign policy, or free speech, or trees, or black people, or whales. Government was a salesman's smile and a gift for phrase.

But it turned out that the lies did make a difference: the lies and the Reagan administration's relentless grasping of illegal and autocratic privilege. Congress offered itself for sale to the highest bidder, and the political action committees bought so many politicians of both denominations that it was no longer possible to tell the difference between a Republican and a Democrat. Nor was it possible to distinguish between the executive and the legislative functions of government. The White House did as it pleased, and Congress asked as few questions as possible. President Reagan and his aides-de-camp on the National Security Council sold weapons to a terrorist regime in Iran in order to finance a terrorist revolt in Nicaragua. The scheme obliged them to make a mockery of the

Constitution and dishonor their oaths of office, yet despite the gross and frequent abuses of power, the Democratic party—i.e., the nominal party of opposition—uttered only the smallest squeaks of objection, and except for a few journals of small circulation, the news media furnished the band music and the floral wreaths. Unimpeded by a coherent opposition, the Reagan administration accelerated the shifting of the bulk of the nation's fortune into the hands of the happy few (i.e., placing as much weight as possible on the monied side of the political balance), and the Bush administration ratified the shift not only by means of its economic and legislative policies, by its Supreme Court appointments and revisions of the banking laws and the criminal code, but also by its definition as the instrument of a privileged class.

The argument between free citizens that was the strength of the democratic idea degenerated into the whine of the courtier cadging favors and coins. Over the course of the last twenty years, and across the span of an extensive acquaintance among the people who enjoy most of the country's advantages—bond salesmen and politicians, as well as publishers, corporate vice-presidents, novelists, lawyers, English professors, and under-secretaries of state—I've noticed that most of the respondents fear and despise both the theory and the practice of democracy. Nobody ever lacks for proofs of civic disorder—the sum of the national debt, riots in the street, the loss of the nation's intellectual capital (in the arts as well as the sciences), the departure of the American competitive spirit—and the complaints become increasingly morose. A stray remark about acid rain or a third-grade textbook can escalate within a matter of minutes into an exchange of insults. Somebody calls Jesse Helms a fascist, and somebody else says that he is sick and tired of paying ransom money to a lot of welfare criminals. People drink too much and stay too late, their voices choked with anecdote and rage, their lexicons of historical reference so passionately confused that both Jefferson and Lincoln find themselves doing thirty-second commercials for racial quotas or a capital gains tax. But although everybody in the conversation bemoans the general decline of the nation's moral and industrial capacity, most of those present imagine themselves being rescued by a friendly tyrant capable of providing "strong leadership."

People who can afford to live on dividends and interest incline to regard themselves as America's guests, and within the polite sectors of affluent opinion last year I noticed that the nervousness of the private conversation matched the alarm in the newspapers. Listening to people talk about their confidence in Perot's ethics or their belief in Clinton's arithmetic, I was struck by their indifference toward any and all questions that didn't bear on their immediate financial interest, and I found myself wondering how is it possible to preserve the democratic spirit in a society distinguished by the absence of democrats. At a dinner in Washington in February I was seated next to a woman who thought that democracy was supposed to be easy, quiet, orderly, peaceful, and safe. She disapproved of the rancor and vulgarity of the primary campaigns, and because the government apparently no longer could afford to provide all its constituents with enough of everything—water, education, justice, appearances in the "Style" section of The Washington Post—she worried about signs of civil unrest. Just that week she had discovered that the setting aside of land for a bird sanctuary in Rhode Island entailed the loss of tax revenue for a township already hard pressed to maintain its schools. The news alarmed her. She had been encouraged to think of democracy as a summer vacation or a matter of consensus and parades. It never had occurred to her that a civil right could interfere with a property right or that the public interest occasionally might require the suppression of a private interest. After listening to her discuss the difficulties for the better part of an hour, I had the impression that she thought that political quarrels somehow did violence to the laws of nature.

Two weeks later, at a wedding reception in one of New York's gaudier hotels, I was surprised to find the ballroom trimmed with American flags. I knew that the father of the bride was a Republican and an admirer of both President Bush and William F. Buckley, Jr., but I hadn't thought that his political enthusiasms could

prompt him to so fervent a show of patriotism. The flag motif
also appeared on the balloons, the matchbooks, and the cake. It
wasn't that I had expected to find myself among malcontents or
doctrinaire leftists. The shrimp was expensive, and so was the
orchestra, and the people present had made a sufficient success of
their various professions (mostly publishing and investment
banking) to assure their stand on the side of the established order.
They were the kind of people who could afford to pay uptown
rents and send their children to private schools, but quite a few of
them had once voted for Jimmy Carter or George McGovern,
and among the women dancing to the medley of Cole Porter
songs I recognized the author who had been briefly famous in the
early 1970s for a book that became the rallying cry for what was
then being called "an equitable redistribution" of the nation's
wealth. At the buffet table I noticed two publishers (one of them a
former patron of Huey Newton and Malcolm X) raising toasts to
"America One," and at a table near the band I spoke to a woman
in a red dress who said that it was about time we understood that
the Arab oil was our own. Four solemn gentlemen standing close
to the champagne informed me that the populace was clearly out
of hand, as was the goddamned liberal Congress, and that if
somebody didn't do something about the debt and the crime in
the streets, not even Alan Greenspan could resurrect the market
in commercial real estate. The gentleman wearing a red bow tie
said that as far as he was concerned the United States already had
become a third world nation all but indistinguishable from Mexico or Czechoslovakia. His associate in the pin-striped suit said
that one had only to compare the airports in New York and Los
Angeles with those in Paris and Singapore (or Düsseldorf or
London or Tokyo) to know that if we wished to retain even the
smallest hope of regeneration, we had no choice but to reform the
banking laws and restrict the government's gifts to the thieving
and ungrateful poor.

A few days before the rioting and fire in Los Angeles, I found
myself at an artist's exhibition on East Fifty-seventh Street, talking to a woman who thought that the police should impose a

curfew on all black people living north of East Ninety-sixth Street. It wasn't that she didn't like black people, and she was sure that their criminal behavior wasn't entirely their own fault, but they were doing too much damage to everybody else, and if we were going to restore the country's social and economic health, well, the work had to begin somewhere. She was a blond and decisive woman in her early forties, artfully dressed and living most of the year in California. She had raised a good deal of money for President Reagan, and she had made a number of speeches on his behalf to audiences in Santa Barbara and Newport Beach. About President Bush she was not nearly so enthusiastic, but like him or not, he was the Republican candidate, and he was certainly preferable to that lying Governor Clinton or that anarchist Jerry Brown. I pointed out that the mayor of New York was himself a black man, as was the chief of police, and that neither gentleman would be likely to recommend a curfew, even if it were generously extended to the permissive hour of 2:00 A.M. The woman from California dismissed the objection with a bright but determined smile. She knew perfectly well that politics were sometimes awkward, she said, but Winston Churchill never permitted himself to become discouraged by hostile criticism. We changed the subject and admired the paintings.

Like the woman worried about the birds and the school-children in Rhode Island, the woman dreaming of Winston Churchill's reincarnation in California had lost interest in the tedious business of self-government. It was too hard, too boring, too complicated. She preferred to leave the arrangements to somebody else, preferably somebody in uniform, and she spoke about what she imagined to be the comforts of autocracy as if she had discovered something as wonderful as an out-of-the-way resort in the Bahamas or a new recipe for monkfish. It didn't occur to her that democratic government is a purpose held in common, or that the idea of democracy is synonymous with the idea of the citizen. The experiment requires the collaboration of everybody present, and if democracy can be understood as a field of temporary coalitions between people of different interests, skills, and generations, then everybody has need of everybody else.

The democratic proposition fails (or evolves into something else) unless enough people perceive their government as subject rather than object, as animate organism rather than automatic vending machine. Such an antique understanding of politics runs counter to the demand for omnipotence or the wish to believe in kings or queens or fairy tales. Ask almost anybody in any street about the nature of American government, and he or she will describe it as something that belongs to somebody else, as a them, not an us. Only advanced students of political science remember how a caucus works, or what is written in the Constitution, or who paves the roads. Every two or four or six years the politicians ask the voters whether they recognize themselves as better or worse off than they were the last time anybody asked. The question is only and always about money, never about the spirit of the laws or the cherished ideals that embody the history of the people. If the 1992 election was remarkable for the popular expressions of disgust with the systems in place, it was equally remarkable for the candidates' silence on the subject of criminal justice, the decay of the cities, the divisions between people of different races, homelessness among the poor, the insolvency of the banks, and the terms of the contract between the citizen and the state.

To the extent that the wish to be cared for replaces the will to act, the commercial definition of democracy prompts the politicians to conceive of and advertise the Republic as if it were a resort hotel. They promise the voters the rights and comforts owed to them by virtue of their status as America's guests (i.e., much the same sort of deal that Louis XIV offered the nobility in residence at Versailles), and the subsidiary arguments amount to little more than complaints about the number, quality, and cost of the available services. The government (aka the hotel management) preserves its measure of trust in the exact degree that it satisfies the whims of its patrons and meets the public expectation of convenience and style at a fair price. The welfare client in hope of free housing or a free meal and the banker in hope of an investment credit or a tax break differ only in the class of their accommodations. A frightened oligarchy and a debased electorate ask of the state what the rich ask of their servants: "Comfort us." "Tell us what to do."[4]

Most of the country's present trouble follows from the blind arrogance of too many people in power and the apathy and lack of objection on the part of too many people out of power. Just as the victories of 1945 tempted the United States to dress itself up in the pretensions of world empire, so also the transformation of the old American Republic into an autocratic nation-state has encouraged the same presumptions of grace that the inventors of the American idea found so offensive among the British upper classes during the years prior to the revolutionary war. Traveling in London in the 1770s, Benjamin Franklin and John Adams were shocked at the gap between the "wealth, magnificence and splendor" of the rich and the "extreme misery and distresses of the poor . . . amazing on the one hand and disgusting on the other." Adams believed that England had reached the same stage as the Roman Republic, "a venal city, ripe for destruction." Franklin opposed a prospective union with the British Commonwealth on the ground that he had no wish to combine with a Britain he thought decadent and hostile to liberty. Writing to Joseph Galloway of Pennsylvania, he remarked on "the extreme corruption prevalent among all orders of men in this old, rotten state" with its "numberless and needless places, enormous salaries, pensions, perquisites, bribes, groundless quarrels, foolish expeditions, false accounts or no accounts, contracts and jobs that devour all revenue. . . ."

Franklin could as easily have been describing the manners and attitudes currently in vogue not only in Washington but also on the thirty-seventh floor of the Time and Life Building, behind the glass walls of quite a few of the country's largest business corporations, and around the tennis courts of Brentwood and Bel Air. How better to describe the savings and loan swindle if not as a sequence of "false accounts or no accounts"? What else was the war in the Persian Gulf if not a groundless quarrel or a foolish expedition? If the late Steve Ross received a salary of $78 million a year for presiding over the economic degeneration of Time Warner and Lee Iacocca a salary of $4.65 million a year for supervising the wreckage of the Chrysler Corporation, do they not illustrate the wonders of a corrupt enterprise swollen with "enormous salaries, pensions, perquisites"?

As both Franklin and Adams also noticed in London in the years prior to the revolutionary war, the scale of unreality implicit in the economic order prompted the holders of great wealth to imagine themselves invulnerable to the assaults of death and time. The ministers of the Crown were so disdainful of the American cause that they never troubled to send a representative, much less one of their own exalted company, to the far shore of the Atlantic Ocean to so much as glance at the cities of Boston or New York. General Thomas Clarke, aide-de-camp to George III, boasted in the presence of Franklin that he would undertake to go from one end of America to the other with a thousand grenadiers and "geld all the males, partly by force, and partly with a little coaxing." Most of the noble lords and ladies in the room received the remark with appreciative nods and condescending smiles.

"The pride and vanity of the nation [Britain] is a disease," said Adams. "It is a delirium; it has been flattered and inflamed so long by themselves and by others that it perverts everything."

A comparable delirium afflicts our own ruling and possessing class, but I'm not so foolish as to suppose that at some idyllic moment in the American past the practice of democracy matched the textbook theory. The Republic always stands at risk, and its enemies, who are many and well fed, always ally themselves with more or less the same mob of selfish fears—with the pride of the rich and the envy of the poor, with the insolence of office and the wish for kings.

Although people like to believe that Washington is the province of knaves and fools, they also like to believe that government is their great and good friend, an abstraction as benevolent as God and capable of curing each and every one of society's ills:

poverty, ignorance, injustice, disease, crime in the suburbs. To
the extent that we cling to this latter belief, we forgive the
politicians their trespasses against us and place our hopes in
some undetermined future when mankind will have been improved beyond recognition and all will be well. Wait for next
year's election, or the miraculous appearance of a right-thinking
leader, or another program of uplifting reform, and then, lo and
behold and just as Abraham Lincoln once said, we will see,
rising out of the mist of lies and television slogans, a government by the people, of the people, and for the people. The hope
is as romantic as it is characteristically American. It is also
extremely convenient to the ambition and self-interest of the
government in residence in Washington, as opposed to the
imaginary government stored in libraries.

The Clinton administration apparently means to define itself as
a television program instead of a government, and although I
admire what I take to be the theme of the show—restoring belief
in the American promise—I don't know how it can please both
its sponsors and its intended audience. The difficulty follows
from the need to protect the interests of oligarchy (i.e., the people
who put up the campaign money) and at the same time sustain the
illusion of popular sovereignty among an electorate hoping for
proof through the night that our flag is still there.

The events attending President Clinton's inaugural might as
well have been chosen as demonstrations of an improbable political theorem. Obliged to reward his patrons and comfort his fans,
the president provided the former with the gifts of office and the
latter with ritual songs and dances. On Capitol Hill the Congress
went about the business of confirming the president's nominees
to the Cabinet—most of them corporate lawyers, several of them
patently unqualified or inept, all of them loyal servants of the
status quo that, as a candidate, the president had so often decried
as timid, self-serving, and corrupt. More or less simultaneously,
the president appeared as the friend of the common man in the
series of *tableaux vivants* staged against the backdrops of Washington's best known monuments—Bill Clinton at Monticello,

departing for the Capitol under the aegis of Thomas Jefferson, and riding through the landscape of the Civil War in a bus bearing the license plate HOPE 1; Bill Clinton by candlelight, approaching the Lincoln Memorial on foot; Bill Clinton ringing a replica of the Liberty Bell; Bill Clinton listening, transfixed, to Diana Ross sing "We Are the World" and to ten saxophonists play Elvis Presley's "Heartbreak Hotel"; Bill Clinton in tears at the Capitol Centre, accepting the badges and emblems of democratic senti-ment at the hands of Barbra Streisand and Michael Jackson; Bill Clinton swearing the oath of office in the presence of Maya Angelou, who read an ode to the multicultural text ("the Asian, the Hispanic, the Jew / The African, the Native American, the Sioux . . . the Gay, the Straight, the Preacher / The privileged, the homeless, the Teacher") of the American soul. The extrava-gant sum of money spent on the inaugural pageant ($17 million provided by the nation's leading business corporations) expressed the degree to which the nation's courtier classes were worried about the resentment still at large in the public opinion polls.

But maybe I speak too soon, and maybe President Clinton's promise of renewal and discovery will prove to be made of some-thing more substantial than the red, white, and blue balloons floating over the heads of the delegates at the nominating conven-tions. The cold war is over, and with it the need to subvert the hope of the future with the fear of the past. Nobody could have foreseen the turbulent political passions let loose in last year's presidential campaigns, and maybe, with or without the help of the Clinton administration, we will find out what we mean to say when we talk about the common American enterprise.

2

The Courtier Spirit

SHOULD A MAN BE APPOINTED TO A NEW POST, PRAISE OF HIM POURS FORTH, OVERFLOWING INTO COURTYARDS AND CHAPELS, REACHING THE STAIR, THE HALL, THE GALLERY, THE WHOLE OF THE ROYAL APARTMENT; ONE'S QUITE SUBMERGED, ONE'S OVERWHELMED BY IT. THERE ARE NO TWO OPINIONS ON THE MAN; ENVY AND JEALOUSY SPEAK WITH THE SAME VOICE AS ADULATION; ALL ARE SWEPT AWAY BY THE TORRENT, WHICH FORCES THEM TO SAY WHAT THEY THINK OR DON'T THINK, OF A MAN, AND OFTEN TO PRAISE ONE WHOM THEY DO NOT KNOW. A MAN OF WIT, MERIT, OR VALOR BECOMES, IN ONE INSTANT, A GENIUS OF THE FIRST RANK, A HERO, A DEMI-GOD. . . .
—*La Bruyère, Characters*

Democracy is better understood as a habit of mind than as a system of government, and among all the American political virtues, candor is probably the one most necessary to the success of the proposition. The energy of the American idea flows from the capacity of its citizens to speak and think without cant, from their willingness to defend their interest, argue their case, say what they mean. As long ago as 1838, addressing the topic of "The American Democrat" in a pamphlet of that name, James

Fenimore Cooper argued that the word *American* was synonymous with the habit of telling the truth. But if the politicians
promote the lying fictions of consensus, and if the citizenry no
longer cares to engage in what it regards as the distasteful business of debate, then the American dialectic cannot attain a syn-
thesis or resolution. The political weather turns pinched and gray.
The institutional directives remain in the safekeeping of the state,
and the popular initiative passes to the demagogues in the streets.
The society falls prey to the extremists of all denominations who
claim alliance with the higher consciousness and the absolute
truth, and the once-upon-a-time eloquence of Daniel Webster or
Henry Clay or Martin Luther King degenerates into the mutter-
ing of Al Sharpton or Pat Robertson or David Duke.

What the founders of the American Republic most detested in
the monarchy of George III was the dance of grace and favor—the
obligatory bending of the courtier's knee to the arrogance of rank
and privilege, the ceaseless bowing and smiling to the presumed
magnificence of an incompetent general or an idiot duke. The
objection was unanimous, and in Philadelphia in 1787 the delegates of all degrees—rich as well as poor, son of liberty or would-
be oligarch—were undivided in their disgust for the stale scent of
flattery that polluted the atmosphere at court. The American
loathing for the condescending and self-important man followed
from the recognition that all those present in the New World had
pledged their lives and bet their fortunes on the same Declaration
of Independence. The American premise is an existential one, and
our political code is moral. We protect the other person's liberty
in the interest of protecting our own, and we hold our fellow
citizens in thoughtful regard not because they are exceptional (or
famous or beautiful or rich) but simply because they are fellow
citizens. The joint venture succeeds to the extent that its citizens
attempt to tell one another the truth—about what they see and
think and know—and to the degree in which they refrain from
using their fellow citizens as subjects of their own vanity or
convenience. What joins the Americans one to another is not a
common nationality, language, race, or ancestry (all of which

testify to the burdens of the past) but rather the participation in a shared work of imagining the future. The love of country follows from the love of its freedoms, not from the pride in its armies or its gross national product. Construed as a means and not an end, the Constitution stands as the premise for a narrative rather than as a plan for an invasion or a monument. The narrative is always plural. Not one story but many stories, and none of them more privileged than others.

As opposed to the presumption of candor implicit in the democratic premise, the courtier spirit consists in the telling of welcome lies. The courtier is a smiling and accommodating man, willing to deny or distort the truth for any expedient purpose, loyal to power in whatever person or institution it makes itself manifest, as cruel or as compassionate as the circumstances might warrant. Counting it his duty to strike attractive poses, to pass vaguely through a room while he displays the loveliness of his good intentions, the courtier makes his career by saying to a succession of masters, "Make of me what you want; I am what you want me to be." He avoids the pitfalls of moral obligation and genuine emotion, and in place of friends he makes connections that can be acquired or abandoned as easily as railroad tickets.

Just as the New World provided unlimited freedom of expression to the democratic spirit, so also it offered equal opportunity to the play of the courtier spirit. Passing through Cincinnati and Nashville in 1831, Alexis de Tocqueville was surprised to find the Americans so adept at the arts of servility. True, they didn't dress as well or as expensively as the ladies and gentlemen in France; their conversation wasn't as refined, and neither were their manners; but they possessed a native talent for ingratiating themselves with anybody and everybody who could do them a favor or grant them a privilege. The effect was often comic—dandies in broadcloth instead of silk brocade, loud in their brag and fantastic in their gestures, bowing and scraping to one another while standing up to their ankles in the muddy street of a wooden town on the edge of a savage wilderness.

Nor did Tocqueville think that the Americans had much use for their well-advertised freedom of speech. He had thought that the citizens of the new democracy would prove to be turbulent and roughhewn people, direct in their actions and forthright in their address. He found them cowed by what he called "the tyranny of the majority," and it occurred to him that never in his travels had he encountered a people so fearful of free expression as the supposedly boisterous Americans. Too many of them were too afraid of losing a fraction of advantage or a degree of self-importance, and so they were very, very careful about talking out of turn and maybe saying the wrong thing.

After considering the paradox for some years, Tocqueville concluded that in a monarchy the courtier spirit was less pervasive and less damaging than it was in a democracy. Even the most arrogant of kings seldom had the gall to speak in the name of the public interest. Louis XIV couldn't impose a military conscription, and he always had considerable trouble with the levying of taxes. The king's interest was clearly his own.

But a democracy claims to serve the interest of the sovereign people, and so the officials who write and administer the laws can claim to act on behalf of anything that they can classify as the common good. The presumption allows for a more expansive arrogation of power than the divine right of kings, and because the figure of the prince in a democracy appears in so many different forms and disguises—as politician, network executive, corporate chairman, town clerk, foundation hierarch, and Washington columnist—the anxious sycophant is constantly bowing and smiling in eight or nine directions, forever turning, like a compass needle or a weather vane, into the glare of new money. A democracy transforms the relatively few favors in the monarch's gift—sinecure, benefice, or patents royal—into the vast cornucopia of patronage distributed under the nominally egalitarian rubrics of tax exemption, defense contract, publication, milk subsidy, tenure. Under the rule of a monarch the courtier spirit crowds in upon the palace, but in a democracy it seeps through the whole of the society, corrupting the arts and sciences as well as the political and commercial orders, and it remains, as Tocqueville noticed, "within easy reach of the multitude" because so many people have so much to gain by prostituting themselves to the mob, to the newspapers, to the wisdom of the rich.

I don't know to what extent the courtier spirit flourished in the United States in the years between 1835 and 1960, but certainly over the span of the last twenty or thirty years it has grown sleek and fat. Maybe I've lived too long in New York City or attended too many academic conferences or lived in too many expensive rooms, but from what I can see and judge of the nation's cultural and political enterprise, I don't think that the premises of democracy have much to do with the *modus operandi* of the institutions that govern the shaping of the American mind. Among the few hundred thousand people who own and operate the country—who write the laws, set the school curricula, and compose the media images—the paths to fortune wind through the maze of sycophancy. At Harvard University or the Public Broadcasting System (as at Condé Nast or Citibank) the candidates for patronage and tenure feel uncomfortable with anything other than the most stylistic representations of democracy, and the art of achieving most forms of credibility or wealth has become the art of attaining a place at court. The attendant paralysis of mind accounts for much of the nation's current distress—for the mounting sum of the debt as well as for the loss of the country's intellectual capital in both the arts and the sciences.[5]

The courtier spirit wears the costume of almost any trade or profession, its characteristic weakness as prevalent among academic poets and television news correspondents as among public relations consultants and undersecretaries of state. What else is the courtier spirit if not the spirit of a society overrun by lawyers? Like the journalist, a lawyer is by definition a courtier, hired to arrange the truth into its most flattering and convenient poses, mediating between his patron and the rudeness of the world outside the palace gates. How else to define the courtier spirit if not as the supremacy of the briefing paper and the interoffice memoranda? We spend our days filling out forms, begging the stamps of official approval and permission, burdened by a federal tax code that now runs to 6,956 pages, currying the favor of a foundation grant, a university appointment, a government contract, or five pages of corporate advertising. The literary and academic guilds shun the risks of direct expression, and the corporations assign nervous committees to the tasks of decision and invention. When I think of the American elites assembled in some conference center or hotel ballroom, I see a great throng of eager and anxious faces—too many to count or to name, but all of them willing to do or to say whatever is required in return for a camera angle or a block of electoral votes, for a tip on the bond market, a letter of credit, a word of praise, all of them applauding the divine wisdom of whatever sponsors happen to be buying the golf balls or the salmon on toast. Very seldom does anybody hazard a guess or an opinion that might harm his or her chance of advancement, and the image that stays in my mind is that of a crowd of flatterers managing their self-interest as deftly as the gentlemen of the king's bedchamber in Louis XIV's palace at Versailles.

Although the expectations of entitlement were firmly in place long before the era of hectic prosperity associated with the Reagan administration, eight years of feckless extravagance raised them to the power of revealed truth, and as the balance of the society's wealth becomes more heavily weighted in favor of a more narrowly circumscribed oligarchy, the arts of obedience become both more galling and more refined. The employees—executives as well as mechanics and anchorpersons—depend upon their corporate or institutional overlord not only for wages but also for the terms of their existence: for medical insurance, pension, country club membership, clothing allowance, and definition of self. As more people become more fearful of losing their place in the world, they become more willing to trade their independence of mind for the price of a second mortgage, a third motorboat, or a new hat. During the early years of the American Republic almost everybody was self-employed, and the citizen whom Jefferson or Madison had in mind was somebody free to tell any other citizen precisely what he thought of his lying contract or his filthy shop. As late as the first decade of the twentieth century roughly 90 percent of the American people were still self-employed. For the most part they lived on small family farms and paid taxes that in the aggregate amounted to less than 5 percent of their annual income. By 1992 only 4 percent of the American people were self-employed, and they paid taxes that in the aggregate (federal, state, city, excise, etc.) amounted to more than 50 percent of their income. If political freedom is conditional upon economic freedom, then the citizen who cannot afford to express an opinion contrary to the opinion of the director of sales—or the deputy secretary or the board of trustees or the executive editor—forfeits an owner's interest in his or her own mind and learns, of necessity, the dance of grace and favor.

The lessons breed resentment, and in the summer of last year the measure of that resentment expressed itself in the sudden flare of enthusiasm for H. Ross Perot. Had Perot been merely rich, he would have been seen as another salesman of economic self-help touring the circuit of the television talk shows in order to hustle his theories of financial redemption ($21.95 in hard cover; $9.95 in paperback; $27.50 for the videocassette), but Perot's fortune exceeded $2.5 billion, and in a society that makes a god of wealth, the rich man inherits the majesty of a king. He can tell everybody else where and when to come or go, and he need never bend the courtier's knee to the pleasure of fools. The vision was immensely satisfying to people who cannot afford the luxury of doing as they please or saying what they think.

The most opulent of the nation's courts resides in Washington, but the country is large enough and still rich enough to sustain a multitude of secondary courts of varying importance and pretension within the citadels of American business as well as in the courtyards of the universities and the studios of the big media. Citibank employs more people than lived in Renaissance Florence, and Michael Jackson holds in his gift more largess than was available to Cosimo de' Medici. Courts form like oyster shells not only around the pearls of great price at CBS News or General

Motors but also around the personae of John Gotti and Barbra Streisand.

Although I cannot measure the courtier spirit as would a tailor—by seam or collar point or sleeve length—I can see it in a gesture or hear it in a turn of phrase. Barbara Walters struck the proper note of subservience when, in the course of interviewing the newly elected president Jimmy Carter in the autumn of 1976, she said, in a breathless and scarcely audible murmur, "Be kind to us, Mr. President. Be good to us." President Bush struck the appropriate note of insolence during the 1988 election campaign when he refused to answer a rude question about an American naval blunder in the Persian Gulf—the shooting down of an Iranian airliner and the abrupt murder of its 242 passengers—on the ground that he would never, "never apologize for the United States of America. . . . I don't care what the facts are." Henry Kissinger's entire career illuminates the character of the courtier spirit—a smiling but invariably treacherous man willing to sacrifice any moral scruple on the altar of his own ambition—and I remember him explaining in the spring of 1979 at a breakfast in New York why he was still busy falsifying so many of his state papers. He was out of office at the time, and because he was eagerly soliciting favor with Ronald Reagan and John Connally (both of them prospective presidential candidates), he worried that his reputation as a statesman might become clouded by too close a study of the written records. His enemies certainly would draw improper inferences, and he felt obliged as a matter of prudence to correct his prior correspondence in a way that proved him to be as prescient as he was infallible. Circumstance, he said, was constantly plotting against him, and he owed his biographers the courtesy of preserving an unblemished image not only in the show windows of the media but also in the mirror of history.[6]

Numerous writers over the last four hundred years have attempted to define the courtier spirit, but none have improved on the course of instruction offered by Baldassare Castiglione's *Book of the Courtier* and Denis Diderot's *Rameau's Nephew*. Both texts take the form of conversations, one of them set in a palace in

Urbino in the summer of 1519, the other in a café in Paris in 1760. Diderot's lesson is the more antic and the more humorous. The author presents himself in the character of a moral philosopher (very dignified, very grave) engaged in a satirical Platonic dialogue with Jean Philippe Rameau, a musician and music teacher who prides himself on his talents as scoundrel, rogue, flatterer, hanger-on, opportunist, hypocrite. The two men talk during the hour before a performance of the opera in the Place de Palais Royale, Rameau berating himself for having committed the stupidity of telling his patron the truth and so having lost his place at his patron's table. He is a wonderfully comic figure, given to sudden and fanciful gesture, often interrupting himself to mime the stance and character of somebody whom he wishes to mock. At one point he performs the beggar's pantomime, the dance that he defines as the perfect expression of the courtier spirit and describes as follows:

> Then, smiling as he [Rameau's nephew] did so, he began impersonating the admiring man, the supplicating man, the complacent man, right foot forward, left foot behind, back bent, head up, looking fixedly into somebody else's eyes, lips parted, arms held out toward something, waiting for a command, and receiving it, and off like an arrow, back again with it done, reporting it. He is attentive to everything, picks up what has been dropped, adjusts a pillow, or puts a stool under someone's feet, holds a saucer, pushes forward a chair, opens a door, shuts a window, pulls curtains, keeps his eyes on the master and mistress, arms at his side and legs straight, listening, trying to read people's expressions. And he goes on, that is my act, about the same as flatterers, courtiers, flunkies and beggars.

If Diderot sketches the humorous facets of the courtier spirit—ingratiating, craven, and absurd—Castiglione describes the less amusing traits of the character, placing particular emphasis on the degrees of calculation necessary to a successful career at court. He offers his book as a manual for the aspiring opportunist, and he sets out the rules of behavior in the manner of Jane Fonda recommending a program in aerobics. The device of the book is a series of conversations among men and women of noble rank who come together over the course of four successive evenings and attempt to define the attributes of the perfect courtier. By the time they finish their discourse and send for the lutes and viols, they have agreed on the following points of character:

— The true courtier avoids "the trap of friendship." Friends implicate one another in emotions, which all too easily can prove inconvenient or impolitic. A friend is a foolish luxury.

— Always display moderation and restraint. Never eat too much or laugh too loudly.

— Conversation is the principal occupation of court, and the courtier who would polish the surfaces of his career always brings something bland and agreeable to say. Never cast oneself as the bearer of a strong opinion, or, God forbid, bad news.

— Dress in an expensive but sober manner. Any doubts on the questions of costume should be resolved in favor of wearing gray or black.

— Shun the pretension of modesty. Only a naïve man waits for the world to recognize his talent. The perfect courtier knows how to promote himself and to claim credit for any deed or thought that wins the favor of his prince.

— Obey the sovereign rule of appearances. A thing is what it seems, and a word well chosen always serves as surrogate for a deed.[7]

During last year's presidential campaign both President Bush and Governor Clinton acted the part of the courtier for anybody and everybody who would reward them with a campaign contribution or a television interview. By late October it was apparent that the story of Bush's life was the story of a man making polite small talk and assembling a résumé that he once described, as proudly as a boy with a stamp collection, as "all these fantastic credentials"—a man born to wealth and privilege, his rise to power dependent upon the gifts of patronage, anxious to please and always remembering to write little notes of thanks and praise, appointed ambassador to China (and then chairman of the Republican National Committee, director of the Central Intelligence Agency, vice president of the United States), willing to revise or discard any thought unsuitable to the occasion, adept at playing the part of bully or toady, passing the tray of watercress sandwiches, laughing at all the rich men's jokes. Clinton was equally accommodating, and late at night, on an airplane while traveling between speeches, he provided his own variation on the theme by Castiglione. To B. Drummond Ayers, Jr., a reporter for *The New York Times*, he set forth what he called "Bill Clinton's Laws of Politics":

1. Always be introduced by someone you've appointed to high office.

2. When you're starting to have a good time, you're supposed to be someplace else.

3. There is no such thing as enough money.

4. If someone tells you it's not a money problem, it's someone else's problem.

5. When someone tells you it's not personal, they're fixing to stick it to you.

6. Nearly everyone will lie to you given the right circumstances.

Governor Clinton's speeches may be letter perfect, but so is his instinct for oligarchy, and the difference between the friends of George Bush and the friends of Bill Clinton seems to be more a matter of style than of substance. Most of the former president's principal advisers and cabinet officials—among them James Baker, the secretary of state, C. Boyden Gray, the White House counsel, Carla Hills, the United States trade representative, Dan Quayle, the vice president, Richard Darmon, the director of the Office of Budget and Management—were born to the security of wealth, all of them endowed with the temperament of the ruling class that they so loyally served and represented, all of them well aware (as were students of human unhappiness as different from one another as J. P. Morgan and Voltaire) that the comfort of the rich requires an abundant supply of the poor.

With only a few modest or senior exceptions, Governor Clinton's surrogates and advisers derive their presumption of privilege from their institutional provenience—not by right of birth but by right of the academic degrees bestowed by Harvard, Oxford, and the Yale Law School. Like their contemporaries in Hollywood and Wall Street, they proved themselves equal to the tasks of self-promotion, and almost without exception they were people whose moral reasoning conformed to the circular design fashionable among the adherents of both Presidents Reagan and Bush—what is good is rich and successful; what is rich and successful is good; I am rich and successful, therefore I am good, and so is my car and my theory of the just society. If the servants of the Reagan and Bush administrations wished to divide the country into an equestrian and a plebeian class, they at least were content to give up the ornaments of conscience in return for the house in Virginia. The friends of Bill Clinton apparently wanted it all—everything in both column A and column B, the Zen garden and the BMW as well as the three-masted schooner and the friendship of rap musicians.

The talented courtier possesses what Plutarch called "the soul of an acrobat," and once instructed in the correct forms of expedient speech, the courtiers in attendance at one court find it a relatively simple matter to perform the same services in other courts. Given the American belief in process and technique, it is not surprising that a man as agile as David Stockman can shift his sophisms from the Methodist Church to the Reagan administration to a Wall Street bank, or that Richard Nixon admired Alexander Haig, his chief of staff, for the general's "plastic capability," or that Henry Kissinger can show up on CBS News in a cameo appearance as the guest weatherman. For the same reasons that the courtier can afford neither convictions nor friends, he avoids the phrase or thought that could be misunderstood as anything other than reassuringly banal. His motto is Prudence, Caution,

Coldness of Heart, and he shows only those emotions that conform to the consensus already present at the conference table. The world consists of only those few people (possibly as many as two hundred) whom one knows, and it is governed by the sovereign rule of appearances. President Clinton ably demonstrated his understanding of the correct sensibility when, three days after he took office, he annulled the appointment of Zoe Baird to the office of attorney general. The woman's dealings with her domestic servants had proved an embarrassment, but because her appointment depended solely on the rule of appearances (i.e., on the need for more women in the new cabinet) she could be replaced as easily as a sofa or a lamp.

Approached by means of a data base instead of by anecdote, the broad outline of American court society might be plotted on a graph that takes into account the boards of directors of the Fortune 500 as well as the trustees of the nation's leading universities, the senior staffs of the major news media, the partners of the larger law firms, the principal figures in the movie business, and the custodians of the prominent policy institutes and philanthropic foundations. The computers would provide the roster of ornamental names that appear on the guest lists for White House dinners and the season's best-publicized charity balls (the names that decorate the gossip columns and sit in the box seats at Forest Hills and the Los Angeles Coliseum), and once the data base had been established, it probably would be safe to say that any name that showed up more than eight or nine times belonged to one or another of the nation's courts. As it would have been fair to say of the company assembled at Versailles, the more visible the personality, the less likely that he or she adds anything but a decorative presence to the sum of the national enterprise. If the water engineers went on strike, cities would become uninhabitable within a matter of hours. Equally unpleasant consequences would attend strikes by the police or fire department, but the media chatter incessantly about the people for whom the society has the least use—about Elizabeth Taylor's wedding, or Jay Leno's contract, or Maria Shriver's hair—and they take little notice of the people or professions on whom the society utterly depends.

As the preferred images of the truth come to take precedence over plain or impolitic fact, the sickly bloom of the courtier spirit produces the predictably feebleminded result across the whole landscape of American thought—in the literary and academic professions as well as in the government, the business corporations, and the army. The agreeable murmur of platitudes is always preferable to the expression of generous or magnanimous feeling, and the din of gossip crowds out the hope of thought. At the expensive literary fetes in New York—the kind of party staged in a gaudy restaurant by the kind of publisher who can pay an author's advance of upwards of five hundred thousand dollars—nobody commits the crimes of candor. What would be the point of saying that a book's success is largely determined by the sum of money assigned to its promotion, that the writing in *Vanity Fair* is really very poor, that if *The New York Times Book Review* almost always devotes its front page to a puff of praise, it is because the *Times Book Review* sets itself the task of supporting an industry rather than providing a frame of critical judgment, that if Simon and Schuster publishes President Ronald Reagan's ghostwritten memoirs under the rubric of autobiography, it is because Simon and Schuster paid an author's advance of three million dollars and sees no chance of recovering its investment if the book is honestly presented as the work of a hired publicist? All the observations might be true, but they would bring little profit or thanks to anybody foolish enough to make a show of them at court. The blurbs promoting new books ("masterpiece," "work of monumental force," "not since the death of Henry James") testify to the diligence of the author's literary friends and connections, not to the book's worth, and the right word in the right ear at the right moment sometimes spawns the birth of genius.[8]

As with the New York literary mises-en-scène, so also with the Washington public policy institutes. Most of the political intellectuals whom I've encountered over the last twenty years might as well be wearing the liveries of their monied patrons—

red brocade and silver piping for the American Enterprise Institute, blue velvet and gold braid for the Brookings Institution. At the symposia convened by the Ford Foundation or the Kennedy School for Government, the initiatives that command the most respect are the ones that are so safe and obvious that they can bear easy translation into the clotted prose of a funding proposal. Once the money is firmly in place, the discussants assembled for the weekend at Aspen or Cambridge proclaim the initiatives "revolutionary." The more elaborate the accommodations—tennis or aerobics between the seminars on Aristotle and the zero sum game—the more uncompromising the adjectives and the more urgent the cries for social reform.

Similarly flattering arrangements of language decorate the annual meetings at which the presidents of the nation's largest business corporations compliment one another for the courage with which they seek out bold financial risks. The more strenuous the after-dinner rhetoric, the more likely that the gentleman making the speech owes his fortune to the grace of his connections. By 1991 the average pay of the average company chairman exceeded the average pay of the average worker by a ratio of 93 to 1, but despite the conventional announcements about a man's worth being measured by his achievement, corporate executives get paid according to the weight of their acquaintance and the number of strata below them in the table of organization.

The gifts of executive compensation follow from the largess of the board of directors, and because the directors owe their places to the corporate chairman—as friends, clients, or patrons—they seldom quibble about another few hundred thousands of dollars in salary, another twenty million dollars in stock options, an improved insurance benefit, or another membership in another golf club because the managers of large corporations remain safely insulated from the owners of the company (i.e., from the rabble of anonymous stockholders whom nobody ever sees). They all too easily become as arrogant as the eighteenth-century French nobility that was as safely insulated from the peasants who worked its lands and paid tributes of taxes and rents. People come to believe what they choose to believe, flattered by their advertising agencies and public relations counsel, confusing the comforts of monopoly with the "rigors of the marketplace." The murmur of ceaseless agreement often produces comic results, and in the early 1970s I remember that before I was introduced to the chairman of the Mobil Oil Corporation (an overstuffed and self-important man named Tavoulareas), it was explained that he sometimes mistook himself for a Renaissance prince and that anybody who hoped to win his favor was well advised to imagine him wearing an ermine cloak and a velvet hat.

During the recession year of 1991 corporate profits fell by an estimated 21 percent, and the firing of common workers took place at the rate of twenty-six hundred a day, but over the same period of time the chief executives of the country's hundred largest corporations improved the value of their holdings of the company's stock (shares, bonuses, and options) by an average sum of $2.63 million. As published in *The Crystal Report* for 1991, the comparison of executive pay with company performance also provided the following gloss on the rigors of the free market:

COMPANY LOSSES FOR 1991		CEO TOTAL COMPENSATION FOR 1991	
General Motors:	$4.5 billion	Robert C. Stempel	$1,600,000
IBM:	$2.8 billion	John F. Akers	$4,900,000
Ford:	$2.3 billion	Harold A. Poling	$1,600,000
Westinghouse:	$1.1 billion	Paul E. Lego	$3,300,000
United Technologies:	$1.1 billion	Robert F. Daniell	$1,500,000

By the winter of 1993 the financial losses reported by General Motors, IBM, and Westinghouse had forced the resignation of Messrs. Stempel, Akers, and Lego. The decision in each instance followed from the agitation of "outside" directors, i.e., people not utterly dependent on the corporation for their livelihood and definition of self. In the business press the writers familiar with the corporations in question spoke of cataclysm and social revolution. The world had been turned upside down, and in their search for reasons and explanations the alarmed witnesses assigned the fault to the abstract forces of historical circumstance—to recession, technological change, and the mystery of global interdependence. Nobody mentioned the corrosiveness of the courtier spirit. Nor did anybody remark on the paralysis of mind characteristic of any institution rich enough to afford, at least temporarily, a private and preferred theory of reality.

At the zenith of the Reagan prosperity in the spring of 1986 I came across an article in the monthly magazine *M* that summed up the presiding sensibility under the title "Those Privileged CEO's and Their Princely Ways." The gentlemen in question were described as "the aristocrats of the age," and the article admiringly noted the favorite topics of conversation (cars, corporate jets, golf, exercise, one's own salary, and the wickedness of the press), the cherished aspirations (the perfect putt, a cabinet post, a first-name relationship with Henry Kissinger, having an article published in the *Harvard Business Review*), and the necessary luxuries (good-looking golf shoes, bodyguards, Mont Blanc pens, quiet wives, and retinues of executive assistants). Elsewhere in the article it was explained that CEOs sometimes have trouble learning "to relate down" to lesser folk in their employ and that families can be best understood as "executive support systems."

The emphasis on court etiquette coincides with my own impression of the corporate gentry, and if I look back over a period of thirty years' acquaintance with presidents of companies and directors of corporations, I see a succession of amiable gentlemen posed around the square of a card table, chatting pleasantly on the thirteenth green, rolling dice from a leather cup in a country club bar. Although they spoke intelligently, sometimes even eloquently, about the specific instances of a specific deal, the conversation beyond the vicinity of their immediate financial interest consisted of pleasantly vacant references to their comfort and their travel plans. A few months prior to the stock market collapse of 1987, I remember talking to the chairman of a New York bank who said that he counted himself fortunate if only 50 percent of his decisions proved correct. He was a man who served on the boards of five corporations and three foundations, and the veneer of his complacence was as immaculate as polished wood. Apparently I showed some sign of confusion or surprise, and when I failed to offer appropriate congratulations, the chairman explained, patiently and as if to a child, the significance of the statistic.

"But you must see how good that is," he said. "That's better than any batting average of any ballplayer. Anybody who can hit five hundred is worth a hell of a lot of money."

He went on to explain that somebody had to make the decisions. The important thing was to do so with an appearance of firm resolve, as if a man knew what he was about.

"Who could know what there is to be known?" he said. "And if somebody did know, then who could possibly know what to do about it?"

If nobody knows but somebody must pretend to know, then the governing of an institution becomes theatrical, and it follows that the people employed by the institution should become preoccupied with the way things look and sound rather than whatever it is they supposedly mean. A good press agent is as necessary as a good tailor, and a thing is so if the right people say it is so. The prince presents a loyal courtier with an honor or a title, and the act of investiture confers upon the loyal courtier the talents or capacities inherent in the honorific language. President Bush pronounces Judge Clarence Thomas "the best person in the country" for a seat on the Supreme Court, and lo and behold (on the instant and in a puff of newsprint), a third-rate jurist attains the stature of Felix Frankfurter or Oliver Wendell Holmes. *The New York Times Book Review* bestows on John Irving and Ann Beattie the rank of genius, and lo and behold (on the instant and in another puff of newsprint), two minor novelists become the peers of Tolstoy.

Similar investitures govern the manufacture of statesmen and military glory. The late Nelson Rockefeller discovered in Henry Kissinger an ambitious sophist and helped raise him to the office of national security adviser; Mr. Rockefeller's brother David accomplished the same marvel with Zbigniew Brzezinski. Although both gentlemen spoke with foreign accents (an advantage as much prized in national security advisers as it is in butlers), neither of them proved much good at diplomacy. Their advice was usually wrong, their judgment skewed to the advancement of their own careers, and their theories of the world twelve or fifteen years behind the train of events; but both gentlemen presented the facade expected of a proper statesman, and their patrons (the national media as well as the Rockefellers) were content to believe that they had imparted the gift of life to Pinocchio.

Against the urgency of the wish for the preferred appearance (whether of great wisdom or great power) facts offer as little resistance as leaves in an October wind. In the spring of 1991 the mass media longed for the return of a great hero, and they found one in the bluff and portly figure of General Norman Schwarzkopf. The general had presided over the suppression of what amounted to a poorly armed mob in Kuwait and Iraq, and he had shown himself to be an efficient traffic manager—by no means a brilliant commander, but convincing at press conferences and competent in the science of logistics. The American army never had to go to the trouble of fighting a battle on the ground, and the American air force never came up against any opposition in the air. General Schwarzkopf's forces conducted a kind of grandiose police raid, killing an unknown number of Iraqis (civilian as well as military) and laying waste to a country roughly the size of California.

But the country wanted to believe that the general had won a great and glorious victory, and the media staged a hero's welcome when he returned from the Persian Gulf in May to address a joint session of a grateful Congress. Standing in the well of the House of Representatives, the general blew up the balloons of self-congratulation: "The prophets of doom, the naysayers, the protesters and the flag burners all said that you would never stick by us. We knew better. We knew you'd never let us down. By golly, you didn't . . . we were the thunder and lightning of Desert Storm. We were the United States military, and we are damned proud of it."

The politicians rose as one person to decorate the general with a standing ovation, and the next day on the White House lawn

President Bush preened himself in the light of the general's new celebrity. Mr. Bush used the occasion to display his courtier's talent for hyperbole by saying of the general's largely untried army in the Arabian desert that it was "the finest fighting force this nation has ever known"—i.e., a finer army than the ones actually engaged in battle under the command of Generals Washington, Scott, Grant, Lee, Sherman, Pershing, Eisenhower, and Patton. *The New York Times* embroidered the pillow of flattery in June, when the general marched up Broadway under a cloud of ticker tape. The *Times* obligingly exaggerated the size of the crowds in the streets (4 million in the *Times*, 750,000 in the opinion of the police), and the reporter describing both the parade and the subsequent show of fireworks was equally generous with the rhetorical sentiment: "Fireworks lighted the velvet skies over the East River with chrysanthemums of red, white and blue, thundering pirouettes of silver and gold. Schwarzkopf crossed the Rubicon into history." By July 4 the general had become synonymous with an advertisement for America the beautiful, land of the free and home of the brave. A New York publisher paid five million dollars for his memoirs, and he posted his lecture fee at sixty thousand dollars and expenses. Less than a year later the war was forgotten, or was understood as a Pentagon trade show staged with live ammunition, and Schwarzkopf's reflections on blitzkrieg proved as worthless as Donald Trump's theories on New Jersey real estate. The result was unimportant. Like the war, Schwarzkopf's military prowess had been made for a moment's diversion.[9]

The commercial premise of the American intellectual markets defines truth as anything that pays the rent and the stockholders, and if this year's fashion has it that the United States has fallen into moral disrepair, then the publishers can hawk the bad news until the fashion changes, whereupon, next year or the year after, they can bring out the revisionist news that the United States is really a very nice place, much befouled by ungrateful literary critics. If in one season Richard Nixon can be promoted and sold as a crouching villain—a secondhand car salesman, an enemy of the people, etc.—in another season he can be promoted and sold as a benign elder statesman—experienced and wise, the soul of probity, etc. Properly marketed, both editions of the man can be processed into headlines, television time, and best-selling books.

Among the several shams promoted last summer by the Republican presidential campaign, the most fanciful as well as one of the most dishonest was the one about "the cultural elite"—the presumably sinister conspiracy of liberal opinion in New York and Los Angeles said to be corrupting the texts of American virtue. Both President Bush and Vice President Quayle described the conspiracy in words unctuously chosen to convey the impression of a vast company of anonymous malcontents whom it would be too dangerous to confront or to name. In answer to a question from Barbara Walters in late June on ABC, President Bush frowned at the camera and said, "I can't define what cultural elite means, but I know it when I see it." Vice President Quayle was slightly more forthcoming with his winks and smiles and brightly polished innuendos. If he provided only a few names—those of Mario Cuomo and Murphy Brown—at least he knew the whereabouts of the conspirators, and he wasn't afraid to say, as countless all-American demagogues have said before him, that they could be found in Hollywood film studios, in university libraries, in the offices of the news media. The Republican caricature of an American cultural elite was as grotesque as the Democratic caricature of the forgotten American middle class. The White House propagandists meant to condemn as wicked and immoral most of what they saw of the nation's intellectual theory and commercial entertainment, but they chose not to make distinctions between the various facets of the mass media, and they assigned to the wrong people the powers of fiends and demons. The manufacture and sale of America's cultural product is the work of very large, very profitable, and very timid corporations—Time Warner, the Washington Post Company, Harvard University, Fox Broadcasting, the Public Broadcasting System, Columbia Pictures. Such corporations define culture as anything that turns a profit—no matter how indecent the photograph or how tasteless the joke—and they seldom take chances with any book, movie, situation comedy, or rap song that fails to drum up a crowd.

The artisans who manufacture the nation's cultural product belong to different guilds—the film producers being bound by different rules and conventions from television anchorpersons or academic literary critics—but at all points on the assembly line they learn to tell their respective audiences what those audiences want and expect to hear. They have no choice in the matter if they wish to make the syndication deal, sell the paperback rights, win through to the safety of tenure. Better understood as courtiers and nervous careerists than as the angry voices of conscience, they could as easily be making sausage or Christmas toys. Many of them feel ashamed of the work made to the specifications of a market survey or a Nielsen rating—ashamed of the perfume commercials brushed with the scent of prurience, ashamed of the books they edit and the music assembled from scraps of pre-recorded sound. But what choice do they have if they hope to advance the token of their career around the Monopoly board of the standard American success? They follow a market or a trend, and very few of them can afford the luxury of an idea of their own.

Although I have spent the better part of twenty years in and around the New York literary bazaars, I have come across only a small number of people who can talk about any particular book at convincing length, and I don't think that I have met more than two or three writers who know much about the specific weights and measures of economics, medicine, history, law, finance, physics, or human anatomy. Their ignorance testifies to the enormous wealth of the United States that has made possible over the last thirty years the existence of a verbal class that needs do nothing but produce objects of language as ornate and often as lifeless and heavy as the jeweled chalices and gold figurines contrived for the greater glory of a Renaissance pope. Construing themselves as guests of the management, the ladies and gentlemen of literary rank define themselves by virtue of their moral and aesthetic attitudes and by their mutual recognition (or, more often, nonrecognition) of the states of refined feeling. Yes, they have read the reviews in the gazettes (usually with feelings of envy and spite), and yes, they can quote the price at which an author's reputation is trading on the literary exchanges, but of the book itself, of what the author actually said or didn't say, they have nothing more than a polite impression. They assimilate books in order to have an opinion, but they do not enjoy the act of reading, which, as every critic knows, interrupts the perfect contemplation of oneself. When writing reviews, the critics tend to award their most generous praise to those writers whom they least fear—to the brilliant young novelist in the provinces who obviously will never write a second novel, to the reliably mediocre historian who can be counted on for a vote in next year's prize committees, to the feminist poet who will think that she has been praised for her talent rather than her politics.

The false investitures synonymous with the courtier spirit debase the currency of the nation's thought in all its denominations (economic as well as aesthetic and political) but they always seem to me most poignant at the nation's better universities. On being asked to give a speech or conduct a seminar, I travel to Harvard or Stanford or the University of Michigan expecting to meet people who still can afford to say what they think. I find instead a faculty preoccupied with the great questions of tenure and preference. Everybody is studying the art of writing grant proposals or worrying about the proper forms of courteous address appropriate to the magnificence of the department chairman. The small talk at the faculty lunch resembles the conversation at the higher elevations of American corporate management, and the preferred jargon is as incomprehensible to the uninitiated as the court gossip in vogue among the residents at Versailles. The freedom of expression proves to be contingent upon the circumstances (permissible in some company, not in others), and the range of acceptable opinion bears comparison with the wingspan of a bumblebee.

The doctrines of political correctness enforce the routine disappearance of words once possessed of a clear or plain meaning, and the language that remains, almost all of it abstract, conforms to a standard of bland generality similar to the one pertaining in the second year of nursery school. The inhibitions reveal themselves as matters of inflection—a discreet pause or a small hesitation in the voice, suggesting that a current of unexamined thought might all too easily carry somebody too far downriver onto the shoals of sexual or racial insult. Everybody must remember what is phallocentric, and who is Eurocentric or Afrocentric, and when it is politic to remain silent. Some professors allow the use of the word *mankind* as a synonym for the human race; other professors insist on the term *humanity* or *humankind*. When pressed for statements of moral or aesthetic intent, almost everybody in the room takes refuge behind the screens of irony.

Probably I've been unlucky in my invitations and academic acquaintance, but I remember once being advised that it might be a mistake to teach a class on the thought and writing of H. L. Mencken. The university in question had just gone to the trouble of composing a "guideline" meant to protect the faculty and students from "verbal harassment," and it was thought that some of Mencken's more pungent statements might be misconstrued by impressionable sophomores. The department chairman was apologetic, but I could well understand his nervousness. Mencken was never a man to take too seriously the pieties of the age (his own or any other), and although I often hear it said that the public conversation would be much improved by Mencken's sardonic return, I expect that the mourners who regret his absence would find ever better reasons to regret his presence. The sage of Baltimore had an unfortunate habit of saying that African Americans (to whom he referred as "Moors") do not think as clearly (or at least along the same lines) as Protestant or Catholic Americans; that homosexuality constitutes a mental disorder rather than a sexual preference; that women, no matter how well meaning or enraged, simply cannot make art or law. None of these opinions would be welcomed with much enthusiasm on the op-ed pages of the nation's better newspapers. Neither would they be deemed appropriate for an appearance at Yale or Stanford University.

The same department chairman who warned me away from Mencken's ghost went on to explain that most academic discourse served the purpose of advancing one's career, and it was wrong to make judgments about the intellectual worth of the volumes of gibbering abstraction published by the university presses. The stuff was meant to be ornamental and inoffensive. Any instructor who made the mistake of provoking an argument was likely to forfeit both his parking space and his hope of tenure. It was much easier to bow to the prevailing orthodoxy (as graciously as possible and with learned allusions to Talleyrand or Francis Bacon) because then everybody could go busily forward with the business of soliciting fellowships and writing op-ed page pieces for *The New York Times*. Jokes, said the chairman, must always be clearly marked (like the surgeon general's warnings on packages of cigarettes), and censorship is a blessing in disguise.

On a train to New Haven in the winter of 1981 the late A. Bartlett Giamatti was even more explicit about what he called "the squalor of the courtier's lot." At the time he was president of Yale University, but he was also a Renaissance scholar, and he once had been an occasional contributor to *Harper's Magazine*. He resigned the column when he became president of Yale because his newfound eminence prevented him from writing or speaking in any language other than what he called "the higher institutional." It was a kind of court language, he said, all euphemism and nonsense, but it was the euphemism and nonsense expected of him, and he couldn't afford the risk of offending anybody who might bestow on the university the blessing of a large sum of money.

Coming across him by chance in Grand Central Station, I noticed that he looked a good deal more depressed than when I had seen him last, and I wondered how and why he had misplaced the offhand brilliance and spontaneity of mind that once prompted him to bursts of eloquence on topics as miscellaneous as Ezra Pound, feminist politics, capital punishment, the Boston Red Sox, and the salons of eighteenth-century France. Before the train cleared the Park Avenue tunnel, he explained that as president of Yale he no longer enjoyed the luxury of making candid remarks on any subject likely to rouse even the faintest murmur of controversy. I don't recall his exact words, but the gist of his melancholy was to the effect that it was the task of a university president to raise money from the alumni (or from the government or the charitable foundations or anybody with the price of a gymnasium), and so he was forever bending the courtier's knee to the ruling prejudices of the age, grinning at every rich man's joke, putting on whatever funny hat of a political cliché the donor of the new library wished him to put on. The thought moved him to bitter and mocking laughter. He had expected a university president to cut a more dignified figure in the world, maybe even that of a man to whom others might look for wisdom or moral example. I can still see his gaunt face clouded in cigarette smoke and the sardonic expression in his eyes as he stared out the window at the rain drifting through the hollow tenements of the South Bronx. "The university president as song and dance man," he said, "stepping lightly through the paces of the beggar's pantomime."

Because the courtier so obviously and so precariously hangs in the trapeze of his connections—at the Harvard faculty club, at the White House, at Citibank or ABC News—the poor wretch can never escape the feeling of weightlessness and dread. If everything is made of appearances, of images and gestures instead of blood or stone or thought, then everything can disappear at a moment's notice. The guests at court—aka "we happy few"—drift through their schedules in an all-but-constant state of panic. As the meaning of their existence becomes synonymous with court ritual and the striking of poses, they know themselves to be superfluous. The poses can be as easily sustained by almost anybody else, even by people as unlikely as Dan Quayle or Al Gore or Nancy Reagan's astrologer. The acute states of anxiety give rise to the urgent need for reassurance, and if the courtier cannot afford to trust his own intellect or his own emotion, then he must set about the great task of collecting badges confirming the news of his importance. In the eighteenth century the demand for the outward proofs of wisdom and magnificence could be satisfied with lands, horses, silk, and architecture. Let the noble lord feel a moment's doubt about his place in the world, and he might order a new coach or another palace. But in twentieth-century America the oligarchy is so bound by the conventions of a nominal egalitarianism that it no longer can flatter itself with a display of limestone or powdered wigs. Only a very few of the higher-ranking grandees can afford the imitations of the old luxury, and the vast bulk of the attendants at court make do with words: with the titles, dignities, and honorary degrees that contribute to the manufacture of a noble name—i.e., a listing at least twenty lines long in *Who's Who in America*.

Anybody who would be somebody thus spends his days accumulating credentials and campaign ribbons, publishing unintelligible treatises in the journals that enjoy the favor of the court (*Foreign Affairs*, the *Wilson Quarterly*, the *Harvard Business Review*, etc.), joining the proper clubs (Cosmos, Century, Duquesne, Pacific Union), making stately progresses to Bildeburg or the Bohemian Grove, worrying about the very best and most significant questions of the day (the environmental catastrophe, the new world order, nuclear weapons escaped from the arsenal of the old Soviet Union), appointing one another to ornamental commissions and boards of review, decorating each other with awards and prizes, traveling to conferences in Colorado or Switzerland for no other reason than that they should be noticed and marked present. It doesn't matter what the courtier has to say (if we assume, of course, that he says nothing offensive or impolite), and it doesn't matter whether he contributes by his going to London or Geneva even the slightest mote of useful service or advice. The important thing is to be seen at the fetes of the prince—whether at Pamela Harriman's dinner party, in Texas for the quail shooting, or writing for *The New York Review of Books*. What matters is one's presence—the name on the list and the picture in the papers.

Like the gentleman at Versailles who hid all night under the bed of the king and Madame de Montespan in hope of finding out what they thought of him, the ambitious American courtier will go to almost any length to secure his place in the light. The life and work of Henry Kissinger are the measure of an age of relentless

self-promotion, but he has many rivals for the laurels of effron-
tery, none in recent memory more industrious than Richard Darman, a Republican courtier of the first rank and as eager in his
search for more honors and higher office as a pig on the scent of a
truffle. Prior to his appointment by the Bush administration as
director of the Office of Management and Budget, Darman performed various services for the Reagan administration, and in
1985, when he moved from the White House staff to the Treasury
Department, he took with him a letter of praise signed by President Reagan. Handsomely framed and prominently displayed on
the wall of his new office, the letter awarded to Darman all the
credit for all the great works of Reagan's first term. Here at last
was the indispensable man, the aide-de-camp without whom the
president could do nothing, not even walk across Pennsylvania
Avenue to Lafayette Park or travel to Georgetown to make a five-
minute campaign speech. Darman composed the letter himself,
and it is worth quoting at some length because it illuminates the
shape of the man's grotesque ego:

> Your abilities, your intelligence, and your willingness to work
> long hours are well known in Washington because they have been
> your trademark for many years. With such an extraordinary com-
> bination of talents, there is no question in my mind that you could
> have been a success in any career you chose. But, while you have
> been successful in both the business and academic worlds, you
> have chosen to devote yourself instead to a career that has chiefly
> been oriented toward public service. Knowing you as I do, I know
> that it is your deep love of America, and your strong belief in its
> future greatness, that has impelled you to make this choice.[10]

Our desperate faith in the smiles and certificates of approval
makes a joke of our mythologies about the freestanding American individual: the American democrat; the child of nature; the
man against the system; the enemy of the status quo; Clint
Eastwood in the rain. We rehearse the phrases in our after-dinner
speeches, but mostly they are made for show. We are a people
who like to belong—to the team, the club, the company—and

more often than not we define ourselves by means of an institutional identity. Gratefully and at the going rates, we sacrifice our independence of mind for an official post, a membership, an appointment, a title. Without an institutional identity, the unaffiliated individual loses not only the desk and the car and the medical insurance but also the claim to credibility. The loss of a title corresponds to a sentence of exile, and I remember that when I was summarily dismissed as the editor of *Harper's Magazine* on an otherwise pleasant afternoon in August 1981, the telephone stopped ringing as abruptly as if the wires had been cut by terrorists in the hills. Most of my colleagues in the New York media trades—newspaper as well as periodical divisions—found it convenient to assume that I had gone to California or Europe. Writers who had effusively praised my judgment when they were hoping to publish their manuscripts in the magazine suddenly acquired the personae of vengeful avant-gardists condemning me as a Philistine who had murdered art. Two years later, when I regained the seals and emblems of office, the same writers proclaimed me the savior of American letters. The institutional identity corresponds to the honorific *de* attached to the names of the French nobility—R. de Mobil Oil, B. du *Washington Post*—and if two businessmen otherwise unknown to each other meet on an airplane or at a suburban wedding, the question, Who are you with? establishes their rank and determines which one owes the other what measures of attention, notice, and respect.[11]

Just as the smile of fortune always turns more easily in the direction of the careerist kneeling at the foot of his patron, the market in kings always has attracted a crowd of eager buyers. The impulse to prostrate oneself before the magnificence of the noble lord was not unknown to the authors of the American Constitution, and a quorum of Federalist merchants wished to confer on George Washington the honor and authority of a crown. Benjamin Franklin, himself an accomplished practitioner of the courtier's art, reminded an apprentice democrat in Philadelphia in the summer of 1776 of its seductions and rewards: "Sir, there are two passions which have a powerful influence on the affairs of men . . . the love of power and the love of money . . . when united in view of the same object, they have in many minds the most violent effects. Place before the eyes of such men a post of *honor* that shall at the same time be a place of *profit*, and they will move Heaven and earth to obtain it."

It is in the nature of human beings to delight in the comforts of flattery and praise (even if the praise is false and the flattery paid for by the publicity department), and it is also in the nature of human beings to honor the sovereign rule of appearances and bestow the gifts of patronage on those from whom they expect a favor in return. We live in a country that prides itself on its salesmanship, on its false architectural fronts and its genius for making something out of nothing. Civil magistrates, as well as corporation presidents, need as much help as they can get, and if they shore themselves up with whatever pomps and hypocrisies come easily to hand, why go to the trouble of condemning their traffic in counterfeit truths? Who can live without lies? If the fabric of authority is torn by revolution, then another tapestry made of the same poor stuff must, of necessity, replace it. What else is the advertising business if not the sovereign rule of appearances? To what other music does the world dance if not to the flutes and drums of the beggar's pantomime? It is a dance in which, at one time or another, we all join hands and bow. How else have we become a nation of talk show guests, skilled at striking poses and quick with one-line commentaries?

The question is one of degree. To what extent does the vaudeville dancing become the substance of a career, a reputation, a war, an economic policy, or a life? For how many more years can the country continue to squander the annual sum of four billion dollars on the fiction of the Strategic Defense Initiative (aka "Star Wars")? To what extent must we debase our schools in order to maintain the pretense that all students can meet the same standards and master the same curricula? The truth is precious, if only in very small amounts, and if thought and language evolve from the transformation of human experience, the systematic perversion of intellect and the routine distortion of language constitute an attack (literally as well as figuratively) on another person's life. People who tell themselves too many lies ("when I am elected . . ."; "when your grandmother dies . . ."; "when my wife gives me a divorce . . .") commit a form of suicide. Failing to hold themselves responsible (i.e., capable of response) to the summons calling them to become more than they thought they could become, they destroy the chance of their own freedom. The same thing can be said of governments, most especially of democracies. More than anything else we have need of a believable story because without a believable story we have no means of connecting the past to the present, the dead to the living, the citizen to the state, the now to the then.

The courtier's art is harmless enough when it is practiced with a degree of self-knowledge—to hustle the book or sell the car. The effect is usually comic, and when I read in the papers that Richard Nixon has been elevated to the rank of statesman (or that Mobil Oil is the avuncular friend of the American people, or that a shirt by Ralph Lauren will certify my admission into the ruling class), the disproportion between the nouns and the adjectives reminds me of the clowns who come running into the circus ring wearing tiny hats and immense sneakers.

The comedy becomes slightly darker when the interested parties begin to believe their own press notices. The television and publishing media award Alan Dershowitz the reputation of an incomparable trial lawyer in homage to his talent for publicity rather than in recognition of his record in appeals cases, which, as of the summer of 1992, stood at nine wins and thirty-nine losses. The sales pitch convinces Mike Tyson and Leona Helmsley, who hire the advertisement and go, more or less directly, to jail. American Express invents the miracle of the Optima card, extending generous credit to those of its customers distinguished by their feats of conspicuous consumption, and within a matter of months the company acquires bad debts in the amount of $2.5 billion. The New York *Daily News* portrays John Gotti as a gangster invulnerable to the nets and snares of the law, and Gotti, admiring his reflection in the mirror of page 1, becomes so

careless of his conversation that he boasts of his crimes in rooms
wired for FBI sound. During President Reagan's two terms in
office the United States borrowed so much money from foreign
creditors that the country was forced to sell a fair percentage of its
assets in order to maintain the illusions of wealth and power and
ease. The reversal of fortune was presented as a victory, and for
eight years the Reagan administration insisted that nothing of
any importance had changed in the world since the glorious
American triumphs in 1945. Precisely at the moment that the
country was going ruinously bankrupt, the court society in
Washington was chattering complacently to itself about the resto-
ration of "America's pride," about Americans "standing tall" in
the company of nations, about America setting the examples of
capitalist thrift for the refugees from a bankrupt communism.

The comedy begins to shade into tragedy when the sovereign
rule of appearances becomes so oppressive as to deny even the
slightest whisper of contradiction. All the accounts that I've ever
read of seventeenth- and eighteenth-century courts—by Swift,
Saint-Simon, Diderot, and La Bruyère—suggest that they were
remarkable for their suffocating conformity as well as for the
pettiness and malevolence of the resident intrigue. The same stale
atmospheres pervade a good many American institutions large
enough and rich enough to sustain their own hermetic systems of
an artificial reality. To the extent that people feel themselves weak
or impotent or small, they assign immense importance to the
rituals of court etiquette, and they learn to speak and think in the
private codes and secret languages known only to themselves.
The pressures of economic recession exaggerate both their fear
and their egoism. The fewer the means and opportunities that a
society allows for generating wealth, substance, and achievement, the more subtle the refinements of the courtier spirit. If a
man cannot make his own estate, then he must steal it or accom-
modate himself to the increasingly exquisite appetites of his
patrons.[12]

In Paris in 1782 Franklin worried that the rumors of ease and
prosperity in the American colonies were likely to attract moun-

tebanks and idle aristocrats, and he took pains to write what he called "An Information for Those Who Would Remove to America" in order to make clear that the sort of people who were wanted in the new country were those who possessed what he welcomed as "any useful art." Not the "gentlemen of quality" who knew how to do "nothing of value." Not courtiers; not the parasitical company of "the explaining classes" insisting on old custom and inherited privilege—but rather mechanics and smiths and carpenters, the sort of people likely to shape their lives and circumstances with whatever materials came readily to hand. Democracy is about the freedom to make and think and build, not about the king's license to plunder and exploit. "As I would not be a slave," said Lincoln, "so I would not be a master. This expresses my idea of democracy. Whatever differs from this, to the extent of the difference, is no democracy."

In the same way that the court at Washington feeds off the productive and regenerative organs still operative elsewhere in the country, so also the camp followers in the palaces of culture consume the stores of art and intellect accumulated by people who weren't afraid of the imagination. The decline of the nation's economic productivity in the last twenty years runs parallel to the loss of vitality in the arts. Deferring to the bias against risk, a generation of business executives submits to the consensus of dithering committees, and a generation of critics polishes the furniture and amuses itself with brilliant glosses on the work of genius long deceased. The fashion in nostalgia bespeaks a fear not only of the imagination but also of the unknown. People who cannot project the future rummage through the past as if through a trunk of theatrical costumes. They exhaust themselves in the frenetic gossip of the auction houses and squander their talents on parody and slander. But no matter how clever their phrases, the court chamberlains have no choice but to stand with the splendor of money and against the creativeness of mind.

The natural antipathy between the courtier spirit and the democratic spirit embodies the old and bitter argument between time past and time future, between the inertia of things-as-they-are and the energy inherent in the hope of things-as-they-might-become. Under a republican dispensation, authority attaches itself to a specific knowledge or skill, and individuals retain their offices only as long as their strategies succeed or their theories meet the proofs of experiment. The more necessary the services of a governing class, the more numerous its numbers and the shorter the span of its dominion.

So volatile a state of affairs is intolerable to the societies at court. The courtier spirit is about the wish to make time stand still, about being, not becoming. The possibility of change—in the arts and sciences as well as in the political or commercial orders—does too much damage to everybody's self-esteem. A ruling class founded on its knowledge or capacity would be too quickly superseded, and the happy few would find themselves too abruptly deprived of the privileges of rank. Whether at Versailles in the eighteenth century or among the American oligarchies in the late twentieth century, the time at court is always noon. Favors come and favors go, and so do wars and presidents, but the court lives forever in the land of the perpetual present, preserved—in Hollywood and the universities as well as in Washington—in the precious amber of incumbency. Nobody ever wants to return to his or her landed estate in Brittany or Oklahoma. On falling afoul of the king's pleasure at Versailles, the French nobles found little comfort in the country. It didn't matter that their estates were spacious and their servants as numberless as the fig trees. Having lost their places at what they deemed to be the center of the world, they thought themselves marooned in a woodcutter's hut, and their letters drooped with a sense of inconsolable loss. A similarly mournful tone drifts through the conversation of deposed company vice-presidents, politicians out of office, and English professors without tenure. During the winter that I met Giamatti on the train to New Haven I remember discovering four former editors of *Newsweek* drinking morosely in the bar at the Century Club, telling each other their melancholy stories about the day on which Katharine Graham had remanded each of them to oblivion. The empty expressions on their faces reminded me of an expression I have often seen on the faces of aging celebrities—the same pathetic hope for a happy return to the klieg lights and the gossip columns. Listening to the murmur of their regret, I could imagine Zsa Zsa Gabor on a gray Sunday afternoon at the wrong end of Wilshire Boulevard, posing as eagerly as an ingenue for the cover photograph of a supermarket flier.

Assuming that they know all the important people in the world, the ladies and gentlemen at court further assume that anybody that they don't know is, by definition, unimportant. God forbid that the world might be changed by some unknown physicist or anonymous computer programmer or by an obscure despot at work somewhere on an island with a name that nobody can pronounce. It is the people at court who shape the clay of events and weave the loom of history, and if they busily come and go from room to room, speaking not only of Michelangelo but also of the Laffer curve, it would be unfair to denounce them as liars and frauds. The attendants at court do not tell calculated lies in the manner recommended by Machiavelli and practiced by Bismarck. I'm sure that President Bush believed in the existence of a new world order, in much the same way that New York literary critics believe in the existence of an American literature or the Hollywood claque at the bar in Spago believes that Oliver Stone is a great movie director.

The courtier believes because he must believe and because acquiescence in the lie or the half-truth is so much easier than thinking for oneself. The courtiers tell themselves stories, like children talking about what they see in the shadows on their nursery walls or like superstitious seamen filling up the empty spaces on their maps with drawings of fabulous beasts. The gentlemen who stand on the left-hand side of the king's bedchamber sometimes use the word *fascist*, but they seldom intend a comparison with Italy in the 1920s. They mean to say that they are mad at the United States and that their names have been left off the king's birthday list. The gentlemen of the right, who mark their maps with red crayons instead of blue, talk about the serpents of government regulation. Like the child who announces that there is a dragon in his bathtub, more often than not they wish to say that they don't want to take a bath.

Not that the court is averse to merit or talent. Nothing so pleases the ambitious courtier as the chance to fawn upon a statesman whom he can mistake for Metternich or a novelist whom he can confuse with Tolstoy. But if he cannot tell the difference between Metternich and James Baker, or between Tolstoy and Philip Roth, he must content himself with the effigies endorsed by the smiling favor of his prince. It is quite possible that somebody might write a good book and even be congratulated for doing so by *The New York Times*; it is equally possible that the Ford Foundation will award a research grant to a scientist capable of useful and original work. Such things sometimes happen. They fall within the category of happy accident, and they justify, at least for the time being and much to everybody's satisfaction and relief, the pretensions of the institution awarding the titles and degrees.

Were it not for the stupidity implicit in the play of the courtier spirit, the stupidity and the fear of the future, the telling of so many welcome lies might play indefinitely as comedy. If given a choice in the matter, who would not rather bring something agreeable to say, distributing money and honors as carelessly as grass seed, admiring the furniture, praising the paintings and the children, reporting the newest gossip, waiting for instructions, handing out prizes and honorary degrees? Unhappily, and as Giamatti, to his sorrow, well understood, people reduced to playing the role of the courtier cannot afford to admit acquaintance with their own thought or their own feeling. Admiring everything and nothing, they conceal a servant's envious rage behind the mask of an ingratiating smile and so abandon not only their courage of mind but also the chance of making a future that doesn't already belong to somebody else.

3

Versailles on the Potomac

AT COURT, PEOPLE EMBRACE WITHOUT

ACQUAINTANCE, SERVE ONE ANOTHER

WITHOUT FRIENDSHIP, AND INJURE ONE

ANOTHER WITHOUT HATRED.

—*Lord Chesterfield*

Like the notables assembled under the king's roof at Versailles, official Washington divides the known world into only two parts. First there is Washington, and then there is every place else. The planes arriving and departing National Airport cross the only frontier of any consequence—the one between the inside and the outside—and all the truly momentous topics of conversation center on only one question, which is always and unfailingly the same: Who's in and who's out? The court might seem to be

talking about something else—about war or peace or racial hatred or the deficit—but the words serve a decorative or theatrical
purpose, and they are meant to be admired for their polished
surfaces, as if they were mirrors or gilded chairs. What's important is what happens in Washington. Yes, it might be interesting
to know that the United States now must pay $292 billion a year
in interest on the national debt, and yes, the poor blacks in the
slums of Los Angeles obviously have their reasons to riot, but
their suffering is far away and in another country, and what
matters is the way in which the story plays tomorrow morning at
the White House or the Department of Defense. Who will come,
and who will go? Who will occupy the office overlooking the
lawn? Who will ride in the secretary's limousine, and who will
carry the president's messages? Court ritual obliges all present to
wear the masks of grave concern and utter the standard phrases of
alarm ("year of maximum danger," "America at the crossroads,"
"the crisis of the cities"), but behind the facade of solemn euphemism, the accomplished courtier conceals the far more urgent
question, What, please, God, is going to happen to *me?*

The masks come loose when the possession of the White
House passes from one political party to the other and the would-
be servants of the new world order parade their ambition in plain
sight. The spectacle is marvelous to behold, and in the days and
weeks following the election of Bill Clinton the news from Washington might as well have been extracted from an eighteenth-
century book of court etiquette. On the Wednesday after the
election the important columnists in town began making their
bows and curtsies by comparing the new president with the
young Jack Kennedy, and the more gracious members of the
troupe professed to see rising from the mists of the Arkansas
River the fabled towers of Camelot. Mo Sussman's, a restaurant
much frequented by the city's principal careerists, added Arkansas Stew to its menu, and at the better markets in Georgetown
the salesclerks murmured their appreciation of fried green toma-
toes and sweet potato pie. The Securities Industry Association
obligingly replaced its executive director, a Republican, with a

Democrat who had known Bill Clinton at Oxford. Similarly abrupt exits and entrances took place in the executive offices of Hill and Knowlton, a consortium of prominent influence peddlers, and at the American Bankers Association.

On Thursday afternoon, less than thirty-six hours after the polls had closed in California, Jack Kent Cooke, the owner of the Washington Redskins, discovered that he was acquainted with a surprisingly large number of Democrats. An invitation to sit in his box at RFK Stadium counts as one of the most visible proofs of rank within the Washington nobility, and during the fat years of the Reagan triumph and the Bush succession the sixty-four seats were comfortably stuffed with personages as grand as Edwin Meese, George Will, and Robert Mosbacher. But on that Thursday, in answer to a question from a correspondent for *The New York Times*, Mr. Cooke remembered that time passes and fashions change: "I'm a Republican, but strangely I have a great many Democrat friends. Dodd. Brzezinski. Greenspan—he's of indeterminate lineage. Sam Donaldson—what's he? Gene McCarthy and George McGovern."

The reporter asked if Mr. Cooke knew of any football fans among President Clinton's circle of dependents and admirers. " 'You must understand,' Mr. Cooke said. 'The box is not used to ingratiate myself with the administration. Please quote me precisely on that. I invite people who are good company, happy, cheerful, good-humored people who love football.' "

Over the first weekend of the new revelation the publications that provide the court with topics of conversation—*The New York Times* and *The Washington Post* as well as *Time* and *The New Republic*—began rearranging the furniture in the drawing rooms of power. Previously resplendent figures much praised for their infallible judgment—among them James Baker, the once-upon-a-time secretary of state—were seen in the light of the Democratic dawn as shabby impostors, as far behind the times as the old baseball glove that President Bush had brought with him from the playing fields at Yale. Together with the work of revision, the court gazettes published the first in a long series of ornamental opinion pieces—from former ambassadors and deputy secretaries of state, directors of policy institutes, eager Harvard professors, and economists in exile—meant to prove their authors deserving of an appointment to Paris or the National Security Council. Other voices in other rooms proclaimed their love of the environment and their interest in the saxophone, and at Wonder Graphics Picture Framing on Vermont Avenue, the owner of the store beheld a vision of prosperity: " 'Everyone's going to have to hang up new pictures in their offices,' [he] said. 'They're going to be putting up new Clinton-Gore glad-handing pictures. They're going to need framing, and we do a very nice job.' "

Through the month of November, as the dance of grace and favor became both more desperate and more refined, I noticed that people long associated with Republican causes, with supply side economics and weekends shooting quail in the company of Senators Simpson and Gramm, proposed themselves as voices of bipartisan conscience. Robert Strauss, the Washington lobbyist whom President Bush had appointed ambassador to Russia, appeared on network television to say that he once had been chairman of the Democratic National Committee and that he had voted, out of conviction and with a whole heart, for Bill Clinton.

Even in New York the conversations often veered off into the niceties of Washington protocol. One morning over breakfast at the Regency Hotel with a government lawyer whom I had last seen in the twilight of the Carter administration, I was surprised to find myself talking about the Roman emperor Marcus Aurelius. The lawyer ordinarily didn't concern herself with events to which she couldn't attach living witnesses as well as a handsome fee, and I remembered her once telling me that history was the refuge of men who were afraid of the world. It wasn't until we had come to the end of the emperor's reign—his stoicism, his persecution of Christians, his bestowal of the empire on Commodus—that she informed me of Clinton's fondness for the late emperor's *Meditations*. She had been invited to a dinner given by one of Clinton's economic advisers, and she wished to make a subtle reference—as if derived from long reflection rather than a quick briefing—to the emperor's noble melancholy.

Three days later, in conversation with a professor of biochemistry at Yale, I was asked to speak for twenty minutes about the significance of Rachel Carson and Yevgeny Yevtushenko. The professor had heard that photographs of those two individuals were to be seen on the walls of Al Gore's office in the Senate, and if he could connect the metaphysical dots between the American environmentalist and the Soviet poet, then maybe, when he went to Washington in a week's time to apply for a post at the Environmental Protection Agency, he might know what else to say after he had made his ritual devotions to the Manchurian tiger and the Japanese crane.

At the court of Louis XIV in seventeenth-century France, people occupied themselves with the great work of making small distinctions: those greeted at the door; those offered armchairs; those deemed worthy of being seen off in their coaches. In official Washington in late-twentieth-century America the court occupies itself with similar distinctions: those assigned government cars; those awarded parking spaces at National Airport; those invited to sit in Jack Kent Cooke's box at RFK Stadium. Against the sum of such tremendous trifles, the questions of yesterday's riot or tomorrow's debt beat as heavily as the wings of moths.

I can admire Washington for its trees, for its monuments and some of its stately public buildings, but I have trouble with the stately inhabitants. So few of them know how to laugh at their own pretension, and so many of them mistake themselves for statues. The court society in Washington was made by the cold war, and my dislike of it, which was as immediate as it was instinctive, was formed in the autumn of 1957, within the first twenty minutes of a conversation in what was then the headquarters tent of the CIA. Dwight Eisenhower was president, and the United States stood at the zenith of its dream of empire. Europe was still in ruins, and the Japanese hadn't yet learned how to make cars or television cameras. Like many other Americans of my experience and generation, I assumed that I had inherited the mandate of heaven. Any American under the age of twenty-five (i.e., somebody young enough to have missed the lessons of both the depression and the Second World War) apparently could do anything he pleased: make war or peace or civilization; become a poet or a statesman; bribe despots; build roads or cyclotrons; finance revolutions; distribute justice and bestow the gift of constitutional democracy on Spanish noblemen and Chinese bandits. Although the gilding on the Pax Americana was beginning to wear a little thin, it was still possible in those days to think that the Communist hordes had to be prevented from sacking the holy cities of Christendom, and the CIA attracted many of the nation's most idealistic young men, all of them eager to leave at once, preferably at night and under an assumed name, for Berlin.

The agency's written examination lasted the better part of a week, and then, after a discreet interval, I was summoned to a preliminary interview with four or five operatives in their early thirties who introduced themselves as "some of the junior guys." The interview took place in one of the Quonset huts near the Lincoln Memorial that had served as the agency's temporary quarters during World War II. The feeling of understated supremacy, of a ramshackle building hastily assembled for both a moral and an imperial purpose, was further exaggerated by the studied carelessness of the young men asking the questions. For weeks I had reviewed the maps and outlines of European history, and I had come to the interview expecting to discuss the Fulda Gap or the risings of the Danube. Instead I found myself being asked the names of the girls who sailed boats off Fishers Island or who had won the golf tournaments in Southampton and Bedford Hills. As the conversation drifted through the course of polite inanity (about "personal goals" and "one's sense of achievement in life"), the young men every now and then exchanged an enigmatic reference to "that damn thing in Laos." Trying very hard not to be obvious about it, they gave me to understand that they were playing the big varsity game of the cold war. Their complacence was as smooth as their matching silk handkerchiefs and ties, and before I got up to leave, apologizing for having applied to the wrong office, I understood that I had been invited to drop around to the common room of the best fraternity in the world so that the admissions committee could find out if I was "the right sort."

The interview at the CIA introduced me to a tone of voice that over the last thirty-five years I've found to be characteristic of the conversation in the E Ring of the Pentagon and the West Wing of the White House as well as of the talk at Georgetown dinner parties and the gossip in the editorial offices of *The Washington Post*. The voice is faintly contemptuous or faintly amused but always as self-satisfied as Vice President Quayle's moralisms or as condescending as David Brinkley's Sunday morning television commentary. It is the voice of Henry Kissinger explaining to the woman seated next to him at dinner that a nation, like an ambitious hostess, cannot afford to invite unsuccessful people to its parties. It is the voice of McGeorge Bundy, who told an audience of scholars in the early 1960s that he was getting out of Latin American studies because Latin America was such a second-rate place. It is the voice of Jeane Kirkpatrick finding something pleasant to say about this year's congenial dictator or the State Department announcing its solidarity with Cambodia and expressing only mild regret about the regime's program of genocide. It is the sign sponsored by the Riggs Bank and posted at National Airport saying, WELCOME TO THE MOST IMPORTANT CITY ON EARTH.

The bland young men in the Quonset hut under the dogwood trees defined truth as an adjective that always modified the nouns of ambition, and the CIA's subsequent performance in Cuba, Vietnam, Iran, and what was once the Soviet Union stands as a lesson in the grammar of political expedience. At the behest of various presidents a succession of compliant CIA directors (all of them made of the same accommodating stuff as George Bush) rearranged the intelligence estimates (about Vietcong troop strength or the geography of the Bay of Pigs, about the military and economic capacities of the Soviet Union, about the Arab oil reserves and the democratic aspirations of the shah of Iran) in order to align the facts with whatever preferred image of the world happened to be in fashion at the White House. Judged by the standards of intellectual honesty, the record is a disgrace; weighed in the balance of Washington politics, the record can be judged a success as great as the savings and loan swindle because the events that followed from the deconstruction of the texts advanced the careers of the court officials who revised or deleted the offending paragraphs.

Over the last thirty-odd years some of the Washington scenery has changed (the newer hotels and office buildings aping the opulence of the Reagan era), and so have some of the political clichés (reduced from twelve words to four), but no matter which administration finds itself in office, the society at court occupies the same hall of mirrors—gazing at its reflection in the "Style" section of *The Washington Post*. The charades and photo opportunities may have become more refined and carefully staged than the alarms and excursions of the early 1960s (Kennedy's Berlin crisis becomes Johnson's Vietnam War becomes Reagan's adventure in Grenada becomes Bush's invasions of Panama and the Persian Gulf), but the attendants at court still prostrate themselves before the majesty of a sovereign appearance, and the decorous and expedient lie still takes precedence over the plain or inconvenient truth. The display of power is the proof of power, and the court is forever measuring the size of a minister's office, counting the number of his adherents, remarking on the space devoted to his image in the newspapers or the talk shows. In 1957 the president of the United States made do with a White House staff numbering no more than 1,218; by 1992 the president couldn't get from one day to the next without a suite of retainers (among them 4 food tasters and 5 florists) that number no fewer than 1,767. The president travels with an entourage (speech writers, Secret Service agents, valets, and newspaper reporters, as well as florists and food tasters) that would have appeased the vanity of Louis XIV.

Comparable degrees of self-aggrandizement describe the

whole enterprise of a government that now employs, in imitation of the magnificence that was once the Palace of Versailles, an opulent household of domestic servants (upper, lower, congressional, regulatory, etc.) comprising as many as three million clerks, functionaries, orators, consultants, briefing officers, press and appointment secretaries, aides-de-camp, weapons analysts, chauffeurs, grooms, speech writers, cooks, media spokespersons, and teachers of aerobics. The splendor of so vast an expenditure flatters the Washington bureaucracies in the belief that the public money is their own. The members of Congress acquire the luxurious tastes of the corporate nobility, in the meantime inflating the sum of the taxpayers' debt (one trillion dollars in 1980; four trillion dollars in 1992); the federal agencies invent more regulations under which the government can exercise the rights of droit du seigneur; the Supreme Court goes quietly and efficiently about the business of changing a civil liberty or civil right into a favor that may or may not be bestowed by a de facto House of Lords.[13]

What John Adams would have recognized as the corollary delirium of pride and vanity becomes more insufferable as the courtiers become more numerous and more accustomed to larger expenses and more expansive claims to privilege. The delirium is often fanciful and almost always absurd, but among its many recent manifestations I like best the one about the delicacy of feeling among the upper servants at the World Bank. The highly placed officials (seventy-four in number) draw salaries averaging $120,000 a year for bringing the blessings of usury to the poorer places of the earth. Three or four years ago, in a moment of thrift or conscience, the bank thought to reduce the cost of sending its officials on charitable missions to countries as destitute as Guatemala and Zaire. A bank official named Michael Irwin returned from a trip to East Africa with the extraordinary news that he had saved $1,900 by flying business class instead of first class. He wrote a memorandum pointing out that the bank would save $12 million a year if its nuncios could bear to subject themselves to a lesser degree of comfort. The response was as prompt as it was indignant. One of the bank's senior vice-presidents dispatched a countermemorandum saying, "My family and I will not feel safe again until Mr. Irwin has been replaced by someone who really cares."

The tone of voice would have been perfectly understood in the galleries of Versailles. So also the servants of the Sun King would have understood Nancy Reagan's special requirements when traveling in state. The lady liked to sleep in her own bed, and she had a passion for the color red. Prior to her departure for a journey of more than three days and two nights in any foreign city, the air force shipped a replica of her bed to the suite of rooms assigned to her use. The workmen who installed the bed were also under orders to paint the walls red (no matter how ancient or beautiful the residence in question) and to rehang all the mirrors in all the rooms and all the corridors at the specific height dictated by Mrs. Reagan's sense of dignified proportion. When she looked into a mirror hung at a normal height, she sometimes saw nothing other than the top of her head. The effect was unflattering. It reminded Mrs. Reagan that she could be mistaken for a dwarf, and her mood for the rest of the day was unlikely to contribute much to the cause of world peace.

The veneers of luxury make more visible the inward presumptions of grace, and it is no accident that among the country's ten richest counties (as measured by per capita income) five comprise the expensive suburbs of Washington, D.C. Over the course of the last thirty years Arlington County, Virginia, and Montgomery County, Maryland, have eclipsed Marin County, California, or Fairfield County, Connecticut, as proofs and symbols of "the good life." The common citizen—i.e., any individual or corporation that cannot afford to hire a friend at court—now works five months a year just to pay his or her taxes—i.e., 42 percent of his income presented as a tithe to a government that in 1990 squandered, by the estimate of its own comptroller of the currency, $180 billion on the luxuries of mismanagement and fraud. Nor does the government feel the least compunction about falsifying its accounts or lying to the electorate about its use of the public money. Prior to the tax and budget summit of October 1990, the Bush administration announced that the granting of a tax increase would reduce the deficit for the following year to the modest sum of $63.1 billion. Six months later, after receiving the favor of the tax increase, the government reported the 1991 deficit at $318.1 billion, and by the end of 1991 the sum had been raised to $384.6 billion—an error of $321.5 billion over the span of a single year's accounting. The numbers speak to the contempt with which the court at Washington regards the American public.

The habit of mind supports the belief, widely held among the ladies and gentlemen at ease on the banks of the Potomac (and openly expressed as the statist bias of the Clinton administration), that wealth is conditional rather than absolute. People elsewhere in the country might imagine that wealth is the product of creative energy and thought or that it belongs to the individuals from whose labor it is derived. Washington thinks otherwise. Wealth is a gift of the state, the product of a tax exemption or a federal regulation, not the work of a carpenter or an engineer or an architect, but something made by the stroke of a functionary's pen, by the inclusion or omission of a single clause in a funding bill, by a word whispered in the ear of one's client or patron. Fortune's smile is the smile of the courtier, the consultant, the lobbyist, the friend of Lloyd Bentsen or Dan Rostenkowski. For the time being the government claims only a little less than half of all the revenues produced by the citizenry, but the gossip in court circles suggests that this sum already has been deemed too small. President Clinton's economic advisers mention the pressing need for more tax money, and officeholders of all ranks complain that they have not been given funds adequate to the monumental works of social engineering. They assume that the national revenue is more appropriately employed by the state, and the money retained by the populace they regard as a donative granted to an ungrateful rabble that scatters the court's largess on idle pleasures and foolish toys. Although admired and excessively praised as an abstraction, the American people, when encountered in person, offend the sensibilities of the court. The American people buy ugly pickup trucks and tract houses in the environs of Duluth; they go to Disneyland and discount stores; they talk to themselves on CB radios and gape at prime-time television. So crass a spectacle sickens the courtiers educated to the exquisite refinement of moral disputes about the meaning of justice or the rights of the unborn. Given their institutional allegiances as well as the urgency of their own ambitions, they identify the national interest with the several interests of the state, not with the multifarious interests of the individuals subsumed under the rubric of "the American people." People die from time to time, but they can be easily replaced. The state is immortal, and so, please God, are the courtiers who stand close to the knee of the prince.

Very early in my acquaintance with Washington I was made to understand the difference between the appearance and the substance of a thing. Appearances were light, and substances were heavy. An appearance could be shifted as easily as a potted palm, and on different days of the week, or in different committees of the Congress, it could be transformed into something that it was not. Substance resembled alimony and steamer trunks. The distinction was explained to me in the first year of the Kennedy administration by a friend from college with whom I had studied the histories of Henry Adams and the novels of Henry James. He had meant to become a professor of nineteenth-century English literature, but he had been caught up in the enthusiasms of "the new frontier," and he had come to Washington with the vanguard of intellectual mercenaries that Kennedy rallied to the banners of moral crusade. Within a few months of his arrival he found himself translated into an administrative assistant on Capitol Hill, and by way of instructing me in the uses of his newfound powers, he received me in the senator's inner office. The senator at the time was traveling in the home counties, and my friend had been left with the authority to hear petitions, answer the mail, and grant the small favors of patronage.

"Letters of recommendation for kids who want to go to Annapolis or West Point," he said. "Intercessions with the Immigration Service on behalf of somebody's cousin in Palermo.

Statements against illiteracy and leukemia. Small stuff. The bone and marrow of democracy."

It was clear that he delighted in his role as tribune of the people, and I noticed that he had cut his fingernails and adopted the habit of wearing a tie. He had kept his beard, but it was neatly combed and trimmed, and even before he offered me one of the senator's cigars, I could see that I was talking to an apprentice statesman and not to an obscure literary hack in a dim and irrelevant library. Despite our prior acquaintance at college, he informed me that he was speaking secretly, "on deep background, you understand," and I still feel bound to the condition that then obtained. He since has become a fairly grand figure in Washington, a Monsieur R. with a long list of titles attached to his name. To the best of my knowledge he has changed his political ideology at least three times during the last thirty years, but he has retained his gift for vituperation and innuendo, and I would not like to bring down on my head the wrath of his policy institute.

Imagine then the young Monsieur R., eager and ambitious and clever, seated with his feet on the senator's desk, smoking one of the senator's cigars, occasionally interrupting the flow of his discourse to answer the phone or sign a letter. He was a vain and self-important man, combining in his own person most of the worst traits of "The McLaughlin Group," but he was no fool, and he had been diligent in his study of the Congress. At college he had the knack for paying attention in class, and during the two years of service to a politician whom he had learned to despise, he had read all the briefing books, all the testimony, and all the tabulations of all the votes.

He had come to understand that the Congress didn't wish to govern. Certainly it didn't want to correct any of the country's more difficult or intractable social disorders. Solutions belonged to the realm of substance, heavy and unpleasant. Somebody had to lose something, give something up, accept the bitterness of limitation, or sacrifice, or restraint. Solutions implied pain, and pain was unacceptable because pain translated into resentment, and resentment lost votes.

It was the summer of 1963, and I was still close enough to my own reading of history to try to refute the argument on the authority of Jefferson. I said something to the effect that the men who had the courage and the self-confidence to write the Constitution accepted both the necessity and the unworthiness of government. I think I even remembered enough of my reading to come up with Jefferson's explicit statement on the subject: "I have no ambition to govern men. It is a painful and thankless office."

The young Monsieur R. shrugged, smiled, nodded, knocked ashes off the senator's cigar, opened his hands in a gesture of amused indifference.

"Which is why we do as little governing as possible, and then only under protest, or if we find ourselves temporarily short of funds."

Many years later I listened to Senator Daniel Patrick Moynihan elaborate the same point with reference to his own reading of the role of senior senator from New York. We had been scheduled to appear on the same radio program, and while we were passing the time in the greenroom, Moynihan echoed the confession of the New York banker who had said that he counted himself lucky if even half his decisions proved correct. Observing that no politician could possibly know or understand everything that his audiences expected him to know or understand, Moynihan ran through the long list of subjects on which he was supposed to be fully and definitively informed—education, health care, foreign policy, highway construction, the multiplication of cancer cells, etc.—and then he laughed at the absurdity of the proposition.

"The thing is impossible," he said, "but I'm not allowed to admit that it's impossible. If the people guessed how little their rulers know, they might become frightened."

Given the expectations of infallibility, Moynihan said, the rulers of the state must pretend to know what they are doing or saying, and so government becomes representative in the theatrical, not the constitutional, sense of the word.

"It's like a fourth-grade Christmas play," he said. "The little boy comes out onstage wearing a crown of paper stars and saying that he's the north wind. I do the same thing when I stand in front of a microphone and answer questions about the intelligence services or what happened to the cold war."

He laughed again, more merrily than before, and when he was called into the studio, he paused in the doorway to strike a theatrical pose. Looking over his shoulder, he said: "Enter the north wind."

Across the span of the thirty years between my encounters with Moynihan and the young Monsieur R., all of the ceremonial displays of government with which I am familiar have met their standards of nursery school pageant. The art of Washington politics consists in the maintenance of the facade of government, and the aesthetic taste of the court shows itself in the promulgation of laws composed in a language so encrusted with the semiprecious stones of legal abstraction as to defy not only the erosion of time but also the understanding of the heathen. Washington is a city of words, but words understood as objects and tokens of power, words as ends in themselves (like marble fountains or fireworks displays), not as a means of expression or thought. The sovereign rule of appearances sets the terms of the conversation at court, and the uses of language bear resemblance to the arts of interior decoration. If rendered in silk or stone, Washington's manufacture of words, its hundreds of millions of pages of notes—documents, briefs, abstracts, speeches, memorandums, studies, bills, circulars, reports, and treaties—would be seen to possess a grandeur surpassing that of the tapestries of Versailles or the mosaics of Byzantium.

What is wanted is not so much a policy, or even money, as the appearance of a policy—a word or an image sufficient to sustain the impression of virtuous authority, of a government that knows what it is about, of people who are in command of events or who at least have some sort of idea in their dignified and well-dressed heads. The court acquires its opinions for reasons of fashion or state, as if they were gilt swords or enameled snuffboxes, bought, at modish expense, from the artificers at the American Enterprise Institute or the Brookings Institution. Nobody cares what the words mean as long as they can serve as scenery appropriate to the performance of the ritual masques and dances presented to the public under the headlines of WATERGATE SCANDAL, or BUDGET CRISIS, or WAR IN THE GULF, or NEW WORLD ORDER. Different opinions come into vogue with different seasons or administrations, and the deft courtier can make a successful appearance at court whether his thought is clothed in a Democratic or Republican style. At Versailles during the reign of Louis XIV the courtiers were required to play cards and scratch on doors with the little fingers of their left hands. Their knowledge in these matters proved their intimate acquaintance with the unutterable mysteries of the universe. At Washington in the late twentieth century the courtiers accomplish a similar purpose by writing op-ed pieces for *The Washington Post* and knowing what to say to CBS News about Medicare or the rioting in Los Angeles.[14]

Before a public that they wish to mislead, the courtiers stage what they hope will be applauded as a convincing charade. The trick is to sustain the illusions of progress and change while preserving the freeze-frame of the status quo. They embrace the platitudes of the moment, speak of "processes," "structures," and "empowerment," impose on any and all political passions the calming principle of "management by objective," postpone decision by referring the questions at hand to another committee, another authorization, another hearing, another signature, define the difficult or dangerous arguments that foreshadow the violence of the American future (i.e., the arguments about race, class, education, injustice, and the environment) as disruptions that must be smoothed over, not as questions that might be answered or responsibilities that must be met. The 102d Congress completed its term last October with an almost perfect record of inaction. Either by neglecting to bring a question to a vote or by passing legislation certain to be vetoed by President Bush, both the Senate and the House successfully avoided difficult decisions on crime, health care, family leave, voter registration, campaign finance, energy policy, and Chinese trade. By way of demonstrating their entire repertoire of false fronts, the

Congress and the White House in the winter of 1991 staged the pretense of a debate about taxes. President Bush submitted a bill. The Democratic majority in Congress submitted a bill. Each of the mock antagonists understood that neither bill stood the slightest chance of passage and that both bills were meaningless. But for fifty days and fifty nights, between the president's State of the Union Address and the roll call votes in both the Senate and the House, all present made an elaborate show of their concern for the public good, belaboring one another with empty phrases about federal spending, surcharges, capital gains, depreciations, and the sorrows of the middle class, wearing their crowns of stars and pretending to be one or another of the changes in the weather.

The obsession with images is as evident in New York and Los Angeles as it is in Washington, but the difference in emphasis is the difference between people interested in thought and expression and people interested in power. It is the business of New York or Los Angeles to manufacture images (whimsically transforming unknown southern governors into presidential candidates), but it is the business of Washington to trade in those images as the currency of political truism. Once having made the image, New York grows bored with it. In Washington the image becomes useful only after it has acquired the stability of the received wisdom, hammered into the brass of a campaign slogan or worked into the lacquer of a cliché, a word or a phrase suitable for an appearance on "Nightline." In New York or Los Angeles a man's thought might cast itself in the form of a play, a legal brief, a dress design, or a merger of companies, but he defines himself by his capacity to attract the paying customer. Washington reverses the sequence. All things follow in the train of political connection, and a man lives not by his works but by his office and his friends, by his talent for "staying in the loop," by an air of knowingness rather than a command of knowledge. Intelligence is conferred as a gift of patronage, and the trick is to know what not to know. A man's star rises or falls not so much by reason of what he does or fails to do as by the courtliness of his manner and his refusal to give or take offense.

Sometimes the charades fail in their intended effect—not often but every now and then—and despite the best efforts of the grand chamberlains of the national news media, the true face of the Washington courtier shows itself to the camera. Within recent memory I can think of no more vivid display of the finery of the courtier spirit than its appearance before Congress in the autumn of 1991 in the persons of Robert Gates, the president's nominee as director of central intelligence, and Clarence Thomas, now associate justice of the Supreme Court. Both gentlemen were confirmed in their new appointments in October, and the hearings, which were televised, showed them to possess the souls of acrobats.

Neither gentleman was qualified for the task at hand, but they enjoyed the favor of the prince (i.e., President Bush), and they had performed long and loyal service to the majesty of Republican money. As deputy director of the CIA between 1981 and 1986 Gates obediently edited the agency's intelligence estimates to fit the ideological fantasies cherished by the late William Casey, then the director, and by the claque of reactionary strategists (among them Edwin Meese and Caspar Weinberger) who commanded the ear of President Reagan. Gates did what he was told and so discovered the conspiratorial motives of the Evil Russian Empire in all the news from Africa, Central America, and Eastern Europe. He discounted or ignored the social revolution taking place in the Soviet Union, and by the spring of 1989 (when President Bush appointed him to the National Security Council) he had shown himself capable of fitting any fact—no matter how stubborn or inconvenient—to whatever story his masters wished to hear.

Testifying before the Senate Intelligence Committee, Gates retained the composure of the accomplished flatterer: Yes, Senator, no, Senator, whatever you say, Senator. It was true, Gates said, that he had made mistakes, but having made the mistakes, he had learned the invaluable lessons of humility, and never again would he trifle with the public trust. His smile was as treacherous as it was thin, but the committee was delighted with his act of contrition, and few of the senators present had the poor taste to pursue a churlish line of questioning.

Judge Thomas proved himself equally skilled at the courtier's arts and graces when he appeared before the Senate Judiciary Committee in October to answer questions about his sexual conduct. For nearly twenty years he had kissed the rings of his Republican patrons (among them Senator John Danforth, Ronald Reagan, Edwin Meese, and George Bush), and he was a man risen in the world not by reason of his merits but because of his connections. By turns polite, indignant, obsequious, and condescending, Judge Thomas revealed himself to be a man who despised the theory as well as the practice of democratic government. His manner was that of an outraged British duke in the reign of George III, and his response to even the smallest whisper of seditious libel about the moral beauty of his soul could have been expressed in the phrase "How dare you?"

On Friday morning Judge Thomas cast himself as a victim, a man who had been forced to endure the unspeakable agony of sitting comfortably in a chair for two weeks and being asked a series of facile questions to which he gave equally facile answers. He went on to say that "no job is worth what I've been through." Like much of the rest of his testimony, the statement was false. He wanted the job so badly that on Friday evening he returned to the witness table armed with the paint pots of racial hatred. Prior to the judge's evening testimony, nobody had smeared the proceedings with reference to anybody's color. The argument was about the abuse of power—about the humiliation that the master can inflict on the servant—but on Friday afternoon the executive producers directing Judge Thomas from the White House apparently told him that his confirmation was not yet certain, and they advised him to get busy with his paints and brushes. The judge did as he was told, and by nightfall he was talking to the television cameras about "bigoted, racial stereotypes . . . racial attitudes about black men and their views of sex."

His technique was that of a demagogue, and by the time he had given his third performance at the witness table it was abundantly clear that Judge Thomas was unfit to sit on the bench of a traffic court in Marina del Rey. He made the case against himself not on the evidence of what he said or didn't say to Anita Hill but on the proofs of his contempt for the entire apparatus of the American idea—for Congress, for the press, for freedom of expression, for the uses of democratic government, for any rules other than his own.

The Senate Judiciary Committee made no objection. Like the British Parliament in the late eighteenth century, the United States Senate in the late twentieth century regards the prospect of social change (any social change) as both an insult and a nasty surprise, and when presented with Professor Anita Hill's report of the sexual advances offered to her by Judge Thomas, the members of the Judiciary Committee were quick to take offense. By turns angry, confused, sullen, or embarrassed, they ignored the historical and existential questions in the room (the ones about the evolution of the society's sexual prejudices) and subjugated any questions of principle or conscience to the rules of Washington protocol. Uneasy with the testimony for reasons of their own, the Democratic senators made no attempt to shape Ms. Hill's observations into a coherent narrative, and the Republicans carried out the White House brief to do whatever was necessary to discredit her experience. They did so with a mean-spirited singleness of purpose that was as effective as it was dishonorable. Senator Orrin Hatch (R., Utah) distinguished himself by virtue of his smirking hypocrisy; Senator Alan Simpson (R., Wyo.), by his ignorance; and Senator Arlen Specter (R., Pa.), by his talents as a sophist and a bully.

The masks again came loose in early January of 1993, during the Senate's confirmations of President Clinton's cabinet. In place of the diverse and unorthodox team of American talent that Mr. Clinton had so often promised, he substituted the familiar trick of labels and tokens ("the Hispanic . . . the African . . . the Gay, the Straight, the Preacher, the privileged . . . the Teacher"), and instead of appointing at least a few citizens remarkable for their courage and independence of mind (i.e., the kind of people who might lend verisimilitude to the impression of change), the President assembled a company of functionaries burdened with an average term of service in Washington of thirteen years. The principal figures in his Cabinet—Warren Christopher, the secretary of state; Les Aspin, the secretary of defense; Lloyd Bentsen, the secretary of treasury—were men grown bleak and pale in the dim basements of politics-as-usual. For twenty-one years as a congressmen from Wisconsin, and chairman of the House Armed Services Committee, Secretary Aspin diligently forwarded the freight of the defense industry. During his 1990 congressional campaign, each of the nation's ten largest military contractors returned the favor with appreciative contributions. As the senior senator from Texas and the chairman of the Senate Finance Committee, Secretary Bentsen consistently supported the banking and insurance lobbies, voting in favor of each of President Reagan's major tax bills. As a corporate lawyer in Los Angeles and deputy secretary of state in the Carter administration, Secretary Christopher earned a reputation for his discreet silence, a man known and relied upon for his unwillingness to offend the consensus of opinion seated at the expensive end of the conference table.

Similar traits of mind and character distinguished almost the whole company of the new cabinet. As a prominent Washington lobbyist, Ronald H. Brown, the secretary of commerce, counted among his clients "Baby Doc" Duvalier, the former Haitian tyrant, as well as the government of Japan. On being raised to federal office, he was so gauche as to demand exemption from the customary rules of pecuniary decency, and it didn't occur to him to discourage the organization of a gala dinner party in his honor that was to have been staged (three days before President Clinton's inaugural) by a quorum of grateful business corporations, among them J. C. Penney, Anheuser-Busch, Sony Music Entertainment, and PepsiCo. Robert E. Rubin, the former co-chairman of Goldman, Sachs & Company, whom President Clinton named chairman of the National Economic Council, was equally careless of appearances. On his way to Washington from

New York, he sent letters to as many as one thousand corporate clients (foreign and domestic), assuring them that both he and his firm "look forward to continuing to work with you in my new capacity."

The too blatant contradictions in terms both embarrassed and frightened the Washington news media, who had thought that Mr. Clinton knew how to stage the play of appearances as adroitly as President Reagan. Certainly as a candidate he had understood that people who would wear the masks of populism must be careful to avoid the shows of vanity. The news media didn't object to the hypocrisy, which is as necessary to Washington as tap water, but they were troubled by the style of the hypocrisy, which was either twenty years out-of-date or five years ahead of its time. It was this latter possibility that compounded their embarrassment with the trace elements of fear.

Away from the cameras and out of sight of the public audience, the court addresses itself to the private questions of "access," and I remember being introduced to the general theory of the right connection during the same autumn of 1957 that I entertained the notion of spying for the CIA. After I had failed the tests of deportment set by the examiners from Yale, I went to the White House to talk to an aide-de-camp named Robert Gray about the chance of a career in politics. Gray subsequently became a successful peddler of Washington influence, but at the time he was President Eisenhower's appointments secretary, a young man in his early thirties, still learning to compose the order of his smiles. I forget how or through whom I arranged the meeting with Gray, but I remember that he was very busy, very energetic, very pleased with himself. He was pressed for time, but he granted me the favor of an audience in the White House barbershop. The White House in those days employed the services of a single barber, who worked in a basement room that resembled a spacious men's room in an expensive golf club. It was not a room that easily accommodated itself to the formality of a state audience. The only chair was the barber's chair, and while waiting for Gray to arrive, I stood anxiously in the doorway, making polite conversation with the barber about the World Series and wondering how and where I would be expected to sit. Gray hurried into the room twenty or thirty minutes late (the crisis had been more momentous than previously supposed), and with an abrupt and impatient wave of his hand he ushered me to a seat on the toilet, which was so placed that my head was level with Gray's shoes. They were, as I remember, very fine shoes, dark brown and polished to a high gloss, shoes in every way worthy of walking on marble floors.

Gray spoke from what seemed like a great height, and his air of urgent hurry I later learned to recognize as a common characteristic among court officials forever coming and going on errands of unutterable significance, always so pressed for time that they dare not speak too plainly about the prospect of global catastrophe or the fate of Western civilization. Gray's advice was as succinct as it was direct. First he allowed me to state briefly my hopes and intentions, and although I cannot now remember the words, I assume that I said something out of a textbook about the "free and open debate," "new ideas," "the democratic process." Gray didn't let me finish. He was, as he said, in a hurry. Interrupting me with another wave of his hand, he said, in effect, that nobody ever learned politics from a book. Join a party, he said, and make connections. Republican or Democrat, it didn't make any difference, as long as I remembered not to change parties and didn't get cute with pretty ideas. Everybody was after the same thing, which was power, and the best way to get power was to do what you were told and make important friends. Nor did it matter what the friends believed. Connections were the beginning and end of it, he said, favors granted and received.

The lesson of Gray's own subsequent career proved him true to his word. He stayed with Eisenhower for two terms, and then, taking with him from the White House a list of telephone numbers and favors granted, he set himself up as one of Washington's most adroit dealers in access. His lobbying firm waxed and prospered over the next twenty-five years, most especially during the Republican administrations of Presidents Nixon, Ford, and

Reagan, and in 1986, sensing a turn in the wind, he sold his name and his connections to Hill and Knowlton, the New York public relations firm. By that time, of course, the court society in Washington had swelled to a size and magnificence undreamed of in the philosophy of 1957, and even the New York money understood that it had no choice but to dance the beggar's pantomime in front of some dull-witted senator or thin-mouthed bureaucrat who could, with a stroke of a pen, eliminate entire markets. Gray remained with the larger company as chief of its public affairs operations in Washington, and in the autumn of 1990 he distinguished himself by managing the deal in which—for a fee of $10.8 million from the feudal monarchy of Kuwait—Hill and Knowlton staged the presentation of false evidence to both the United Nations and the United States Congress and mounted an advertising campaign meant to sell the American people the bauble of a foreign war.

If Gray, in 1957, provided the general theory, my observations of Washington over the last thirty years have provided the specific proofs and instances. Since the revision of the campaign finance laws in the late 1970s, most of the candidates don't even take the trouble to court the good opinion of the voters. They speak instead to the other people at court—to the PACs, to the lobbyists who can fix the money for campaigns costing as much as $350,000 (for the House of Representatives) and $4 million (for the Senate). The rising cost of political ambition ensures the rising rate of incumbency (47 percent of the present U.S. Congress was in office in 1980, as opposed to 4 percent of the Supreme Soviet). The sponsors back the safe bets and receive the assurance of safe opinions.

A democracy supposedly derives its strength and character from the diversity of its many voices, but the politicians in Washington speak with only one voice, which is the voice of the oligarchy that buys the airline tickets and the television images, and on Capitol Hill I never hear the voice of the scientist, the writer, the athlete, the teacher, the plumber, the police officer, the farmer, the merchant. I hear instead the voice of only one kind of functionary: a full-time politician, nearly always a lawyer, who spends at least 80 percent of his time raising campaign funds and construes his function as that of a freight-forwarding agent redistributing the national income into venues convenient to his owners and friends.

Together with the lobbyists in the city, the regulatory agents have multiplied at the prevailing rates of inflation. The latter company now comprises no fewer than one hundred thousand officials of various weights and measures—government administrators as well as corporate facilitators—who trade or bestow favors expressed as the price of corn, the permissible levels of air or water pollution, the rules of automobile safety, or the chemical structure of chewing tobacco. As recently as 1979 only 117 of the nation's health care organizations maintained lobbyists in Washington; by 1986 the number had swelled to 502, and by 1992 to 741. Similar improvements took place across the whole stage of American industry. For a period of about eighteen months in 1985 and 1986 I never once traveled to Washington (whether on the Metroliner or a plane) without finding myself seated next to an expectant contractor with whom I could discuss the prices paid for access and connections in the form of a campaign contribution or a legal fee. The gentlemen understood that they were on the road to court. None of them first thought of themselves as democrats or of the United States as a democracy.

The cost of access has kept pace with the cost of the champagne at the Four Seasons Hotel, and in April 1992, on reading the price schedule for a dinner given by the Republican National Committee, I remembered an apprentice real estate tycoon who had boarded a train in Philadelphia. He had borrowed ten thousand dollars from his mother-in-law in order to sit on a dais with Senator Hugh Scott, and in return for that flattery he expected to receive subsidized loans for a prospective row of town houses fronting on Penn's Landing. So paltry a sum as ten thousand dollars didn't buy much prominence at the 1992 Republican dinner at the Washington Hilton. Tables for ten sold for between fifteen and twenty thousand dollars. The buyer of two tables received an invitation to a reception on Capitol Hill with Senator Robert Dole (the Republican majority leader) as well as the option to request the presence of a congressman at one table and, at the other table, a senator or senior official in the Bush administration. Anybody who contributed ninety-two thousand dollars received the additional benefit of a photo opportunity with the president and the chance of being seated at a head table, either with the president or with Vice President Quayle.[15]

Just as the cost of a friend at court prices most Americans out of the market for political expression, so also the rule of grace and favor exempts the government from the nuisance of obeying its own laws. If the well-placed bribe can so easily rescind the will of Congress, then we might as well be ruled by George III or the emir of Kuwait. From the point of view of most of the government functionaries whom I've known in Washington, the shift to monarchy would require nothing more difficult than a change of costume.

The observation is by no means new or exceptional. Various journalists writing about Washington politics over the last thirty-odd years have described at considerable length the mechanics of what has become a mock democracy. In the spring of 1992 William Greider, the national correspondent for *Rolling Stone*, published a book entitled *Who Will Tell the People,* in which he cited numerous examples of the customs at court, but the scene that I thought especially fine was his conversation with Stuart E. Eizenstat, formerly a policy adviser to President Jimmy Carter and now a prominent lobbyist and lawyer. Greider was asking Eizenstat about the ways in which the Office of Management and Budget routinely employed the jargon of cost-benefit analysis to annul any regulatory laws deemed harmful to a well-connected corporation's gross profits. Apparently he was surprised by Eizenstat's cynicism—in much the same way that I had been surprised by Gray's cynicism—and Eizenstat, like Gray, lost patience with the civics lesson. "Of course, the law's up for grabs!" he said. "The law's always up for grabs. That's why you win elections and appoint judges. . . . [T]hat's what having political power is all about, for Chrissake!"[16]

The prevailing atmospheres of deception by common consent account for Washington's failure to produce a novelist of rank or even a first-rate satirist. For years I used to wonder why this was so in a city glutted with wealth and populated by as wonderful a cast of fools and knaves as could have been dreamed of by Shakespeare or Molière. On the evening news I would hear rumors of some grand absurdity—the chairman of the House Ways and Means Committee in a reflecting pool with a striptease dancer, another of President Nixon's justifications for the Vietnam War, Alexander Haig's hysteria on contemplating his possible accession to the presidency when Ronald Reagan was shot, the Pentagon theory of "Star Wars," etc.—and then I would look through the next day's editions for the ribald laughter or the deadly insult. It was never there. Not a flash of wit or a squeak of rage. Nobody but Art Buchwald, or somebody else as harmless as Art Buchwald, making a cute and inoffensive witticism.

I once asked an old and cynical newspaper editor why this was so, why he didn't assign a reporter to write about Congress in the manner of Ambrose Bierce. If the reporter understood that he was writing about the human comedy, and if he avoided the pious claptrap about the issues, he never would lack for incident, and along the whole length of Pennsylvania Avenue the mere mention of his name would prompt a nervous fluttering of fans. The editor looked at me with the same sort of weary smile that I saw several years later drifting across the gaunt face of Bart Giamatti on the train to New Haven. The thought had occurred to him, he said, but so had the prospect of bankruptcy. The paper would never be invited to dinner at the White House or to the cocktail parties in Georgetown, and how would he explain the omissions to the advertisers who expected to see their products in the company of the best people? He reminded me that Saint-Simon's memoirs of Versailles were published only after the duke's death.

The court temperament can enjoy the malicious character

sketches of Maureen Dowd and Alessandra Stanley or admire the
stately admonitions of orators in the Roman tradition of Walter
Lippmann, Joseph Alsop, or George Will, but it cannot abide the
angry voices worked in the skeptical tradition of Mark Twain,
Thorstein Veblen, or I. F. Stone. The staleness of the result is
never more obvious than when the Washington press corps attempts the feat of humor at its annual Gridiron Dinner. The
resident journalists invite various politicians and government officials to what is supposed to be an evening of unleavened comedy. The politicians make fun of themselves, and the journalists
tell inside jokes. But almost everybody's lines have been written
by professional comedians, and the laughter is as forced as the
laugh track on a network sitcom. The politicians spend their time
working the room, canvassing an opinion or seeking to change
the angle of a perception, and most of the journalists present
wonder why they're not sitting at the same table with Ben
Bradlee or Sam Donaldson. Like every other party in Washington, the dinner is about improving one's place at court, and the
effort is so earnest that before laughing at the hired jokes, everybody has to look to see that the president (or Bob Strauss or
George Mitchell or Jay Rockefeller) is also laughing. Who can
afford to say anything that might injure one's chances of advancement? Somebody important might take offense, and then what
would become of one's invitations to the Sunday morning talk
shows? Better to stay safely with "the issues," with supercilious
analysis of polls and trends, with innuendo and sophism and the
occasional snubbing of somebody already well on the road to
oblivion.

An equivalent absence of direct statement distinguishes most
of the memoirs published by the country's principal statesmen -
books brought out under the names of Nixon, Carter,
Brzezinski, Clifford, Kissinger, Ford, Nitze, Reagan. Even on
leaving the precincts of government, the most splendid court
officials cannot bear to tell the truth. Too long accustomed to the
habit of euphemism, the authors (or, more likely, their hired
surrogates) sound as if they were making an after-dinner speech,

and as often as not their use of the language betrays a genuinely terrifying emptiness of thought. Although I've read many memoirs by many high-ranking Washington officials over the last thirty years, no text has seemed to me more depressing or more fairly representative of the customary tone of voice than a book review by Caspar Weinberger published in 1987 in *The Wall Street Journal*. Weinberger at the time was the secretary of defense, and the book under review was Tom Clancy's geopolitical romance *Patriot Games*. Within the space of a few hundred words the secretary said as much about the sentimental ignorance of the Reagan administration as did all the volumes of memoirs published by people like Michael Deaver and Donald Regan.

Weinberger began the review with a fanfare of praise for what he called "a spine-tingling narrative drama": ". . . 'Patriot Games' is a story of bravery, great skill and villainous Irish terrorists, who are as fully as dangerous and despicable as their Iranian brothers. The plot is superb. Mr. Clancy has created a particularly plausible tale of an authentic hero, retired navy officer Jack Ryan. . . . Ryan has the leading role in 'Patriot Games,' and he is in the classic mode of the modest, skillful, brave warrior with all the virtues."

Mr. Clancy is a man of many talents, but creating "a particularly plausible tale of an authentic hero" is not one of them. His characters are made of wood, his plots as preposterous as those in a movie starring Sylvester Stallone or Chuck Norris. On reading the secretary's review, I could imagine him being led like a child through an air base or a naval installation, uttering small cries of wonder and surprise on being allowed to touch the nose cone of an F-16. Together with President Reagan, Weinberger apparently thought of an aircraft carrier as a kind of floating military theme park. How simple it must have been to tell ghost stories (about arcs of crisis, domino theories, and windows of opportunity) to a secretary of defense who, writing of Clancy's fable, could say, with boyish delight, "the villains are all satisfactorily ruthless, contemptible, and in urgent need of extermination." Were the secretary a schoolboy, or even a professor of sophomore English, the callowness of his thought might have been forgivable, or at least bearable. But he was a minister of war for the most heavily armed nation on earth, a man entrusted with the keeping of the final weapons, and his failure of imagination aroused the feeling of dread.

Once having ruled inadmissible any evidence of creative thought or candid expression, the court can talk to itself only in the whisper of gossip. The languid young men at the CIA in 1957 were explicit on the point: The gossip about whom one knows or sleeps with is always more important than the news from Indochina or the Black Sea. The court resides at a great distance from the realm of common necessity, and this results in a feeling of terrible emptiness. The space has to be filled with something, and so the attendants at court collaborate in the great work of making trompe l'oeil. They must persuade themselves that the world they see and know is equivalent to the vast sum of the universe. Anybody who spends his time going to ceremonies and reading the court gazettes obviously doesn't have the chance to study politics or art, let alone particle physics or Chinese. He has no choice but to make something miraculous of what he does see and know—the other people at court.

On my numerous passages through Washington I've invariably been struck by the distance between the public and the private conversation. The front-page news is about the Cuban missile crisis or the Vietnam War, but the backstairs gossip is about Jack Kennedy's pander or Ronald Reagan's horse. Through the spring and summer of 1991, in the midst of the dissolution of the Soviet Union and the end to forty years of American geopolitical theory, *The Washington Post*, Ted Koppel, and the hostesses on P Street were preoccupied with the far greater questions of John Sununu's travel plans, Robert Mosbacher's awning, the trial of Teddy Kennedy's nephew, and Kitty Kelley's biography of Nancy Reagan. Was it true that Nancy had received Frank Sinatra in the White House and there astonished him with what was rumored to be a Hollywood talent for fellatio? Would Sununu fall from grace at Kennebunkport, and if so, who would replace him? Would the Kennedys never come of age? Among all the stories then in vogue, I liked best the ones about Sununu's travels and Mosbacher's awning.

Then the White House chief of staff, Sununu couldn't bear to travel on commercial aircraft, and he believed himself demeaned unless he could be carried around the country in the equivalent of a sedan chair. When he wished to keep a dentist's appointment in New Hampshire or go to Colorado for the skiing, Sununu summoned an air force plane. If he was invited to give a political speech in the American hinterland (Ohio, say, or Tennessee), he demanded a plane from a corporation or a trade association, and once, when he was in a hurry to go to New York City to buy stamps at a collectors' auction, he requisitioned a White House limousine.

When the proofs of his vanity eventually made the news, Sununu justified his pretensions by saying, in effect, that he was indispensable. Unless he was "constantly in touch" (i.e., available by phone in the plane or the car), the American government almost surely would collapse. Nothing could happen without his knowledge or permission. Remove Sununu from the circle around President Bush, and it was possible that the world might come to an end.

Mosbacher is a caricature of the fatuous and overstuffed plutocrat. A friend to George Bush in the Texas oil business, born rich and accustomed to the shows of deference, he arrived in Washington with the new administration in 1989 and discovered that not enough people appreciated the true proportion of his magnificence. Apparently he wasn't received with enough applause or his name didn't appear often enough in the "Style" section of *The Washington Post*. Within the bureaucratic maze of his own department he felt himself slighted by the custom of extending to the secretary the same sort of egalitarian courtesy extended to a telephone operator or a file clerk. Ordinary people greeted him casually in the corridors, and their familiarity affronted his dignity.

Anxious to show everybody who was who and what was what, Mosbacher devoted the first nine months of his ministry to the great project of magnifying his own entrance to the building. What had been a public or common entrance on Fifteenth Street Mosbacher appropriated to his private use, decorating it with a red awning (red because Secretary of State James Baker had a blue awning) and furnishing the adjacent lobby with an extravagant show of flowers. When the work was completed, Mosbacher announced that the new entrance was reserved for the comings and goings of only six people: himself, his chief of staff, his private secretary, his lawyer, his deputy, and his wife.

The effect was very grand but still not grand enough. After a few weeks of walking in and out of the building in a stately manner, Mosbacher took a strong dislike to the long corridor between his new lobby and his private elevator. The corridor was too narrow. Too many doors opened into offices in which Mosbacher could see ordinary people bent over their work—people in shirtsleeves, minor people, noisy people, black people, yellow people, unimportant people. The sight offended him, and he ordered the corridor enlarged and the offices removed.

It is the vanity of the court that eventually proves its ruin. Not the extravagance or the fraud or the sexual disorder, but the dreams of self that encourage the rose-red courtiers in the White House garden to imagine themselves situated at the center of the world, blessed with the gifts of limitless wisdom and power. R. W. Apple, chief of the Washington bureau for *The New York Times*, struck the preferred tone of self-congratulation in a front-page column on the day after President Bush sent American troops to the Persian Gulf. For some months official Washington had been worried about losing its status in the world. In June of that year the Russian premier, Mikhail Gorbachev, had been presumptuous enough to hold a summit meeting with the German chancellor, Helmut Kohl, without first asking the Americans for permission. President Bush was being seen as a "wimp," and the nation's intellectual riffraff in New York were writing tracts about America's bankruptcy and decline. Apple welcomed the president's show of military resolve as an invigorating tonic, and he was proud to report that all the dreary talk about America's future was just so much trendy, sniveling rot. What had returned to Washington, he said, was the sense of its own deserved magnificence, "the heavy speculation and avid gossip, the gung-ho here's where it's happening spirit that marks the city when it grapples with great events." Apple's burbling enthusiasm was seconded by Ben Wattenberg, another loyal servant of the court, in *The Washington Times*. Wattenberg published his word of gratitude for the crisis under the headline THANKS SADDAM, WE NEEDED THAT.

President Clinton's arrival in Washington last winter was welcomed as yet another proof of the city's sublime importance—more avid gossip! more gung ho spirit! more great events!—and the incessant din of applause reconfirmed the residents at court in the belief that they exist at an exalted remove—either beyond or above—anything so paltry and confining as common necessity. Even on rainy days they tell one another that their understanding surpasses the understanding of the common people, and they find it easy to believe that because they are who they are, they can do as they please. The stupidity implicit in that last proposition defines a governing class that cannot tell the difference between what is true and what it chooses to say is true. As wish becomes synonymous with action, and reason interchangeable with desire, the drivel of a demented deputy secretary of defense becomes "strategic weapons policy," and the ravings of a bigoted senator become "a return to family values." The treasury squanders twenty-five billion dollars on the child's fantasy of the Strategic Defense Initiative, the National Institute of Mental Health dismisses its director for being so careless as to make a remark about apes and slums deemed politically incorrect, and the federal government blithely orders state and municipal governments to provide public services—for health, education, the environment, water purification, etc.—without giving so much as a moment's thought to how the states and cities might raise the money to pay for those services.[17]

The formulation of public policy as drama in the theater of the self produces grotesque results throughout the whole enterprise of government, but the vanity of bureaucrats shows to its worst and most foolish effect in the arenas of foreign policy. For a few years in the immediate aftermath of the Second World War the United States bestrode the world like a colossus, and the delusions of grandeur were mistaken for proofs of immortality. The CIA, under the direction of Allen Dulles (aka "the Great White Case Officer"), enjoyed a brief moment of triumph in a world still largely in ruins, at a time when the military and economic supremacy of the United States went largely unquestioned. The American intelligence services placed a number of agents behind Communist lines in Europe; recruited émigré armies to recapture the lost kingdoms of Poland, Bulgaria, and Ukraine; and assisted with the removal of governments thought to be subversive in Iran (1953) and Guatemala (1954).

Within a very few years the victories proved to be illusory or, at best, ambiguous. Advance scouts for the émigré armies parachuted into the Slavic darkness and were never seen or heard from again. By overthrowing a popular but socialist regime in Iran (at the behest of the Anglo-Iranian Oil Company), the United States opened the way to the vanity and ignorance of the shah of shahs (who had trouble speaking Farsi), to the quadrupling of the Arab oil price, and to the revolutionary zeal of the ayatollah Khomeini.

By the end of the decade the American variations on themes of subversion had acquired the character of farce. With the hope of eliminating Achmed Sukarno as the president of Indonesia (because he permitted Communists to take their elected posts in his government), the CIA in 1957 armed a cadre of restless Sumatran colonels and engaged a Hollywood film crew to produce a pornographic film. Entitled *Happy Days*, the film purportedly showed Sukarno (played by a Mexican actor wearing a mask) in bed with a Soviet agent (played by a California waitress wearing a wig). The coup d'état failed, and the film was understood as a joke.

In 1961 the bungled invasion at the Bay of Pigs (aka "the glorious march through Havana") ensured Fidel Castro's Communist authority throughout Latin America. The invasion was conceived in Washington by American intelligence officials who didn't know—or didn't want to know—the difference between fact and fiction. To the Cuban exiles in its employ, the CIA supplied false information, not enough firepower, and the wrong tactics. As drawn on a briefing officer's blackboard in Washington, the invasion was a perfect success; as enacted by a crowd of amateur soldiers on a narrow beach, the invasion was a textbook calamity. On precisely the same night and at precisely the same hour that Castro, dressed in a military uniform and smoking a cigar, was urging his troops forward into the Zapata Swamp, President Jack Kennedy, wearing white tie and tails, danced at a White House ball to the tune of "Mr. Wonderful."

By encouraging the assassination of Ngo Dinh Diem in Saigon in 1963, the United States allied itself with a policy of realpolitik no less cynical than the one against which it was supposedly defending the principles of justice. Four American presidents defined the expedition in Vietnam as a prolonged covert action and systematically lied to the American people about the reason for our presence in a country with which we never declared ourselves at war. As a result of our effort to rid Indochina of communism, Vietnam became a unified Communist state. As a result of our effort to teach the world the lessons of democracy, we taught a generation of American citizens to think of their own government as an Oriental despotism.

President Nixon compounded the aura of royal fantasy with his imitations of Ludwig, the Mad King of Bavaria. He wished to rule by decree and interoffice memorandum, and he was forever scribbling furious directives in the margins of the daily press summaries, instructing his courtiers to rid him of his real and imagined enemies. His verbs were always violent—"Get someone to hit him," "Fire him," "Freeze him," "Cut him," "Knock him down," "Dump him"—and he entertained fantastic notions of his own character. Prior to his first meeting with the Russian premier Leonid Brezhnev in the spring of 1972, Nixon directed Kissinger, who preceded him to Moscow, to announce him as a man who was "direct, honest, strong." He was, in fact, devious, dishonest, and weak, a sly and cunning man constantly brooding about the worth and beauty of his own image. On the eve of another of his departures for Moscow he compared himself with both William the Conqueror and Dwight Eisenhower on the morning of D Day.

By the late 1970s the conversation within the sealed and cloistered rooms of Washington's diplomatic establishment had begun to resemble the dialogue in a play by Samuel Beckett. The privy councillors were ceaselessly worrying about America's pride and credibility, about the sending of signals and "bomb-o-grams," about the symbolism of the fleet, about perceptions, analogies, and the importance of French or Russian opinion. At dinner one night I remember hearing a government official say of a Central American state that he was depressed by "the quality of the regime." It would have been possible to assume by the tone of his voice that he was talking about a second-rate wine or a Hyatt Hotel gone to seed in a town no longer attractive to the brokers of business conventions. The official wasn't concerned about the nation's capacity to harm the United States; the army was small and ill equipped, the mineral assets not worth the cost of a first-class embassy. Nor did the official think the governing junta particularly adept at exporting "the virus of Marxist revolution." What troubled him was the "indecorousness of the regime." The country was in bad taste.

With the arrival of Ronald Reagan in the winter of 1981 the formulation of White House policy descended to vaudeville. The administration made no secret of its contempt for anything so chickenhearted and un-American as the due process of law, and its characteristic tone of voice was that of the adventurer and the zealot: Attorney General Edwin Meese operating the Justice Department as if he didn't think the Constitution relevant to the expediencies of the state; White House communications director Patrick Buchanan proclaiming the president and Colonel North heroes because they had the guts to do what they damn well knew was right; the CIA justifying its invasions of Central America as works of noble conscience; the Justice Department subverting the law in order to eliminate any impurities likely to appear in the citizenry's urine or speech. Instead of advocating conservative habits of thought, which imply a decent regard for the established rights of individuals as well as institutions, the president's companions construed their victory at the polls as a coup d'etat. They seized the spoils of government with the swagger of brigands, as secure as Clint Eastwood in their knowledge of the good, the true, and the beautiful. The games of imperial "let's pretend," which in many ways resembled the toy realpolitick popular in France during the Second Empire of Napoleon III, culminated in the Iran-contra arms deal. Preening themselves on their righteousness, the road show Machiavels allied the purity of their cause with a Middle Eastern consortium of thugs, sharpers, bankrupts, arms smugglers, cutthroats, swindlers, and disbanded soldiers. Congratulating themselves on their shrewdness, they bargained in languages that none of them understood, traded the diplomatic currencies of the United States for worthless promises, and discredited the government they hoped to defend. The plot followed the lines of an episode of "The A-Team," and on being discovered in their criminal charades, all present conducted themselves in the manner traditional among thieves: Everybody professed his own innocence and assigned the fault to a friend. Secretary of State George Shultz and Vice President George Bush moved fastidiously upwind from any prior knowledge, and those who could do so (among them Vice Admiral John Poindexter and Lieutenant Colonel Oliver North) offered to incriminate one or more of their companions in return for immunity and safe passage into the nearest book deal.

The president, meanwhile, drifted amiably through the scenes and stage sets provided by his scriptwriters, speaking his lines with flawless inflection and always knowing precisely where to stand. He conceived of the presidency as a starring role in a major motion picture directed by Cecil B. De Mille, and as between the texts of the common and the preferred reality, he never knew, or cared to know, the difference. He cried when he first saw the television commercials announcing that it was "Morning in America." Riding in the limousine to the first Economic Summit

Conference in 1983, he was asked by James Baker, then secretary of the treasury, if he had read the briefing book. Reagan looked at Baker with an expression of genuine bewilderment and concern, as if he had been asked a question to which all right-thinking people already knew the answer.

"But, Jim," he said, "*The Sound of Music* was on last night."

Like President Reagan, President Bush inhabited a world out of time, and in January 1992 he departed on a fool's errand to Japan, fully persuaded that the year was still 1945 and that if the pomps and ceremonies of his Oriental tour had conformed to his inward state of mind, he would have arrived in Tokyo Bay on board the USS *Missouri*, dressed in a white naval uniform and very pleased to present the Japanese people with the sight of his squared jaw and gold braid. As conceived by the Washington designers of photo opportunities, the pageant was meant to show a vigorous American president coming to Japan to demand economic justice from the old and duplicitous *keiretsu*. The spectacle seen in the theater of the news presented the American president as a failed suppliant instead of a conquering hero—an ailing and pathetic figure dismissed with the smile of pity and the gift of some sweet candies shaped as miniature sculptures of the president's two dogs.

The embarrassment followed from the disjunction in time. In the autumn of 1945 it would have been hard to imagine that one day the United States might find itself pressed for cash or that the lines of credit would run from East to West. Tokyo was in ashes, and the emperor had been informed by General Douglas MacArthur that he was no longer a god. The common wisdom held that everybody's image of the future looked like an American postcard. How was it possible to think otherwise? Was it not true that democracy, capitalism, and social progress were all part of the same wonderful idea? Who could fail to embrace the American systems of value and the American theories of fair trade?

President Bush formed his understanding of Japan as a navy pilot in World War II, and apparently nothing in his subsequent experience obliged him to amend his first impression. This lack of development is fairly common among people born to the assumptions of wealth and rank. They can afford to believe what they choose to believe, and they seldom find it necessary to revise the texts of the preferred reality. The president and his companions declined to acknowledge any realities other than the ones they chose to acknowledge. In the courtyard of a palace in Kyoto Mr. Bush thrust himself into a game of *kemari* (a ball game he'd never seen before and didn't understand), and after a few moments of aimless play he said to his attending courtiers, "We won." He told various microphones that "world leadership is at stake" and made himself memorable to the Japanese public by fainting at a state dinner and vomiting on Prime Minister Miyazawa's suit. His journey to the East ended as burlesque. Attempting to portray himself as a politician who cared about American domestic issues, he lost much of his stature as a statesman presumed to know something about foreign issues. On his return to Andrews Air Force Base the president made a virtue of his ignorance. Because he had steadfastly refused to learn even the smallest lesson of experience, he could say to the assembled cameras that the journey had been a triumph. It was still 1945, now and forever, and he had carried the flag of the American workingman to the uttermost ends of the earth.[18]

Every administration has no choice but to confront the world's violence and disorder, but the doctrines of American grace oblige it to do so under the banners of righteousness and in the name of one or another of the fanciful pretexts ("democracy," "civilization," "humanity," "the people") that preserve the conscience of the American television audience. The electorate expects its presidential candidates to feign the clean-limbed idealism of college sophomores, to present themselves as honest and good-natured fellows who know nothing of murder, ambition, lust, selfishness, cowardice, or greed. The pose of innocence is as mandatory as the ability to eat banquet food, but it gets confused with the dream of power, and pretty soon, usually within a week of the inaugural address, a new president discovers that the American political system allows for the parallel sovereignty of both a permanent and a provisional government. The permanent government—the

Congress, the civil and military services, the media, the legion of Washington lawyers and expensive lobbyists—occupies the anonymous hierarchies that remain safely in place no matter what the political truths voted in and out of the White House on the trend of a season. It is this government—sly and patient and slow—that writes the briefing papers and the laws, presides over the administrative routine, remembers who bribed whom in the election of 1968 and why President Carter thought it prudent to talk privately to God about the B-1 bomber.

Except in the rare moments of jointly opportune interest, the permanent government wages a ceaseless war of bureaucratic attrition against the provisional government that once every four or eight years accompanies a newly elected president to Washington. The amateur government consists of the cadre of ideologues, cronies, plutocrats, and academic theorists miraculously transformed into cabinet officials and White House privy councillors. Endowed with the virtues of freebooting adventurers, the parvenu statesmen possess the talents and energies necessary to the winning of elections. Although admirable, these are not the talents and energies useful to the conduct of international diplomacy.

The president and his confederates inherit a suite of empty rooms. The media like to pretend that the White House is an august and stately institution, the point at which all the lines of power converge, the still center of the still-American universe. The people who occupy the place discover that the White House bears a more credible resemblance to a bare stage or an abandoned cruise ship. The previous tenants have removed everything of value—the files, the correspondence, the telephone numbers, the memorabilia on the walls. The new repertory company begins at the beginning, setting up its own props and lights, arranging its own systems of communications and theory of command, hoping to sustain, at least long enough for everybody to profit from the effect, the illusion of coherent power.

All other American institutions of any consequence (the Chase Manhattan Bank, say, or the Pentagon) rely on the presence of senior officials who remember what happened twenty years ago when somebody else—equally ambitious, equally new—proposed something equally foolish. But the White House is barren of institutional memory. Maybe an old butler remembers that President Eisenhower liked sugar in his tea, but nobody remembers the travel arrangements for the last American expedition to Iran. Within a week of its arrival in Washington the provisional government learns that the world is a far more dangerous place than anybody had thought possible as recently as two months ago, when the candidate was reciting the familiar claptrap about nuclear proliferation to an airport crowd somewhere south of Atlanta. Alarmed by the introductory briefings at the Defense Department, the amateur statesmen feel impelled to take bold stands, to make good on their campaign promises, to act. Almost immediately they find themselves checked by the inertia of the permanent government, by the maze of prior agreements, by the bureaucrats who bring up the niggling reasons why a thing can't be done. The sense of frustration incites the president's men to "take it inside" or "move it across the street," and so they make of the National Security Council or the White House basement the seat of "a loyal government" blessed with the will to dare and do. The decision inevitably entails the subversion of the law and excites the passion for secrecy. The technological possibilities presented by the available back channels, map overlays, and surveillance techniques tempt the would-be Metternichs to succumb to the dreams of omnipotence. Pretty soon they start speaking in code, and before long American infantrymen begin to turn up dead in the jungles of Vietnam or the streets of Beirut.

Under the title *The March of Folly* the late Barbara Tuchman in 1984 published a set of instructive essays addressed to what she called the "surpassing woodenheadedness" exhibited by various states bent on the destruction not only of their own best interests but also of their existence. She divided what Adams had called the delirium of pride and vanity into four cautionary tales: Troy's welcoming of the Greek wooden horse; the misrule of six successive Renaissance popes, who, by virtue of their spendthrift tastes for luxury and murder, incited the Protestant Revolt and Reformation; Britain's loss of North America in the late eighteenth century; and the American defeat in Vietnam.

Fairly spectacular proofs of woodenheadedness show up throughout much of the American oligarchy—most recently in the corporate boardrooms of IBM and General Motors—but I can think of few more specific statements of the presiding stupidity than the ruling handed down by the Supreme Court in May 1991 in which it was announced that people who accept government money must say what the government wishes them to say. The ruling followed from the Court's interpretation of *Rust v. Sullivan* and forbade mention of the word *abortion* in any of the forty-five hundred clinics that receive federal funds. The clinics provide advice and care to as many as four million women in the United States, many of them frightened and most of them poor, but few of the members of the Court have had much experience of the citizenry in whose name they compose the laws. Seven of the present justices never have been required to impose a prison sentence, and only two (Justices Sandra Day O'Connor and David Souter) have served as trial judges. Impatient with any set of circumstances that cannot be construed as sublime abstraction, the Court in the matter of *Rust v. Sullivan* relied on a line of reasoning (supplied by Chief Justice William Rehnquist) that defined speech as a function of congressional subsidy. Because the government doesn't choose to fund the practice of abortion, then doctors accepting government funds cannot talk about the practice of abortion. Speech becomes a privilege instead of a right.

The four justices who joined Rehnquist's opinion (Justices Souter, Scalia, Kennedy, and White) presumably shared his inclination to recognize only those truths that appear in court with an acceptable financial statement. If the viewpoint is funded, it may be discussed; if the viewpoint is not funded, it cannot be introduced in polite company. A clinic retains permission to talk about abortion only on condition that it does so in a separate building under the disguise of a separate program that receives none of its funding from the federal government.

The Supreme Court decision in the matter of *Rust v. Sullivan* satisfied Tuchman's criteria for an act of folly by asserting that the myopic desire of a petulant oligarchy is synonymous with judgment and reason and that words can be made to stand as surrogates for deeds. Rehnquist spoke for a majority, not only of the Court but also of the American governing and possessing classes, when he ruled that the democratic experiment had gone far enough and that the Republic no longer could tolerate the risk implicit in the freedom of speech and the freedom of thought. Henceforth, said the Court, the truth is a function of dogma, and the government will pay to hear only what it wants to hear. Any statement that fails to conform to the prerecorded political or religious announcement isn't welcome at the White House dance.

President Clinton on his second day in office overruled, by executive order, the Court's reading of *Rust v. Sullivan,* but he did so by fiat, without debate in the Congress or the press. Affirming the same divine right of kings, he attempted to rescind, also by executive order, the ban against homosexuals in the military services. Once again, the law was the stuff of wish and dreams, and human nature a text that could be as easily deconstructed as a campaign promise or a poem.

Let reason and desire become one and the same, and the possible stupidities become as infinite as the number of the fixed stars. Isidore of Seville affirmed that menstrual blood was a fluid dispensed by the devil and that the merest touch of it caused blossoms to fade, grasses to wither, iron to rust, and brass to turn black. In colonial America anyone caught eating mince pie was suspected of royalist sympathies. The host of beetles that ravaged the vineyard of St. Julian were commanded to appear in king's court, and when they neglected the summons, a lawyer was appointed to speak on their behalf. The art of tyromancy divines the future in the coagulation of cheese.

Sooner or later, of course, the foolishness and greed of the ruling class become so overbearing that the people lose respect for the name and image of authority. When the people also lose respect for the idea that their rulers supposedly serve and represent, the march of folly becomes a rout.

4

Rosencrantz and Guildenstern

[A FREE PEOPLE HAS] AN INDISPUTABLE,
UNALIENABLE, INDEFEASIBLE, DIVINE
RIGHT TO THAT MOST DREADED AND EN-
VIED KIND OF KNOWLEDGE, I MEAN OF
THE CHARACTERS AND CONDUCT OF
THEIR RULERS.

—*John Adams*

At least once a year for the last twenty years I have attended some
sort of solemn conference at which various well-placed figures
within the hierarchies of the American news media attempt to
calibrate the precise degree of their own importance. For two or
three days the discussants come and go, praising the view of the
mountains or the sea, admiring their names on the program,
puffing contentedly on pipes, saying that they must be careful to
use their vast and godlike powers only in defense of liberty or for

the benefit of mankind. All present begin with the assumption that the media are very, very powerful—maybe omnipotent. They address their remarks to the ancillary questions, Just how does the power of the media make itself manifest, and what is the effect of that power on a sometimes unappreciative public? The discussants frown and take thoughtful notes with small gold pencils, and every now and then one of the ranking magnificoes makes a high-flown speech describing journalists as men against the system, tireless champions of liberty ferociously pacing to and fro on the ramparts of freedom.

The image is comical. The organizations represented at the banquet tables and on the speaker's dais belong to the small number of media syndicates that deliver 90 percent of the nation's news—the three television networks and CNN, three news-magazines, and maybe four or five newspapers (*The New York Times*, *The Washington Post*, *USA Today*, the *Los Angeles Times*, *The Wall Street Journal*)—and anybody who rises to prominence in their ranks—as editor, political columnist, publisher, anchorperson, theater critic, or foreign correspondent—learns to think along the accommodating lines of an expectant courtier in any other large corporation. Their timid and reactionary temperament seems to me so self-evident that I find it hard to argue with people who talk about something that they insist on naming "the liberal press." I might as well be arguing with people who believe that the earth is flat. The characterization of the press as "liberal" might pertain to a few columnists writing for journals as marginal as *The Nation* or *The Village Voice*, but the stock character more nearly personifying the soul of the major American news media would be that of the dandy or the fop—Rosencrantz or Guildenstern, an anxious and smiling gentleman, pathetically eager to please, forever worrying about the quality and number of his dinner invitations, glad to do the king's bidding, quick to repeat the gossip heard on the palace stairs, a credulous and servile little friend to all the world.

If the sketch seems somewhat at odds with the official portrait, it is because the media, together with their owners and political

overlords, find it convenient to pretend that the free and courageous voice of conscience defends the American people against
the darkness of tyranny and injustice. The media do nothing of
the kind, but the disguise is as flattering as it is profitable, and it
conceals the function of the media as the first and foremost of the
nation's courtiers. The big media identify themselves with wealth
and privilege and the wisdom in office. They preserve the myths
that the society deems precious, reassuring their patrons that all is
well, that the American truths remain securely in place, that the
banks are safe, our doctors competent, our presidents interested
in the common welfare, our artists capable of masterpieces, our
weapons invincible, and our democratic institutions the wonder
of an admiring world. By telling their audiences what they assume they already know, the news media reflect what the society
at the moment wants to believe about itself. Yes, say the media,
the Vietnam War was a holy crusade (no, say the media, the
Vietnam War was a cruel imperialist hoax); yes, say the media,
homosexuality is a life-style (no, say the media, homosexuality is
a disease); yes, say the media, the Kennedys are demigods (no,
say the media, the Kennedys are beasts); yes, say the media,
America is indestructible (no, say the media, America has lost its
resolve). Yes, Virginia, there is a world out there, and it not only
can be vividly described but also looks just the way you always
wanted it to look. Throughout the late spring and early summer
of 1991, in the brief but euphoric interval that followed the
victory in the Persian Gulf, the news media were busy telling
their audiences that they were the happiest and freest people ever
to walk the face of the earth, triumphant in war and magnanimous in peace. The fine phrases didn't alleviate the sorrows of the
domestic economy, and within the space of nine months the
public mood turned melancholy. The media obligingly changed
their f-stops and cast the middle class in the comfortable and
familiar role of a citizenry betrayed. The timeless prophets of the
age (among them the principal columnists for *The New York
Times* and *The Washington Post*) put on the robes of hired
mourners, cherishing the wounds of the American body politic as

if they were the stigmata of the murdered Christ. The expressions of self-pity were understood as a kind of compliment. No matter how severe the adjectives, the emphasis remained fixed on the subject of supreme interest and importance—the beauty of the American self, once glorious and now lost.[19]

By arranging the ambiguity of events into polite abstractions, the media compose the advertisements for a preferred reality, and their genius consists in the agility of the courtier spirit that allows them to serve, simultaneously, two masters: the demos, whom they astound with marvels and fairy tales, and the oligarchy, whose interests they assiduously promote and defend. The trick is by no means easy. It demands the skill of the juggler and acrobat, but few of the well-paid adepts admit to talents they associate with carnivals and fairs. They prefer to cast themselves as dignified, professional gentlemen trading at par value with physicians, lawyers, and professors of theology. Their vanity stands at odds with their self-interest, and at the awards banquets and on the annual pilgrimages to the mountains, nobody mentions the media's embarrassing resemblance to a chain of cut-rate department stores. Like all arrivistes jealous of their prerogatives at court, they scorn their clumsy and ill-bred relations who don't know how to attend a photo opportunity or when to ask a question in the White House Rose Garden, and nothing so excites the passion of the assembled company as the vulgarity of "the supermarket press"—those awful people selling cheap sensations in *The National Enquirer*—common people like Donahue and Oprah and Geraldo, willing to drag a presidential candidate through the mud of a sexual malpractice suit.[20]

It isn't that the news media object to displays of immoral conduct but rather that they think it their duty to protect the rulers of the state from the howling of the mob, to preserve them (for as long as is decently possible) as images of wisdom and power. Once the politician has left office, it is perfectly appropriate to dismember his reputation in an unauthorized biography, but not while the gentleman still must sustain the illusion of a virtuous and a well-ordered commonwealth. The news media's devotion to the status quo accounted for their active and unanimous endorsement of Governor Bill Clinton during the final months of last year's election campaign. No other candidate seemed likely to preserve both the fictions of democracy and the interests of oligarchy. The public opinion polls had turned against President Bush, and Perot—whether he was a genuine populist or a cleverly disguised despot—clearly was no friend to Ted Koppel. Clinton was one of the media's own, a politician fluent in the ritual language of the issues and careful to observe the pieties embodied in the editorial pages of *The Washington Post*, and the journalists at court expressed their gratitude by favoring him with easy questions and prominent photo placements.

The upper servants of the American news media possess the instincts of an English butler, and as long as they have reason to fear the administration in office, they can be counted upon to maintain the decorous facade of government. Prior to last year's adoration of Governor Clinton, I can think of no better demonstration of the news media's chronic servility than their figurative wringing of hands when Judge Clarence Thomas appeared before the Senate Judiciary Committee in October 1991 to answer questions about his sexual conduct. If politics consists in the ceaseless and bitter argument about who has the power to do what to whom, at what price, for how long, and with what chance of redress, here at last were people waging that argument in plain sight, telling one another the self-interested lies that they ordinarily manage to hide behind closed doors or disguise in the language of polite euphemism.

The hearings provided the American people with John Adams's "most dreaded and envied kind of knowledge," but the major American news media didn't want any part of it. Testimony began on Friday of the Columbus Day weekend, and the next morning on the front page of *The New York Times*, R. W. Apple bemoaned the "lurid, gut-wrenching" scenes on Capitol Hill, and on Sunday, still appalled by "horrifying events" and "excruciating detail," he was suggesting that maybe the Congress should conduct its confirmation hearings in secret or at least come to some sort of prior arrangement with the White House about the kind of nominee who could be relied upon to refrain from embarrassing the children and the servants. The following Tuesday in New York I found myself at lunch with several television and newspaper correspondents who were worrying about what they called "the unseemliness" of the proceedings on Capitol Hill. The tone of their conversation was indignant. The gentleman seated nearest to the ferns referred to "the spectacle of degradation." A woman dressed in silk said that she was "disgusted" by the "sordid" lines of questioning. All agreed that the hearings were "a national disgrace," that "something must be done" to correct a system of government so patently vile that it discouraged the participation of the good and true Americans (presumably present in large numbers somewhere west of the Alleghenies) who refused to descend into the sewers of politics. I noticed that I was the only journalist present who hadn't already appeared on a talk show to ask (molto serioso and while gloomily shaking the head) what was to become of a country in which louts, madwomen, and irresponsible gossipmongers could foul the temple of government with scurrilous rumor. Somebody quoted Judge Thomas (or maybe it was George Bush, or David Broder, or Senator John Danforth, or R. W. Apple) to the effect that the scenes on Capitol Hill were "intolerable . . . not the America we know."

But the America represented by the Senate Judiciary Committee was, of course, precisely the America we do know—the America of the savings and loan swindle and the fraudulent defense contract, the America defaced by its crowded prisons and its wretched schools, the America that lies to itself about the wonderful prosperity certain to derive from an economic policy that places an intolerable burden on the weak, the old, the poor, the ignorant, the young, and the sick. If the hearings were sordid or degrading, it was because the argument was lost to the champions of oligarchy, not because of the sexual aspects of the testimony or because of the slanders brought by the Republican senators against the character of Professor Anita Hill. As both

Jefferson and Lincoln well knew—possibly because they were subjected to slanders far more vicious than those addressed to Clarence Thomas—the advancement of civilization is never a pretty sight. But we can't know what we're about, or whether we're telling ourselves too many lies, unless we can see and hear one another talk.

Against the abuses of power available to any government—the monarchy of George III as well as the oligarchy currently in office in Washington—the best defense is a raucous and belligerent press. A democracy stands in need of as many questions as its citizens can ask of their own stupidity and fear, and the virtues of a free press inhere in its character as a necessary affliction rather than as an exemplary comfort. It is necessary precisely because it is an affliction, for exactly those reasons that require of its practitioners little refinement and less compassion, no sense of aesthetics, and the gall of a coroner. Like history and Lear's Fool, journalism is better able to diagnose than to cure, and when it is faithful to its purpose, it presents society with a rude measure of the distance between the graceful images of an approved reality and the awkward facts of the matter. By and large, and certainly in its more useful aspects, journalism is not a fit occupation for the landed or intellectual gentry. The press draws its strength from its nature as a loudmouthed crowd in the street, and it betrays itself when it attempts diplomacy or feigns philosophy, when its practitioners construe themselves as oracles or undersecretaries of state and imagine the business of government as a stately pageant in which benign statesmen wearing white gloves pass noble documents to one another on silver trays. The courtly pretensions leach the blood out of the animal and make it an easy prey for those of its enemies who would gag its mouth with cinnamon and apples.

The education of an American journalist is a courtier's education, and the ladies and gentlemen who do well at the business define the world as the sum of their acquaintance and obey Castiglione's sovereign rule of appearances. I received my own instruction in the trade as a reporter for the *San Francisco Examiner*

and *The New York Herald Tribune* and then, some years later, as
an occasional columnist for *The Washington Post.* I went to work
for the *Examiner* in the late autumn of 1957, and within a matter
of eight or nine months I understood that nothing was to be
gained by thinking for oneself. What was true was what somebody important said was true, preferably somebody who could
certify the afternoon's revealed wisdom with a seal or stamp of
authority—the police, the coroner's office, the Department of
Parks, the congressional committee, the presidential commission, the chairman of the insurance company. Only on rare
occasions did the newspaper question the substance of an official
proclamation. If the statement could be attributed to an individual or institution with appropriate credentials, the paper was
content to publish nonsense. Itself a bureaucracy, the press retains a devout faith in bureaucratic paper, and much of the news
therefore takes the form of official statements slightly revised to
meet the expectations of the marketplace. City officials in both
San Francisco and New York routinely made announcements
easily recognized as bald-faced lies—announcements about the
integrity of the budget, about the exemptions granted to a real
estate developer, about the time and cause of death. As a reporter loyal to the orthodoxy of "objective journalism" I was
bound to accept the press release as the last and best word on the
subject. I once asked an observant night city editor about the
game of "let's pretend," and I remember that he was surprised at
my stupidity. Where had I been for nine months, and what did I
think I had been doing? The newspaper business, he said, was a
matter of telling stories, some of them more interesting than
others, all of them subject to revision on short notice. The
official announcements could be construed as a series of fantastic
tales (embodying at best a plausible hope or a remote possibility), and they would be soon followed (preferably in time for
the next edition) by denials, contradictions, further explanations, and more fantastic tales. All the stories were straw with
which to make the bricks of the news. In answer to my objection that journalism wasn't much different from popular fiction,

the editor reminded me that most of the information that most people received in the course of a week or a year—in newsletters, gossip columns, stock market reports, medical diagnoses, or travel advertisements—sooner or later proved to be a figment of somebody's imagination.

Nor was there any profit in independent inquiry or investigation. The work took time and money, and when it was done, where were the honor and applause? The result undoubtedly would embarrass or infuriate the institutional sponsors of the news; the journalists in question would dull the smiles of welcome at City Hall, and their readers seldom could tell the difference between the official and unofficial version of events. Worst of all, the paper risked the chance that its own conclusion might prove wrong. Next to the expression of a blunt emotion or a genuinely new idea, nothing so terrifies the media as the prospect of being made to look ridiculous—precisely the same terror that governs any and all societies at court. [21]

The corps of correspondents at the *Examiner* in the late 1950s understood that most of the news in the paper constituted a kind of stage play in which police detectives, Russians, and flood victims all appeared as stock figures in an American *commedia dell'arte*. It was also understood that the most satisfying stories (the ones about the mayor's sexual perversity or the police commissioner's deal with the governor) never were ushered into the light of print. Nobody objected to these omissions because the possession of what was thought to be secret knowledge inflated one's sense of self-importance and sustained the illusion of being "on the inside." In the absence of decent pay, the flattery compensated the reporters for the work of rewriting press releases.

After two years on the *Examiner* I thought the fault was with the paper, not the profession, and I left for New York and the *Herald Tribune*, believing that what was then one of the most influential newspapers in the country might encourage the practice of independent thought. The hope was misplaced. As at the *Examiner*, the habit of dependence proved to be chronic and pervasive. The conversation took place in a slightly more elevated sphere—solemnities about the cold war instead of the crime in Oakland—and the institutional bulletins arrived on more expensive paper under more impressive letterheads—the Ford Foundation and the State Department instead of the Geary Theater or the Golden Gate Bridge Authority—but the rules were the same, and so was the craving to know what the public didn't know (or what one thought the public didn't know) about politics, art, sin, Europe, Greenwich Village restaurants, and John F. Kennedy's mistresses. The assumption of access to privileged information expressed itself as an air of knowingness, which, as in San Francisco and later in Washington, concealed the loss of the reporter's freedom of mind.

None of the senior officials at the paper needed to go to the trouble of explaining the codes of self-censorship. The stories that made page 1 were the stories that confirmed the preferred definitions of the news, and an attentive reporter learned within a matter of weeks which subjects and points of view were rewarded with headlines. Like every other important newspaper in the country, the *Tribune* didn't concern itself with the routine injustices committed by the people who owned the wealth of the country—for the logical and very good reason that the same people owned the press. Nor was the paper much interested in poverty, hunger, the inequities of the tax laws or prisons on days when the inmates neglected to riot. A related order of value determined the differences between a murder in Scarsdale and a murder in Spanish Harlem. If the Scarsdale murder took place at a good address and the victim, preferably a woman, belonged to a family socially prominent and decently rich, news of the crime remained on the front page for as long as the ingenuity of the city desk could contrive supplemental rumors and further speculation. The report of an otherwise identical crime in economy class on East 134th Street seldom received as much as two inches of type on page 41 in an early edition.

Two years at the *Tribune* taught me that I had the wrong temperament for the major news media. The rewards and honors of the profession accrued to the accounts of people who could dress up the wisdom of the moment in the costume of a clever phrase, and the man who would be Anthony Lewis or Sam Donaldson was obliged to believe the images in the mirrors of the news. If he couldn't do so with unreserved enthusiasm, then he would be condemned as an eccentric—unfit, irresponsible, clearly incapable of arranging the intellectual scenery ("missile gap," "new frontier," "third world") into the social or political meanings deemed suitable for a presentation at court.

I worked for the *Tribune* from the winter of 1960 through the early spring of 1962, and it was during that same brief interval that the national news media became enamored of their roles as instruments of government. In 1960 most of the people working at the seven newspapers in New York City understood that they had more in common with vagabond poets than they did with diplomats, soothsayers, or court chamberlains. Many of them were self-educated, and because they had come of age in the 1930s and 1940s, they were schooled in the lessons of poverty and given to a sardonic turn of mind. They hired themselves out as journeymen, not as immortal artists, and they tended to identify with the crowd in the bleachers rather than with the swells in the box seats. With a few exceptions on the order of Walter Lippmann and Joseph Alsop, none of them would have described themselves as gentlemen, and if asked to state their occupation, they would have said "reporter" or "newspaperman." The term *journalist* pertained only to Englishmen and would-be novelists. My own presence in the city room was understood as an anomaly, both by myself and by those of my companions who urged me to quit the business and study law or investment banking. About six months before John Kennedy was elected president, at a cocktail party on the Upper East Side, a young woman recently descended from Radcliffe asked me what I did for a living. With a feeling of some pride, I told her I was a newspaperman. At first she thought I was joking, and then she asked me what I meant to do when I grew up.

Kennedy's glamorous arrival in the White House coincided with the dawning of the age of glamorous media, and within a year of his election the suddenly respectable "profession of journalism" was attracting volunteers from Harvard and Princeton. The new recruits arrived with bound volumes of the absolute truth, and they regarded themselves as the social equals of the politicians and movie stars about whom they were obliged to make popular romances. A few of them made their entrances under the aegis of their prior service as government functionaries, and most of them knew more about the pleasures of Paris or London than they did about the sorrows of Brooklyn or Queens. The rates of pay kept pace with the expanding wealth of the communications industries, and by the end of the decade the higher-priced operatives earning upwards of five hundred thousand dollars a year found it easy to see themselves as the friends and peers of oligarchy. The ambiguity of the Vietnam War compounded the confusion, and just as the moralizing elements of the media came to imagine that they were better qualified to govern the country than the candidates elected to public office, so also they dressed themselves in the mantles of righteousness. The affectations were often very grand. If a person has been graduated from an Ivy League college, and if he or she wants to keep up with the latest dances and the most important people, and if a person goes to dinner with the secretary of state and conducts spacious discourse on the fateful issues of the day, then a person doesn't like to be reminded of his or her resemblance to a fop or, in Prince Hamlet's phrase for Rosencrantz and Guildenstern, a gilded waterfly. To the extent that the government and the media have learned to promote and flatter each other by inflating the importance of their mutual interests, the media have become increasingly vain. By and large they have made the mistake of believing their own reviews—the media as keepers of the nation's conscience, the media as consorts to royal celebrity, the media as the patrons of freedom, etc.—and they have renounced their character as a necessary affliction.[22]

By 1965 I had become a contract writer for the *Saturday Evening Post*, and in April of that year the editors sent me to Washington to write about President Lyndon Johnson. The magazine at the time was still one of the important facets of the national media, and the senior Washington politicians were as pleased to be seen in its pages as on NBC's "Meet the Press." Johnson was embarking that spring on the first term of the presidency to which he had been elected in his own right, and now that he had emerged from the shadow of President Kennedy's assassination, the editors of the *Post* wanted to know what kind of man would he show himself to be and what did he mean by "The Great Society." Like the network news divisions in later years, the *Saturday Evening Post* in those days spent money on a scale commensurate with its exalted station as one of the country's leading manufacturers of public opinion. I took a room at the Hay-Adams Hotel, across Lafayette Park from the White House, prepared to stay for whatever period of time proved necessary to the task in hand.

During my first week in the White House press lobby I remember being surprised to discover that the terms of service were the same as those in effect in the San Francisco police precincts and New York's City Hall. The correspondents in residence did what they were told and took what they were given, and in return for their courtesy and good behavior they were granted the illusion of thinking themselves situated at the still center of the turning world. They counted among their company thirty or forty permanent representatives from the major news organizations (the television networks, *The New York Times*, *Time* magazine, etc.), who mostly sat around on the comfortable couches and chairs in the West Wing of the White House, reading the papers, exchanging rumors, complaining about the ignorance of their editors, and deploring the credulity of the American public. Four or five times a day the news was brought to them from the office of George Reedy, the presidential press secretary, who conducted morning and afternoon briefings and arranged for the correspondents to attend one or more of the events listed on the president's daily calendar. The invitations were delivered by one of Reedy's senior assistants, a severe and sometimes sarcastic woman in her middle thirties who wore her blond hair in a tight bun. At random intervals throughout the day she suddenly would appear in the lobby, raising her voice to the pitch of a public announcement.

"Attention, reporters," she would say. "Attention. I have news. Over here, reporters."

I can still hear the sound of her voice, which was high and clear and peremptory, a voice that brooked no disobedience or delay. All of us rose more or less smartly to our feet and followed wherever she led—to the Rose Garden for a photo opportunity with the prime minister of Ghana, to Reedy's office for the daily briefing, to the theater in the basement to hear a general explain a map, to the South Lawn to watch the president play with his dogs. During the whole of my sojourn among the White House press corps I never could escape the impression of a flock of ducks—plump and well-kept ducks, ducks worthy of an emperor's garden, waddling back and forth to the pond on which the emperor's gamekeepers cast the breadcrumbs of the news.

Within a few days of my arrival in the press lobby I told Reedy that I didn't intend to recognize the distinctions between what was said "on the record" and what was said "off the record." Because I was writing only one article for the *Saturday Evening Post* (i.e., because I was passing briefly through the White House and never coming back), I could afford to ignore the protocols meant to guarantee continued access and favor. Reedy made no objection. He knew that I was unlikely to come across anything that his office defined as news, and he wasn't interested in the descriptive writing then being promoted under the label of "the new journalism." My defection from court etiquette was not so well received by the White House press corps. Some of the senior members expressed varying degrees of indignation and outrage, and in early May two of them took me to dinner at Duke Zeibert's Steak House to instruct me in the higher mysteries of responsible journalism—for my own good and the good of the profession, in order that I might not find myself shunned as an outcast on the trips to Texas as well as in the interest of maintaining a united front against the red-necked critics of the media, who, given the least encouragement or provocation, stood willing to wreck the delicate porcelain of the First Amendment. When even so well intentioned a sermon failed to win me to the cause of hints and whispers, the White House press corps denied me the privilege of a long-term pass to its lobby. Every morning for three months I was obliged to apply for a day pass at the west gate, running through the same half-hour security drill with one or more of the same guards.

As it turned out, I stayed in Washington through April, May, and June 1965, and during those few months President Johnson played the White House press corps for a crowd of hapless fools. The sleight of hand was easy for me to see because I didn't have to meet the daily deadlines of a three-hundred-word newspaper story or a thirty-second television broadcast. The press corps couldn't afford the luxury of keeping silent, and nobody had the time to compare the statements made on Monday with the statements made on Wednesday and Friday. The ease with which the stories could be changed became embarrassingly apparent over the span of the Dominican crisis in the first week of June. On four successive days President Johnson summoned the reporters to urgent and private briefings in which he presented them with four different justifications for the presence of American marines in Santo Domingo. All his confidences were theatrical, and all of them were false. The newspapers advertised each successive specious reason as revealed truth, and by the end of the week even James Reston and David Broder didn't know which phrases to believe. They resolved the difficulty by believing each and every one.

The indolence of the White House press corps was most plainly seen when it was traveling out of town, and after several excursions in the presidential entourage I understood why the Washington media were so unwilling to give up their comforts for something so unreliable as an idea of their own. Late in the afternoon of the day prior to departure, the austere blond woman posted a schedule of the forthcoming adventures and entertainments. If the correspondents could manage to get themselves and their luggage to the White House the next morning at the appointed time, they were assured of spending the next two or three or four days in a state of suspended animation. Military servicemen (usually air force personnel, but sometimes infantry or marines) carried the luggage to a chartered plane at Andrews Air Force Base, and at the point of arrival (in Texas or California or Florida) other military servicemen arranged the luggage in each of the correspondents' hotel rooms. Because Johnson liked to spend several days a month on his ranch near Austin, Texas, the press corps was in the habit of bringing golf clubs and tennis rackets, and when I first saw the ritual of departure on a morning in early April, I remember thinking of big-game hunters going off on safari with a procession of native gun bearers. Each of the correspondents received an identification tag (worn around the neck in the manner of children on a nursery school outing), and the bus proceeded directly to the steps of the plane, in those days a 707, waiting on the runway behind Air Force One. From the moment they left the White House until the moment they were returned to the same door, the correspondents never had to think for themselves. Herded through the sequence of photo opportunities, supplied with press releases, briefed once or twice a day, provided with telephones, flattered by their proximity to the chief of state and the staff officer carrying the briefcase with the nuclear weapons codes, the ladies and gentlemen of the White House press corps did as they were told and said what they were expected to say. What was depressing was their sense of self-importance. They mistook the pomp and majesty of their travel arrangements as proofs of their ennoblement, and those of their company who had traveled too long and too often with the president's entourage (i.e., for more than six months) began to imagine that without their good opinion the sun would die and the government would fall.

Like people rich enough to buy the best seats to the tennis matches or the opera, the ladies and gentlemen of the press have seen everything once. They can afford not to look too closely at the spectacle under consideration because they assume that there always will be something else to look at—another presidential candidate or a victim of repression, another opening night or sexual revolution in California. Transported from place to place at high speeds, talking incessantly about their connections and travel arrangements, the ranking American journalists devote their energies to questions of technique and to the relief of boredom. On the assumption that they have received their systems of ideas with the tickets of admission, they have no further cause to think. They can concentrate their attention on the logistics of getting inside the White House, on the excitements of riding around in airplanes with the candidates, or on the ceaseless repetition of gossip and the description of scene. But when, after prodigious labor, they find themselves at the signing of the peace treaty or the inaugural ball, they can think of nothing to say. They have no idea what any of it means, only that it is there and somehow very, very important and very, very glamorous or very, very sad.

From the White House press corps I learned the lesson of the emperor's ducks—i.e., that the media's principal voices were passive and that their principal agents were the kind of people willing to trade the capacity to act for the security of being acted upon. Washington measures a journalist's stature by the number and importance of his connections—sources, dinner invitations, friends in high places, etc.—and so the best journalist is, by definition, the journalist who best knows how to dance Diderot's beggar's pantomime. As with politicians and oil company lobbyists, access is all, and no journalist in Washington over the last twenty years has played the courtier's part more gracefully than Bob Woodward, a managing editor of *The Washington Post*, the famous author of many books, the model of the heroic journalist played in the movies by Robert Redford. Woodward's work and reputation rest on his gift for ingratiating himself with anybody in office or power with whom he can trade the favors of secrets kept and rumors revealed. His celebrity as an investigative journalist (i.e., the tireless champion of liberty pacing ferociously to and fro on the ramparts of freedom) is one of the better jokes of American journalism.[23]

Servile by need, the media become servile in spirit. The reason is not lost on people who take the time to reflect on the media's duties as court chamberlain and archflatterer. Lyndon Johnson referred to the Washington press corps as a troupe of "puppets . . . who simply respond to the most powerful strings." Some years ago in a conversation published in *Harper's Magazine*, Tom Wicker, a former columnist and Washington bureau chief for *The New York Times*, said of the media:

> In the end we are still part of the league of gentlemen. The people who run the press—particularly the metropolitan, largely capitalized institutions of the press—are part of it, along with the people who run the government and the major businesses and the big corporations . . . we don't want to be out in front, to attack the establishment, to criticize major institutions, to be accused of endangering national security . . . sure, someone could write a two-line memo tomorrow and change the news policy of the *New York Times* to be more skeptical and challenging of established institutions. But they don't do it, not because they couldn't do it, not because they don't have the power to do it, but because they don't want to suffer more than the minimal necessary disapproval of the league of gentlemen.

The longing for respectability makes the upper servants of the media especially vulnerable to the polite attentions of the political gentry in the drawing room, and when the eminent correspondent finds himself asked to dinner in Georgetown by an undersecretary of defense, he is as careful with his silences as he is with the wineglasses and the spoons. The correspondent and his source remark upon the weather and exchange the expected gossip about the provincialism of New York. Eventually the talk veers around to the affairs of state, and the undersecretary discourses at circuitous and euphemistic length about a shift of policy in Latin America or the Middle East. The correspondent doesn't take notes. Accustomed to the polite forms of "deep background," he knows that the undersecretary expects him to publish, without attribution, an abridged report of the conversation. A few days later, preferably in the context of a coup d'etat in Guatemala or an election in Israel, the story receives prominent display in the correspondent's newspaper. The correspondent assigns his information to a "high government source," and he knows enough to omit any reference that might embarrass or identify the undersecretary. Neither does he pursue, either in print or by further questions, all the implications of the story. He wishes to retain the dubious confidence of his source, and for the time being he has accomplished his purpose. Only in an indirect and subsidiary way does his purpose have anything to do with "the people's right to know." The correspondent has been rewarded with his name in the paper, praise from his editors, the envy of his peers, and the comfortable assurance that he enjoys access to the wellsprings of political power. Correspondents do not sell themselves for money. They traffic in the currency of vanity in order to preserve the illusion that they speak with the voice of history. They inhibit the circulation of any news that doesn't enhance the self-importance or the self-interest of their suppliers. The reporter who agrees to deal in protected information transforms himself into a press agent. The more the secrecy, the more the balance of power shifts in favor of the source. The substance of power remains with the source, the appearance of power with the journalist. How can a reporter challenge a man he cannot name? Unless the journalist translates himself into a sycophant, how can he reach the upper tiers of authority? Who would have any use for his company? Certainly not the White House or the senior management of the corporations; nobody in the investment banks, the Pentagon, or the front offices of the National Football League.

The dependence on the rule of grace and favor gives rise to states of acute anxiety. Having resigned the habit of independent thought—for the perfectly good reason that there's no money in it—the ladies and gentlemen of the fourth estate know that they are interchangeable. Rosencrantz is Guildenstern, is Rather, is Jennings, is Brokaw, is Guildenstern, is Rosencrantz. To the editor of the paper or the producer of the evening news it makes no difference which of his servants brings the bulletins from the king's army or the gossip from the queen's bedchamber. But any loud or prolonged objection to the wisdom in office, any violation

of the rule of what Wicker called the "minimal necessary disap-
proval," results almost at once in ostracism, leaks to competitors,
an absence of invitations to appear on "Crossfire" or "The
McLaughlin Group." The contacts vanish like the dew of the
morning, and at next week's important cocktail party on P Street
or next year's Gridiron Dinner, Kay Graham no longer remembers
one's name.[24]

The ceaseless anxiety that attends a courtier's comings and
goings accounts for both the arrogance and the credulousness of
so many journalists of large reputation. Knowing that they live
well beyond their moral and intellectual means, they quiet their
fears by insisting on the privileges of corporate rank (first-class
hotel and airline accommodations, chauffeured cars, the deference of waiters) and by exaggerating their claims to social conscience. The latter pretension might be more willingly forgiven if
the media made the slightest show of giving heed to their own
piety, but they continue to shove microphones into the faces of
dying men, to acquiesce to the advertising interests, to insist on
their own privileges without conceding comparable privileges to
anybody else, to consider themselves beyond question or re-
proach. The pose is neither surprising nor damnable, but it is ill-
becoming to those who would anoint themselves with the oil of
sanctimony, and most people find something unconvincing about
journalists who agree to set forth on a quest for truth only after
they have received large promises of money and been assured of a
suite at the Beverly Hills Hotel.

The credulousness of the media follows from the courtier's
assumption that nothing of importance takes place beyond the
horizon of his acquaintance. Believing itself omniscient, the
corps of court journalists constantly finds itself surprised. The
figure of H. Ross Perot rises and falls in the public opinion polls,
and the news media fail to anticipate or understand either event.
Saddam Hussein appears, disappears, and reappears, and the
news media wonder if he is the reincarnation of Adolf Hitler or
the Thief of Baghdad. At least once a week for the whole of the
twenty years after Richard Nixon made the unctuous speech in

which he defended his honor by declaring his love for his dog Checkers, every national columnist of rank reviled the man as a charlatan, a used car salesman, a Tartuffe devoid of conviction or scruple. And yet, when it came to pass that the taped transcripts of Nixon's Watergate conversations appeared in print (thus proving him worthy of all the prior characterizations), the columnists expressed shock and stunned disbelief. James Reston wondered what had happened to the awe and majesty of the office of the presidency; David Broder wished that he hadn't been told. To this day nobody knows why the burglars rifled the safe in the Watergate Hotel, or who was Deep Throat, or who shot Jack Kennedy. Nor, apparently, do the news media care to know. They prefer the effects of melodrama to the uses of history, and their recent promotion of two fraudulent wars—the war on drugs and the Persian Gulf War—exemplifies both their credulity and their delight in patriotic masques and pageants. In both instances the media composed advertisements for reality meant to confirm the moral beauty of the government in Washington and to assure their several audiences that God was in his heaven and all was right with the world.

President Bush proclaimed the war on drugs in September 1989 with the drums and flourishes of a rhetoric that was as cynical as it was dishonest. It was a genuinely awful speech, rooted at the beginning in a lie, directed at an imaginary enemy, sustained by false argument, proposing a policy that already had failed, playing to the galleries of prejudice and fear. The first several sentences established its credentials as a fraud. "Drugs," said Bush, "are sapping our strength as a nation." "The gravest domestic threat facing our nation," said Bush, "is drugs." "Our most serious problem today," said Bush, "is cocaine." None of the statements met the standards of either minimal analysis or casual observation. The government's own figures at the time showed that the addiction to illegal drugs troubled a relatively small number of Americans and that the current generation of American youth was the strongest and healthiest in the nation's history.

But the audience that President Bush most wished to impress—i.e., the politicians and their fuglemen in the big media—welcomed both the speech and the specious war on drugs as gifts from a gracious heaven. Because the human craving for intoxicants cannot be suppressed—not by priests or jailers or acts of Congress—the politicians can bravely confront an allegorical enemy rather than an enemy that takes the literal form of the tobacco industry, say, or the oil and banking lobbies. The war against drugs provides them with the appearance of moral conviction, requires them to do nothing difficult, and allows them to postpone, preferably forever, the more urgent and specific questions about the state of the nation's schools, housing, employment opportunities for young black men—i.e., the conditions to which drug addiction speaks as a tragic symptom, not a cause. They remain safe in the knowledge that they might as well be denouncing Satan or the rain, and they can direct the voices of prerecorded blame at metaphors and apparitions which, unlike Senator Jesse Helms and his friends at the North Carolina tobacco auctions, can be transformed into demonic spirits riding north across the Caribbean on an evil wind. The war on drugs thus becomes the perfect war for people who would rather not fight a war, a war in which the politicians who stand so fearlessly on the side of the good, the true, and the beautiful need do nothing else but strike noble poses as protectors of the people and defenders of the public trust. The norm of cynicism was implicit in President Bush's arithmetic. In his September speech he asked for $7.9 million to wage his "assault on every front" of the drug war, but the Pentagon allots $5 billion a year to the B-2 program—i.e., to a single weapon. Expressed as a percentage of the federal budget, the new funds assigned to the war on drugs amounted to 0.065 percent.

The drug war, like all wars, sells papers, and the media, like the politicians, ask for nothing better than a safe and popular menace. The campaign against drugs involved most of the theatrical devices employed by "Miami Vice": scenes of crimes in progress (almost always dressed up with cameo appearances by one or two prostitutes); melodramatic villains in the Andes; a vocabulary of high tech military jargon as reassuring as the acronyms in a Tom Clancy novel; the specter of a crazed urban mob rising in revolt in the nation's cities.

Like camp followers trudging after an army of Crusaders on its way to Jerusalem, the media in the summer of 1989 displayed all the garish colors of the profession. Everybody who was anybody set up a booth and offered his or her tears for sale—not only Geraldo and Maury Povich but also, in much the same garish language, Dan Rather (on "48 Hours"), Ted Koppel (on "Nightline"), and Sam Donaldson (on "Prime Time Live"). In the six weeks between August 1 and September 13 the three television networks combined with *The New York Times* and *The Washington Post* to produce 347 reports from the frontiers of the apocalypse—crack in the cities, cocaine in the suburbs, customs agents seizing pickup trucks on the Mexican border, smugglers named Julio arriving every hour on the hour at Key West.

Most of the journalists writing the dispatches, like most of the columnists handing down the judgments of conscience, knew as much about crack or heroin or cocaine as they knew about the molecular structure of the moons of Saturn. Their ignorance didn't prevent them from coming to the rescue of their own, and the president's, big story. On "World News Tonight" a few days after the president had delivered his address, Peter Jennings, in a tone of voice that was as certain as it was silly (as well as characteristic of the rest of the propaganda being broadcast over the other networks), said, "Using it even once can make a person crave cocaine for as long as they [*sic*] live."

So great was the media's excitement, and so determined their efforts to drum up a paying crowd, that hardly anybody bothered to question the premises of the drug war. Several of the more senior members of the troupe wrote diatribes against any dissent from the received wisdom in the same hysterical tones of voice that they brought to bear last summer on the impious presidential candidacies of Governor Jerry Brown and H. Ross Perot. A. M. Rosenthal, on the op-ed page of *The New York Times*, denounced even the slightest show of tolerance toward illegal drugs as an act of iniquity deserving comparison to the defense of slavery. William Safire, also writing in *The New York Times*, characterized any argument against the war on drugs as an un-American proof of defeatism. Without notable exception, the chorus of the big media tuned its instruments to the high metallic pitch of zero tolerance, scorned any truth that didn't echo their own, and pasted the smears of derision on the foreheads of the few people, among them Milton Friedman and William Buckley, who had the temerity to suggest that perhaps the war on drugs was both stupid and lost.

The story of the drug war played to the prejudices of an audience only too eager to believe the worst that can be said about people whom they would rather not know. Because most of the killing allied with the drug trade takes place in the inner cities, and because most of the people arrested for selling drugs prove to be either black or Hispanic, it becomes relatively easy for white people living in safe neighborhoods to blur the distinction between crime and race. Few of them have ever seen an addict or witnessed a drug deal, but the newspapers and television networks keep showing them photographs that convey the impression of a class war, and those among them who always worried about driving through Harlem (for fear of being seized by mythic gangs of armed black men) or who always wished that they didn't feel quite so guilty about the socioeconomic distance between Fairfield, Connecticut, and South-Central Los Angeles can comfort themselves, finally and gratefully, with the thought that poverty is another word for sin and that they or, more likely, their mothers were always right to fear the lower classes and the darker races. To the extent that the slums can be seen as the locus of the nation's wickedness (i.e., a desolate mise-en-scène not unlike the Evil Empire that Ronald Reagan found in the Soviet Union), the crimes allied with the trafficking of drugs can be classified as somebody else's moral problem rather than one's own social or political problem. The slums become foreign, nations on the other side of the economic and cultural frontiers.

The deliberate confusion of geography with metaphysics turns out—again to nobody's surprise—to be wonderfully convenient for the sponsors of the war on drugs. The politicians get their names in the papers, the media have a story to tell, and the rest of us get off the hooks that otherwise might impale us on the obligation to confront with questions of conscience.

The recruitment of the media to the banners of the Persian Gulf War was even easier than the swearing of their allegiance to the war on drugs. The summer of 1990 began as a disappointment for the syndicated Washington journalists fretting about America's lost place in the sun, and the Iraqi invasion of Kuwait in early August roused the court to the glory of urgent headlines. Within a matter of hours everybody who was anybody was waving a flag or beating a drum. *The New York Times* applauded the return of the "gung-ho, here's where it's happening spirit" of a city grappling with "great events," and "Nightline" set up interviews with the first in what proved to be a long procession of generals.

The advantage of hindsight suggests that President Bush and his nearest privy councillors resolved to go to war almost as soon as Saddam Hussein made the mistake of invading Kuwait. If the war could be quickly and easily won, then the administration might gain a number of extremely desirable ends, among them the control of the international oil price, a revivification of the American military budget, a diversion of public attention from the sorrows of the domestic economy, a further degradation of what passes for the nation's political opposition, a cure for the mood of pessimism that supposedly had been undermining Washington's claims to world empire. But none of these happy events could be brought to pass unless a credulous and jingoistic press could convince the American people that Hussein was a villain as monstrous as Adolf Hitler, that his army was all but invincible, that the fate of nations (not to mention the destiny of mankind) trembled in the balance of decision. It wouldn't do any good to send the grand armada to the Persian Gulf if the American people thought that the heavy guns were being wheeled into line to blow away a small-time thug.

The trick was to make the sitting duck look like a six-thousand-pound gorilla. Much later in the proceedings Lieutenant General Thomas Kelly could afford to say, amid applause and self-satisfied laughter at the daily press briefing at the Pentagon, that yes, sending B-52s to carpet-bomb a single Iraqi Scud site was, come to think of it, "a delightful way to kill a fly." But in the beginning the generals were a good deal more careful about the work of disinformation. As early as August 3 Washington was besieged with ominous reports—about Hussein's chemical and biological weapons, about the price of oil rising to fifty or one hundred dollars a barrel, about the nuclear fire likely to consume the orchards of Israel, about the many thousands of body bags being sent to Saudi Arabia to collect the American dead. All the reports derived from government sources, all of them proved to be grossly exaggerated, and all of them were eagerly believed by Rosencrantz and Guildenstern. Most of the prominent columnists in the prominent newspapers faithfully repeated the cant about Hussein's resemblance to Hitler, and the networks portrayed him as a bandit escaped from a B movie or a lunatic asylum.

By August 7, less than a week after Iraqi troops occupied Kuwait, the United States had mustered the largest military parade to be sent overseas since the Vietnam War. President Bush did his best to dress up the motive in the language of conscience and virtue. Explaining the national purpose to the American people, he said that the time had come for the United States "to stand up for what's right and condemn what's wrong, all in the cause of peace." His manner was that of a sincere and boyish scoutmaster, trying not to use too many big words, his earnest smile meant to convey an impression of goodness. A villain had arisen in the desert, a villain guilty of an "outrageous and brutal act of aggression," and the villain had to be punished. "America," the president said, "has never wavered when her purpose is driven by principle." He ended his speech by inviting his fellow countrymen to pray.

The media never subjected the administration's statements to cross-examination, in large part because the administration so deftly promoted the fiction of a "liberal press" bent on the spiteful negation of America's most cherished truths. The administration well understood the profoundly conservative bias of the news media (as well as the profoundly conservative sympathies of the prime-time audience), and so it knew that it could rely on their complicity in almost any deception dressed up in patriotic costume. But for the purposes of the autumn sales campaign it was necessary to cast the media as an antagonist as un-American as Saddam Hussein. If even the well-known "liberal press" (i.e., the same straw man known as the cultural elite in the 1992 presidential campaign) could be brought into camp, then clearly the administration's cause was just. The Pentagon's campaign against the American media, like the campaign against the Iraqi Army in the Arabian desert, relied on superior logistics and control of the systems of communication. Both campaigns were directed at enemies so pitiably weak that their defeat was a foregone conclusion.

The media loved the story lines (especially the ones about their own dread magnificence), and by Christmas every network and every magazine of respectable size had designed for itself some kind of red, white, and blue emblem proclaiming its ceaseless vigilance and its readiness for war. At the end, as in the beginning, the bulk of the writing about the events in the Persian Gulf War was distinguished by its historical carelessness and its grotesque hyperbole. The bombardment of Baghdad began on January 17, and within a matter of hours the newspaper and television correspondents had abandoned any claim or pretension to the power of independent thought. It was as if they had instantly enlisted in the ranks of an elite regiment, sworn to protect and defend whatever they were told to protect and defend by the generals who presented them with three or four paragraphs of yesterday's news. The Iraqi troops were forced to suffer the admonitions of gunfire, but the American media surrendered to a barrage of propaganda before the first F-16 fired its first round at an Iraqi tank.

The Pentagon's invitation to the war carried with it a number of conditions: no reporters allowed on the battlefield except under strict supervision, and then only in small task forces designated as "press pools"; all dispatches submitted to military censors for prior review; no unauthorized conversations with the allied troops; any violation of the rules punishable by expulsion from the theater in the sand. The media accepted the conditions with scarcely a murmur of protest or complaint. Who could afford to decline even so ungracious an invitation? The promise of blood brings with it the gift of headlines, audiences, single-copy sales, Nielsen ratings, Pulitzer prizes, and a swelling of the media's self-esteem. A television network on assignment to a war imagines itself outfitted with the trappings of immortality. The pictures, for once, mean something, and everybody has something important to say.

On the fourth day of the bombing Dan Rather confirmed the Pentagon's contemptuous opinion of media cheaply bought for a rating point and a flag. He appeared on a CBS News broadcast with Connie Chung, and after reading the day's bulletin, he said, "Connie, I'm told that this program is being seen [by the troops] in Saudi Arabia. . . . And I know you would join me in giving our young men and women out there a salute." Rather then turned to the camera and raised his right hand to his forehead in a slightly awkward but unmistakably earnest military salute.

The salute established the tone of the media's grateful attendance at what everybody was pleased to call a war. Had anybody been concerned with the accurate use of words, the destruction of Iraq and the slaughter of an unknown number of Iraqis—maybe 50,000, maybe 150,000—might have been more precisely described as a police raid, as the violent suppression of a mob, as an exemplary lesson in the uses of state terrorism. Although the Iraqi Army had been much advertised as a synonym for evil (as cruel as it was "battle-hardened," possessed of demonic weapons and a fanatic's wish for death, etc.), it proved, within a matter of hours, to consist of half-starved recruits, as scared as they were poorly armed, only too glad to give up their weapons for a cup of rainwater.

But the American media, like the American military commanders, weren't interested in the accuracy of words. They were interested in the accuracy of bombs, and by whatever name one wanted to call the Pentagon's trade show in the Persian Gulf, it undoubtedly was made for television. The parade of images combined the thrill of explosions with the wonder of technology. Who had ever seen—live and in color—such splendid displays of artillery fire? Who could fail to marvel at the sight of doomed buildings framed in the glass eye of an incoming missile? Who had ever seen the light of the Last Judgment coursing through a biblical sky?

Most of the American correspondents in Saudi Arabia experienced the war at more or less the same remove as the television audience in Omaha or Culver City. They saw little or nothing of the battlefield, which was classified top secret and declared off limits to the American public, on whose behalf the war presumably was being waged. The military command provided the media with government issue images roughly equivalent to the publicity stills handed around to gossip columnists on location with a Hollywood film company. Every now and then the government press agents arranged brief interviews with members of the cast—a pilot who could be relied upon to say hello to all the wonderful folks who had made the plane and the ordnance, a nurse who missed her six-month-old son in Georgia, an infantry sergeant (preferably black) who had discovered that nothing was more precious than freedom—but even this kind of good news was subject to official suspicion. A reporter who said of some pilots that their excitement upon returning from a mission had made them "giddy" found the word changed to "proud."

The Pentagon produced and directed the war as a television miniseries based loosely on Richard Wagner's *Götterdämmerung*, with a script that borrowed elements of "Monday Night Football," "The A-Team," and "Revenge of the Nerds." The synchronization with prime-time entertainment was particularly striking on Super Bowl Sunday. ABC News intercut its coverage of the game in progress in Tampa with news of the bombing in progress in the Middle East, and the transitions seemed entirely in keeping with the spirit of both events. The newscasters were indistinguishable from the sportscasters, all of them drawing diagrams in chalk and talking in similar voices about the flight of a forward pass or the flare of a Patriot missile. The football players knelt to pray for a field goal, and the Disneyland halftime singers performed the rites of purification meant to sanctify the killing of the desert. The televised images defined the war as a game, and the military command in Riyadh was careful to approve only those bits and pieces of film that sustained the illusion of a playing field (safe, bloodless, and abstract) on which American soldier-athletes performed feats of matchless daring and skill.

Like the sportscasters in the glass booth on the fifty-yard line, the newscasters standing in front of the palm tree or the minaret understood themselves to be guests of the management. Just as it never would occur to Frank Gifford to question the procedures of the National Football League, so also it never occurred to Tom Brokaw to question the ground rules of the war. When an NBC correspondent in Israel made the mistake of talking to New York about an Iraqi missile falling on Tel Aviv without first submitting his news to the local censors, the Israeli government punished his impudence by shutting down the network's uplink to the satellite. The embargo remained in force until Brokaw, at the opening of "NBC Nightly News," apologized to Israel for the network's tactlessness.

Between representatives of competing news organizations the protocol was seldom so polite. The arguments were about access—who got to see whom, when, why, and for how long—and the correspondents were apt to be as jealous of their small privileges as the hangers-on attached to the entourage of Vanilla Ice. When Robert Fisk, a reporter for the British paper *The Independent*, arrived at the scene of the fighting for the town of Khafji, he was confronted by an NBC television reporter—a

licensed member of the day's press pool—who resented the in-
trusion. "You asshole," the television correspondent said. "You'll
prevent us from working. You're not allowed here. Get out. Go
back to Dhahran." The outraged nuncio from NBC summoned
an American marine public affairs officer, who said to Fisk,
"You're not allowed to talk to U.S. marines, and they're not
allowed to talk to you."

Even under the best of circumstances, however, print was no
match for television. The pictures shaped the way the story was
told in the papers, the newsmagazines, and the smaller journals of
dissenting opinion. Although a fair number of writers (politicians as well as scholars and plain citizens) took issue with the
Bush administration's conduct of the war, their objections
couldn't stand up to the heavy-caliber imagery delivered from
Saudi Arabia in sorties as effective as the ones flown by the tactical
fighter squadrons. *Time* and *Newsweek* followed the pictures with
an assault of sententious rhetoric: "The greatest feat of arms since
World War II. . . . Like Hannibal at Cannae or Napoleon on a very
good day."

Through the five weeks of the aerial bombardment and the
four days of the ground assault, the version of the public discourse presented in the media turned increasingly callow. *Time*
and *Newsweek* published posters of the weapons deployed in the
Persian Gulf, and the newspapers gave over the majority of their
editorial page space to columnists gloating about the joy of kick-
ing butt. Andy Rooney on "60 Minutes" struck what had become
the media's preferred note of smug self-congratulation. "This war
in the gulf," he said, "has been, by all odds, the best war in
modern history. Not only for America but for the whole world,
including Iraq probably. It was short, and the objectives of victory were honorable. In spite of all the placards, the blood was
not for oil. It was for freedom. We did the right thing."

The return of the nation's mercenary army was staged as a
homecoming weekend for a college football team, and the troops
arriving in Georgia and California found themselves proclaimed,
in the words of *Life* magazine, "Heroes All." Many of them had

spent several uncomfortable months camping in the desert, but few of them had taken part in any fighting. The number of American casualties (125 dead in action, 23 of them killed by "friendly fire") once again posed the question of whether America had gone to a war or to a war game played with live ammunition. It was a question that few people cared to ask or answer. Several months after the end of the Persian Gulf War, even so faithful a servant of power as Dan Rather was moved to reflect on his status as an expensive publicist. Speaking to John R. MacArthur, the publisher of *Harper's Magazine*, Rather said: "We begin to think in terms less of responsibility and integrity, which get you in trouble . . . and more in terms of power and money . . . increasingly anybody who subscribes to the idea that the job is not to curry favor with people you cover . . . finds himself as a kind of lone wolf. . . . Suck up coverage is in."[25]

Suck-up coverage was always in, even as long ago as 1960, when I was introduced to the protocols in place on the third floor of the *Herald Tribune*, but I think it's probably fair to say that the toadying character of the national news media has become considerably more pronounced over the last thirty years, a consequence as much of the expansion of the national security state as of the ascendant spirit of oligarchy. Given the historical and economic circumstances, I doubt that anybody had much choice in the matter. As most of the newspapers that were once independently owned have been sold to large media syndicates, and as those syndicates in turn have become fewer in number, the always narrower concentrations of wealth and decision suppress the instincts for dissent. The fifteen or sixteen owners of the bulk of the nation's media could sit quite comfortably around a fairly small conference table. None of them thinks of a free press as a necessary affliction. The taste for oligarchy communicates itself to the expensive editorial operatives—anchorpersons, publishers, columnists, news directors, senior correspondents—receiving annual salaries of as little as three hundred thousand dollars and as much as two million dollars for work that in 1960 paid between forty thousand and two hundred thousand dollars a year. Just as the atmospheres of privilege encourage the dance of grace and favor, so also the judgments of the bottom line evoke the fear of libel suits and reward the use of words and images that cannot be mistaken for anything other than a compliment. To the extent that the nominally democratic press allies itself with the interests of the oligarchy, the ritual of democratic government becomes self-defeating as well as farcical. Denied knowledge of the character of its rulers, an uninformed citizenry becomes a credulous mob, and a sycophantic press, mistaking its faults for its virtues, learns to discourage the right to free speech; to rely more heavily on the corporate or government spokesman; to submit, more graciously, to the censorship imposed by the Pentagon, the managing editor, the White House, or the director of advertising; to play, more courteously, the parts of Rosencrantz and Guildenstern.

Some years ago *The New York Times'* editorial page expressed the complacent notion that "great publications magnify beyond measure the voice of any single writer." The statement is misleading. The instruments of the media multiply or amplify a voice, serving much the same purpose as a loudspeaker in a ballpark or a prison. What magnifies a voice is its character, its compassion, honesty, or intelligence. Unfortunately for all concerned, the major American news media all too easily relinquish their courage and freedom for the privilege of a court chamberlain who opens and closes the doors of publicity. The lesser power is by no means sovereign, but it is a visible and officious power—the power of a headwaiter or a master of ceremonies—and to people who don't know any better, who mistake the appearance of power for the substance of power, the media seem to play the part of God or time, welcoming the happy few into the warm and well-lighted ballrooms of celebrity, as indifferently ushering the anonymous many into the attics of oblivion.

5

The Wish for Kings

STARS DON'T GET TO *DO* ANYTHING.

STARS ONLY *ARE*. THEY'RE A STATE OF

MIND.

—*Whoopi Goldberg*

The founders of the American Republic entertained few illusions about the perfection of human nature, but as an advance over the pagan belief in a pantheon of gods and heroes, they proposed the countervailing ideal of a civil government conducted by mere mortals. They put their faith in the resourcefulness and self-discipline of the free citizen. No man was deemed indispensable. Given the instruments of the law, and the institutions directing the use of those laws, otherwise ordinary men were presumed capable of conducting the business of the state. The authors of the Constitution recognized in themselves and their fellow men the familiar vices of vanity and greed, but they preferred the risks of freedom to the assurances of monarchy. Thomas Jefferson preached the virtues of a genial anarchy, explaining that "Government is either needless or an evil and that with enough liberty, everything will go well." Not only Hamilton and Madison but also Adams and everybody else in Philadelphia in the summer of 1787 thought the laws by no means perfect, but at least they gave men the means of rescuing themselves from megalomania and self-hatred. The mechanism of checks and balances placed as many obstacles as possible in the way of the fears or passions of the moment, and by so doing, it preserved the principle of freedom against the promise of miracles and the wish for kings.

The proposition was as courageous as it was optimistic, but it doesn't meet the expectations of an age that worships celebrity and defines itself as the sum of its fears. To the extent that the world comes to be seen as a more dangerous and complicated place than was dreamed of in the philosophy of Walt Disney, people become impatient with rulers in whom they all too easily can recognize the corruption of the merely human. The rising levels of perceived risk lower the levels of tolerance for the norm of human fallibility. The news broadcasts swell with rumors of catastrophe—murder in the suburbs and rioting in the cities, poisoned apples at the headwaters of the Columbia River, and nuclear weapons in the hands of madmen—and an anxious public yearns for the shows of omnipotence, not only on the part of its rulers but also from its scientists, its ballplayers, its divorce and bankruptcy lawyers. Omnipotence doesn't exist in a state of nature. It must be manufactured, and the supply increases with the demand. Authority vested in institutions gives way to authority vested in persons, and on the great stage of the national political theater, the cast of democratic magistrates gives way to a procession of miraculous mandarins offering prayers to the sun or the moon.

The wish for kings is an old and familiar wish, as well known in medieval Europe as in ancient Mesopotamia, but its recent and cringing appearance in late-twentieth-century America, in a country presumably dedicated to the opposite premise, coincided with the alarms and excursions of the cold war, with the presidency of John F. Kennedy, and with the emergence of the theater of celebrity. At a moment in time when America enjoyed the prospects of limitless economic and geopolitical triumph, President Kennedy happily embodied the wish for kings in the person of a young man who seemed to make of government a synonym for a good time. An adoring media translated what Jefferson had called "the thankless task of governing men" into the legend of Camelot, and Kennedy appeared as the figure of an American prince of the realm, glittering in the eye of the world like the sun at noon playing on a wall of glass. So gracefully did he content himself with the best of everything that America had to offer—with its moral idealism as well as its expensive summer cottages, with sailboats and Harvard professors and pretty girls—that he endowed inherited privilege with an aura of redeeming social purpose. Among a restless or disappointed people ceaselessly striving to become something else, the spectacle of a man content merely to be has a soothing effect. Men endowed with wealth presumably can afford the luxury of inner repose, their exemption from existential doubt and common necessity presumably allowing them to notice, possibly even to comfort and assist, people less fortunate than themselves. Kennedy understood that princes of the realm do nothing but stand as symbolic figures (i.e., the sum of their appearances) in the midst of as much pomp and ceremony as can be decently arranged within the constraints of a republic nominally democratic. They grant audiences and receive petitions, in the meantime indulging themselves in pleasures demonstrably royal. Kennedy did what was expected of him, reciting noble phrases, squandering his inheritance among bawds and panders, casting the blessing of his countenance on the poor, displaying a connoisseur's interest in justice and the music of Pablo Casals. His death marked the passing of America's unquestioned supremacy on the stage of world events, a star turn that was supposed to last a century but played to cheering audiences for less than twenty years—from August 12, 1945, until November 22, 1963. Camelot vanished in a mist; the sun passed the zenith; the idealism of the American people was never again so brilliantly reflected in the mirror of the state.

Kennedy came and went so quickly that the memory of him is like a flash of light that still blinds the public eye to the mundane politics of trial and error in which mortal men make the usual mistakes and offer the usual self-serving excuses to cover the nakedness of their failure. Nor were Kennedy's successors as fortunate in the role of benign prince. President Johnson had too voracious an appetite for power, and he didn't know how to conceal his ambition behind the napkin of aristocratic disdain. He was constantly showing people his wounds and trophies, proving that even while sitting on the toilet at the morning levee in the White House, he could make policy and scourge his enemies in Washington and Vietnam. Nixon was too obviously a bourgeois figure, a crouching and literal-minded man whose pretensions to sovereignty were as ridiculous as the uniforms that he designed for the White House guards. As a plausible image of wisdom and power President Jimmy Carter proved even more disappointing than President Nixon. The media bestowed the favors of publicity in the hope that Carter would reward them with the semblance of a king, but he went about the business of government with the earnestness of a pious clerk, uneasy with the displays of extravagance and mumbling about the symptoms of what he called "America's malaise." Kennedy had the good manners to flatter his audiences by saying, in effect, "You are so good that you are fit to follow me." Carter weakened the compliment, by saying, in effect, "You are so good that I am fit to follow you."

The advent of Ronald Reagan restored to the White House the aura of celebrity. The effect was garish and made mostly of tinsel, but we were grateful for the flags and banners of geopolitical romance. Like Kennedy, Reagan expressed the serene calm of a man content merely to be, and he had the same gift for confusing the world of men and events with the rituals of flattery and play. It didn't matter that the operetta was paid for with borrowed money or that Reagan knew almost nothing about the workings of democratic government. He was a man who loved a parade, and we forgave him his ignorance for the sweetness of his actor's voice and the radiance of his actor's smile.

President Bush couldn't sustain the image of godlike ease. Without the operatic stage set of the cold war, the American national security state was hard pressed to define its purpose, and the American people were beginning to understand how much money and poetic imagination had been invested in the making of the Communist menace. The Soviet Empire apparently had been as important to our economy as General Motors or Iowa corn, as fundamental to our freedoms as the First Amendment. As enemies of the first resort the Russians had the shambling and clumsy demeanor of familiar trolls—unspeakably sinister, of course, but so thoroughly incompetent as to allow for the hope of escape. They came, as good villains should, from the land of ice and snow, and they never spoiled a good story by trying to make it come true. President Bush did his best with military productions in Panama and the Persian Gulf, but he was too obviously a nervous functionary and too much the anxious courtier, never at peace or at rest, forever pointing into the wind of the expedient sentiment and the seasonable truth. As the economy weakened through the second half of his term, the public turned from him in fear and disgust. The general feeling of revulsion for a figure no longer deemed magical—i.e., for a politician seen as merely mortal—prompted the enthusiastic welcome briefly granted to H. Ross Perot. The failures of the economy bid up the prices for gods and heroes, and Perot arrived on the political stage from the enchanted garden of celebrity portrayed in the supermarket tabloids—from the realm of Elizabeth Taylor's marriages and the resurrection of Elvis Presley. Vast wealth is itself celebrity, a presence so luminous that the individuals through whom it makes itself manifest serve as vessels for its glory. Perot's fortune of $2.5 billion introduced him to the television talk show audience as the figure of wealth incarnate, the instrument of economic deliverance, the revelation of the Godhead capriciously expressed in the person of an East Texas computer salesman armed with an album of golden platitudes.

The sudden and spectacular rising of Perot's image over the horizon of the news testified to the hope of miraculous rescue, and until Perot withdrew from the campaign in July, both President Bush and Governor Clinton suffered in the comparison with the dream of immortality. After Perot's withdrawal, the comedy of the proceedings followed from the attempts to fit the two remaining candidates with the costumes of celebrity. At their respective nominating conventions in New York and Houston, Governor Clinton and President Bush dutifully invoked the holy names of God and Elvis Presley, and it was clear from the tenor of their remarks that between the two deities they placed their greater trust in the one with the rhinestones and the electric guitar. It was equally obvious that neither they nor their stage managers would have had much trouble with the question of endorsements. Offered a choice of photo opportunities, they plainly would have preferred to appear with the king at Graceland than with Christ at Golgotha or Gethsemane.

Both candidates descended bravely into the wells of bathos, submitting to the ordeals of public confession at the feet of Donahue and Barbara Walters. Both offered tales of emotional distress (George's maligned children, Bill's alcoholic stepfather) as testaments to their status as genuine human beings worthy of pity and love. Both embraced the memory of the newly canonized Harry Truman as proof of their acquaintance with the virtue of the common man. Bill played the saxophone for Arsenio Hall, and Arnold Schwarzenegger wandered around the country as a latter-day Hercules attesting to the truth that George was "no wimp." When all else failed, and the polls showed the electorate still sullen with resentment, both candidates sought to explain and reveal themselves by means of cultural metaphor or through their nominees in the popular media: the Simpsons versus the Waltons; Murphy Brown versus Bruce Willis; late-night jazz clubs as opposed to Sunday mornings in church; Barbara Bush's chocolate chip cookies against Hillary Clinton's chocolate chip cookies.

But although both candidates stood willing to accept any indignity and bear any expense, to smile stage right or stage left, to say whatever the issues director of the focus group told them to say, neither they nor their press agents could make a living star from a dead moon. At the end, as at the beginning, they couldn't escape their characters as petty magistrates skilled in the arts of subservience. Like Bush, Clinton was too easily shaped by the results of yesterday's opinion poll, another Washington courtier forever making excuses about his trouble with women and the army.

If both President Bush and Governor Clinton failed to achieve the rank of celebrity, it was not only because they lacked theatrical presence but also because they spoke a language no longer intelligible to a large and distracted audience. Each of them knew a good deal about the mechanics of government in late-twentieth-century America, but they tended to phrase their remarks as statements of policy, and sometimes they made the mistake of being seen to think. The emotional vocabulary of the mass media doesn't lend itself to the discussion of complicated political issues, much less to moral ambiguity or moments of doubt. The television camera demands prophetic certainty and a sentimental script, and over the course of the last thirty years the amplification of images increasingly has shifted the weight of magical personality against the play of ideas and the uses of thought. During the second presidential debate (the one in Richmond, Virginia, that entertained questions from the audience and had the feeling of a daytime talk show) a very sincere and sweet-spoken gentleman at the back of the auditorium cast himself and his fellow voters in the role of needy children. Confessing his weakness to all three of the candidates, he said: "The focus of my work as domestic mediator is meeting the needs of the children that I work with . . . and I ask the three of you, how can we, as symbolically the children of the future president, expect the two of you, the three of you, to meet our needs . . . could we cross our hearts; it sounds silly here, but could we make a commitment?"

The gentleman was asking for a king to whom he could assign his soul as well as his vote. As mortal politicians in thrall to the opinion polls, none of the candidates could make any commitment likely to last longer than a week, but once Clinton had been elected president, the media promptly set about the task of answering the gentleman's prayers. The promise of compassion was redeemed in the coin of pious gesture and sentimental prose. On the instant and in a puff of newsprint, the candidate who had been seen as a timid frog was turned into a courageous prince.

As recently as 1960 it was still possible to make distinctions between the several forms of what were then known as the lively arts. The audiences recognized the differences between journalism, literature, theater, the movies, and politics, and it was understood that the novelist wasn't expected to double as an acrobat or a sage. The distinctions dissolved under the technical and epistemological pressures of the next ten years, and as the lines between fact and fiction became as irrelevant as they were difficult to distinguish, the lively arts fused into the amalgam of forms known as the media. News was entertainment, and entertainment was news, and by 1970 network television was presenting continuous performances on the stage of events with a troupe of high-definition personalities who shifted their mises-en-scène as easily and as abruptly as the actors in a Shakespearean play, to Dallas, Vietnam, Chicago, Vienna, Washington, and the Afghan frontier. The special effects were astonishing, and by 1980 the theater of celebrity had replaced the old religious theater in which Poseidon and Zeus once staged cataclysmic floods and heavenly fires with the effortless aplomb of ABC's "Wide World of Sports."

The postmodern imagination is a product of the mass media, but as a means of perception it is more accurately described as post-Christian. The vocabulary is necessarily primitive, reducing argument to gossip and history to the telling of fairy tales. Like the old pagan systems of belief, the mass media grant the primacy of the personal over the impersonal. The ancient Greeks assigned trace elements of the divine to trees and winds and stones. A river god sulks, and the child drowns; a sky god smiles, and the corn ripens. The modern Americans assign similar powers not only to whales and spotted owls but also to individuals blessed with the aura of celebrity. Whether in Washington hearing rooms or Hollywood restaurants, names take precedence over things, the actor over the act. On television commercials and subway signs, celebrities of various magnitude, like the nymphs and satyrs and fauns of ancient myth, become the familiar spirits of automobiles, cameras, computers, and brokerage firms. Athletes show up on television breathing the gift of life into whatever products can be carried into a locker room, and aging movie actresses awaken with their "personal touch" the spirit dormant in the color of a lipstick or a bottle of perfume.

The greater images of celebrity posed on the covers of our magazines impart a sense of stability and calm to a world otherwise dissolved in chaos. The newspaper headlines bring word of violent change—war in Yugoslavia, near anarchy in Moscow, famine in Somalia, moral collapse in Washington—but on the smooth surfaces of the magazines the faces look as vacant and imperturbable as they have looked for twenty years, as steady in their courses as the fixed stars, as serene as the bronze Buddha in the courtyard at Kamakura. There they all are—Liz and Elvis, Madonna and the Kennedys—indifferent to the turmoil of the news, bestowing on the confusion of events the smiles of infinite bliss. Like minor deities or a little crowd of unpainted idols in a roadside shrine, they ease the pain of doubt and hold at bay the fear of change.

The average American household now watches television for roughly seven hours a day, and soap opera stars receive as many as one hundred thousand letters a week, in which their devotees confess secrets of the heart that they dare not tell their wives, their husbands, or their mothers. The loss of distinction between who is real and what is fictitious sustains the market for movies on the order of Oliver Stone's *JFK* and books in the manner of E. L.

Doctorow's *Ragtime,* for the art of lip sync and the New Age dreams of a shaman's return from the lost continent of Atlantis. As the traditional narratives of the recent past lose their coherence and force, Ross Perot can commission Ken Follett to write a heroic version of his life under the title *On Wings of Eagles,* and Gloria Steinem, always a bellwether of the going trend, can align the passion for witchcraft with feminist political doctrine: "The healers and wise women of pagan times knew what they were doing when they made covens of thirteen witches—small enough so everyone could talk, large enough for diversity and an uneven number so decisions were not deadlocked."

Over the course of a generation the popular worship of images has become so habitual that we find it easy to imagine celebrities enthroned in a broadcasting studio on Mount Olympus, idly conversing with one another on an eternal talk show. It doesn't matter that they say nothing of interest or importance. Neither did Aphrodite or Zeus. Celebrity is about being, not becoming, about the indefinite postponement of death and time, and by reason of their existence in a realm of weightless images, celebrities need not trouble themselves with the rules of cause and effect. Any statement is equal to every other statement, and the question of what Mikhail Gorbachev said to Ronald Reagan about thermonuclear war at a summit meeting in Iceland is of no more or less consequence than the question of what Madonna ordered for breakfast—raspberries or strawberries—in a suite at the Château Marmont on the morning after her marriage to Sean Penn. What matters is the presence of immortality. Elvis lives, and so does anybody else who can transform the corruptions of the private flesh into the incorruptibility of the public image. The presence of celebrity comforts the faithful with the hope of a temporary exemption from the laws of chance and fate.[26]

The belief in the magical powers of licensed personality afflicts even presumably stolid business executives who ask themselves and their public relations people, What is the point of running a company richer than Venezuela if nobody knows your goddamn name? Why remain within the shadow of anonymity if the company employs enough people to fill the seats in Yankee Stadium? The dispirited executives look at ballplayers selling hair spray or actors hustling jogging shoes, and they wonder at the injustice of a world that casts so much light on persons of so little substance. It's all very well to be rich or talented or beautiful or brave, but unless one is known to be rich or talented or beautiful or brave, one cannot be a celebrity, and if one isn't a celebrity, one might as well be dead. The nobility in seventeenth-century France entertained similar feelings for the brilliantly lit society at Versailles. They believed themselves invisible unless they could make a show at court, but before they could appear at court, they had to know how to walk and curtsy and speak an artificial language that would fall pleasingly on the ear of a duchess.

In the United States in the late twentieth century, gentlemen of great wealth or polite intellectual attainment—novelists and university presidents as well as candidates for political office—attend "media training sessions," meant to furnish them with the supreme gift of a public image. The apprentice aristocrats learn to refrain from fidgeting in their chairs, to wear their hair at modish lengths, to walk gracefully through the aisles of the accounting department, to keep their fingers from drumming on the lectern, to speak forcefully, and, above all, to avoid raising their voices when exchanging civilities with the ladies and gentlemen of the press. These latter personages open and close the doors to the ballrooms of celebrity, and unless one knows how to conduct oneself in their august presence, even the richest of businessmen or the wisest of authors must vanish into the pits of anonymity and ridicule.

Two years ago I attended one of these lessons in court protocol administered to the chairman of a large insurance company encumbered with the embarrassment of indictment for fraud. The gentleman had been invited to an interview on network television, and he had reason to be anxious. His company hadn't been receiving the best press notices, and for the modest sum of ten thousand dollars he had hired public relations counsel for a one-day lesson in studio etiquette. The chairman arrived promptly at

9:00 A.M., uneasy and nondescript despite the expensive tailoring of what was obviously a new suit. He was accompanied by seven assistants: the vice-president in charge of political affairs, two secretaries, a speech writer, a statistician, a consultant, and a valet. About the same number of people represented the public relations firm.

Everybody shook hands with everybody else, and the company arranged itself around a long and highly polished table. A producer named Bernie came briskly to the business at hand. He introduced a troupe of "communications specialists" who would play the part of the television journalists, and then, speaking to the chairman, he said: "What you have to bear in mind is the simplicity of the medium and the stupidity of the hosts. Never answer their questions. Never be seen to think."

The chairman nodded complacently, delighted to hear Bernie confirm his dearest prejudices. Bernie made a few more observations—about dictating the terms of the interview and keeping one's fingers out of one's nose—and everybody moved into an adjoining studio for the first performance. The chairman settled himself into a chair opposite the surrogate host, an aggressively affable young man named Mort, and waited confidently for the first question.

His self-assurance didn't last thirty seconds. Mort smiled a greasy smile and said: "Perhaps you can tell us, Mr. Chairman, why your company gouges people with the viciousness of a Mafia loan shark?"

The chairman's mouth opened and closed like the mouth of a netted fish. Mort accepted his silence as a concession of guilt and went unctuously on to the next question: "I can't say I blame you, Mr. Chairman, but maybe you can tell us why your company robbed its own stockholders of five hundred million dollars last month to prevent the merger with E. F. Hutton?"

By an obviously heroic effort, as if struggling with giant snakes, the chairman achieved the victory of speech. It wasn't coherent speech, of course, and none of it resembled the notes on the index cards in the chairman's coat pocket—wonderfully succinct little statements about his company's benevolent service to the American people. Gasping with rage, he managed to say, not very distinctly but distinctly enough to be heard on camera: "You're a dirty, lying son of a bitch."

Bernie stopped the camera. In a voice almost as breezy as Mort's, he said: "Yes, well, I can see we have a lot of work to do."

The rest of the day wasn't easy. Mort was sent away, replaced by a woman who wasn't quite so rude. The valet trimmed the chairman's hair; the speech writer typed the prepared statement in capital letters; the secretary reminded the chairman that he was one of the richest men in the world. By six o'clock in the afternoon the chairman was capable of getting through five minutes in front of the camera without committing the theatrical equivalent of suicide. His retainers helped him out the door, mopping his forehead, steadying his shoulders, murmuring reassurance in his ears. Watching him depart, Bernie said: "Believe it or not, he was better than most."

And then, after the door had closed: "It's a wonderful world. Fifty years ago I could have been teaching debutantes to dance."

If the media succeed with their spectacles and grand simplifications, it is because their audiences define happiness as the state of being well and artfully deceived. People like to listen to stories, to believe what they are told, to imagine that the implacable forces of history speak to them with a human voice. Together with the expansion of a national security state over the last thirty years, the society so enlarged and complicated its acquisition of knowledge—political, scientific, economic, technological—that the public has become desperate for easy and authoritative answers. Harassed by data of all denominations, surrounded by a din of images, people revert to a primitive exchange of signs. Given too much to read, they tend to read as little of it as possible. It is easier to watch "Monday Night Football" and to hope that at the next conference or cocktail party somebody will turn up with an authoritative bit of gossip descended from Kevin Costner or William F. Buckley. Despite the prodigies of the new data bases and computer systems, we seem to know less than we did when we sealed letters with wax and waited eight months for a reply from London. Fewer and fewer people find the time even to glance at the papers. The periodicals gather like unwelcome cousins in the hall; the memorandums, the books, the abstracts, the briefing papers collect in briefcases that people would rather not open. Even a middle-level executive at a middle-level brokerage firm receives five hundred household advisories a week (not to mention the subscriptions to trade journals or the daily and financial press); dossiers of equivalent bulk circulate at every level of authority within the corridors of any American institution large enough to boast of its presence in the twentieth century. Thus the sense of confusion and loss. What does any of it mean? Who has the time to read what he or she has to read? Where and how to find—at a price of seventy-five cents or less—not only violent sensations and high-minded sentiment but also baseball scores, moral instruction, accurate weather forecasts, and the truth? The more complicated or ambiguous the circumstances, the more desperately people fall back on prophetic certainty.

Our politics becomes synonymous with advertising—a procession of images notable for the strict separation of cause and effect—and the inanity of the American political debate follows from the reduction of the words to wands with which to perform the rituals of omnipotence. The less that people understand of what politicians do, the more urgent their desire to appoint politicians to the ranks of the immortals. In the absence of any discernible moral or intellectual difference between the Republican and Democratic parties, elections proceed by means of ideographs and holograms—John F. Kennedy as Prince Hal; Jimmy Carter as Christ the Redeemer; Ronald Reagan as John Wayne or Old King Cole; Bill Clinton as the down-home democrat. The image of the president (or any other politician) corresponds to what the country wants to believe about itself, and as the occasion arises every two or four or six years, those among the Washington gentry who actually stand for public office hire a retinue of literate squires (speech writers, policy advisers, pollsters, et al.) who outfit them in an armor of slogans heavy enough to withstand the blitzkrieg of an election campaign.

The candidates come and go within a burning arc of klieg lights, pursued by the inquisitions of the press, weighed in the daily balance of the public opinion polls, their voting records and childhood memories sifted through the labyrinths of computer analysis. The sophistication of the technology has the paradoxical effect of reducing the campaign to a barbarous entertainment. The more that is known, the less that can be said. Never before in the history of the world have so many people had so much access to so much information about their prospective rulers, but the accumulated data apparently give them small comfort, and so they rely instead on what has become a trial of physical strength, as if they were hoping for a proof of divine or supernatural favor. Medieval chroniclers tell of princesses who sent Christian knights in search of dragons, requiring them to recover bits and pieces of the True Cross and to wander for many days and nights in heathen forests. Toward the end of the twentieth century, in a country that prides itself on its faith in reason and the wonders of its science, candidates for the presidency wander for months and years through the ballrooms of Holiday Inns, answering, in twenty words or less, questions that cannot be answered in a hundred thousand words, smiling steadfastly into the lens of the camera that never sleeps, and displaying, in the manner of surgeons and generals, not the least sign of fear or disgust. President Clinton proved his worthiness in last year's election campaign less by what he said or didn't say than by his capacity to endure insult and humiliation. All the speeches, all the fine phrasing and rephrasing of domestic economic policy were as nothing compared with the doggedness with which he withstood the questions about his romance with Gennifer Flowers and his avoidance of the military draft.[27]

The transformation of politics into soap opera makes nonsense of the sham distinctions between Democrat and Republican, liberal and conservative. If authority is invested in persons instead of ideas or institutions, then the politician stands on no platform other than the scaffolding of self-dramatization. The rule of love supplants the rule of law, and instead of addressing fellow citizens, the politician who would be king seeks to recruit fans. When President Bush first introduced Judge Clarence Thomas to the television cameras at Kennebunkport in July 1991, he didn't say a word about the nominee's understanding of the law. He presented the media with a celebrity biography. Praising the nominee as a "delightful and warm, intelligent person, who has great empathy and a wonderful sense of humor," the president concluded his endorsement with an inspired non sequitur. "Judge Thomas's life," he said, "is a model for all Americans, and he's earned the right to sit on this nation's highest court." The two clauses had nothing to do with each other. By virtue of the same false syllogism, the president as easily could have submitted the name of Michael Jordan or Oprah Winfrey.

Judge Thomas responded on key and in kind. He announced himself as an exemplary proof of the coming to pass of the American Dream, and his remarks could have served as the acceptance of an Academy Award. Instead of talking about the nature of the office for which he had been nominated, about the weight and spirit of the laws or his countrymen's hope of justice, he thanked the wonderful cast that had "helped me to this point and this moment in my life—especially my grandparents, my mother, and the nuns, all of whom were adamant that I grow up to make something of myself. I also thank my wonderful wife and my wonderful son." Judge Thomas told the story of a poor black boy born in a Georgia slum, deserted by his father at the age of seven, who learned his letters from Catholic nuns, and who, by dint of his spiritual faith and moral effort, triumphed over the evil of segregation and went on to win fame and fortune in the imperial city that was Ronald Reagan's Washington. The judge glistened with egoism (seldom a good sign in a magistrate), but he spoke with tears in his voice, and the effect enhanced the photo opportunity.

As with President Bush's encomium, it was the story of the life, not the temper of the thought, that justified Judge Thomas's place on the Supreme Court. He could as easily have been made of straw or wood. The media obligingly supplied the trappings of human character. Writing in *The Washington Post*, the columnist George Will discovered in Judge Thomas a man who "could have stepped from the pages of those novels 19th-century readers loved, novels of astonishing upward mobility by strivers who succeed by pluck and luck." Writing in *The Wall Street Journal*, Peggy Noonan (once-upon-a-time speech writer to both Presidents Reagan and Bush) abandoned herself to the language of twentieth-century soap opera: "Clarence Thomas made it in America because he was loved. His mother loved him. And when she could no longer care for him she gave him to her parents to bring up and they loved him too. . . . He got love and love gave him pride and pride gave him confidence that he had a place at the table."

The parade of celebrity invariably silences the voices of conscience or thought, an effect of which I was forcibly reminded in May 1990 at the Cathedral of St. John the Divine in New York City, on an evening when a choir of celebrities staged the political analogue of an Academy Awards ceremony in honor of Vaclav Havel. In December 1989 Havel had become the president of Czechoslovakia, and the proofs of his eloquence and courage had evoked the admiration of a good many people in countries other than his own. The last of the day's light faded before the cathedral doors opened, and I found a seat in the nave, about half the distance between the west door and the pulpit. As the immense and dimly lit neo-Gothic space gradually filled with people come to pay their respects to a brave man, I studied the mimeographed program promising remarks by Milos Forman and Eli Wiesel, readings from Havel's speeches by Paul Newman and Gregory Peck, songs by Dizzy Gillespie and Roberta Flack, and a good many orchestral performances of music by Dvorak and Mozart. Across the aisle, about four rows nearer the camera and the pulpit, I noticed one of New York's wealthier literary agents in conversation with an author noted for his patriotic fictions on the theme of America the Invincible and America the Good. They looked as sleek and soft as otters, both of them expensively manicured and glittering with gold jewelry, and it occurred to me that neither would have had much trouble serving the Communist *ancien régime* in Prague. Nor, if the times demanded a change of ideology and a rearrangement of the political furniture, would they find it difficult to serve any other regime (fascist or monarchist or social democratic) that generously rewarded them for their hired loyalty and praise. I was estimating the likely speed of their change of costume when Havel entered the cathedral through a side door, forty-five minutes late, invisible in a crowd of friends, dignitaries, and Secret Service agents. He was so far away that I was aware only of blurred movement, as if I were watching a wind passing through distant grass. Although almost nobody else in the cathedral could see him any better than I, the entire congregation, maybe as many as one thousand people, instinctively rose and applauded.

The program began with a fanfare played on a herald's trumpet and the ringing of the cathedral bells. Milos Forman spoke a few words of welcome to his longtime friend and fellow dramatist, Placido Domingo sang an Agnus Dei written by Bizet, and Paul Newman read a brief passage from one of Havel's reflections about the difference between the uncomfortable truth and the expedient lie.

Newman read the lines with an emphasis and inflection better suited to a bad movie, and yet, much to my astonishment, the words rang true. Listening to the voices in the cathedral for the next hour (Susan Sarandon reading Havel's letters from prison, Arthur Miller addressing Havel as the first avant-garde president), I thought that it might yet be possible to invent or discover a politics expressed in a language capable of telling a straight story. The Brooklyn Philharmonic Orchestra played a passage from Mozart's *Don Giovanni* (which was first performed in Prague in 1787), and I thought, if the Czechs can slip the bonds of cynicism and cant, then might not the Americans make good their own escape? All that would be required would be a few people willing to say what they meant and to bear the responsibility for their own voices.

The current of generous feeling in the cathedral failed on the instant that Henry Kissinger appeared in the pulpit. A man seated directly behind me shouted, "Murderer," and in the echoing distance of the sanctuary I could hear people shouting boos and catcalls. Prior to Kissinger's arrival, the evening had passed without embarrassment; the music was good, the emotion genuine, the speakers brief and to the point. All of them had tried to describe the shape of an idea larger and higher than themselves, looking, at least figuratively, upward. Kissinger looked down, condescending to bestow on the congregation the favor of his advice. Instead of talking about Havel, he talked about himself. "When I was in Prague in 1968," he said, "I tried to warn my good friends the Czechs, but they wouldn't listen to me. . . ." He continued in the same manner for more than five or six minutes (nobody else having spoken for more than one or two minutes), and the effect was turgid and pompous.

Kissinger was followed by Barbara Walters and Saul Bellow, two other self-important figures at court, who, like Kissinger, spoke adoringly of themselves. Walters said that she had been thrilled to be in Prague last Christmas, in time for the wonderful, thrilling experiences associated with the collapse of a Communist regime. Bellow was glad to know that when Havel was in prison, he had remembered to read Bellow's novel *Herzog*. As a reward for Havel's intelligence and taste, Bellow had brought an autographed copy of the novel which he hoped the obviously perceptive president of Czechoslovakia would accept as a token of his esteem.

The evening collapsed inward on itself like a dead star, and it ended on a sustained note of mummery—with the presenting to Havel of a meaningless "spirit of freedom award," with the passing around of candles for everybody in the cathedral to light, and with the playing of Aaron Copland's disingenuous *Fanfare for the Common Man*.

The theater of celebrity favors the worship of power over the uses of freedom, and I remember the distinction being very clearly drawn on another evening in New York, at a reception for Michael Jackson at the American Museum of Natural History. To a gathering of celebrities as impressive in its bulk as the stuffed elephants and the polyurethane whale, the president of Columbia Records introduced Jackson as "the greatest artist of all time"— not the greatest recording artist of all time, not the greatest pop singer or dancer of all time, but, simply and unequivocally, the greatest artist of all time. The hyperbole seemed excessive, and at first I thought that the gentleman from Columbia Records merely wished to say that Jackson was extremely rich. This form of politeness is so prevalent in New York and Los Angeles that if a performer in any venue earns an income that can be counted in eight figures, he or she becomes, as if by royal proclamation, an artist. But even the magnificence of Michael Jackson's fortune didn't adequately explain the phrase "the greatest artist of all time." Why not merely "a sublime artist" or "one of the greatest artists of all time"?

Eventually it occurred to me that the president of Columbia Records, like so many of his peers in both the weapons and the entertainment industries, identified art not with talent or inspiration, not even with skill or ingenuity, but with power. I thought of Adolf Hitler at Nuremberg in the 1930s, experimenting with the twentieth-century forms of *son et lumière* and presenting himself as the first of the modern rock stars. He set the scenes of his speeches as artfully as the producers of music videos arrange the visual accompaniments for songs, and in *Mein Kampf* he observed that the object of all propaganda was the "encroachment upon man's freedom of will." Toward this end he recommended techniques likely to "whip up and excite . . . the instinctive." The impresarios look for the same effect, and by art they mean, more often than not, the Dionysian burst of feeling that draws a crowd, burns the Reichstag, elects a president, or sells forty million copies of *Thriller*.[28]

The belief in the transfiguring power of personality derives its modern and egalitarian bona fides from Jean Jacques Rousseau's romantic pastoral of man as a noble savage at play in the fields of the id, of man set free from laws and schools and institutions, free to set himself up as his own government, free to declare himself a god. Rousseau was acutely conscious of the subjugating power of fame, and in a spirit that would be well understood by the editors of *People* magazine, his writings constantly allude to his desire to complete other people's lives, to walk into a room and seize the instant and universal approbation of everyone present, to focus upon himself all eyes, all praise, all sexual feeling.

Precisely the same desire denominates the character of President Clinton. He is a man defined by his voracious appetite, for more friends, more speeches, more food and drink, more hands to shake, more hugs. His eagerness to please—to complete other people's lives by presenting himself as the world's most obliging talk show host—suggests the emptiness of a soul that knows itself only by the names of what it seizes and consumes. So insatiable is the president's lust for center stage that on the night before the inauguration, during the gala presented in his honor at the Capital Centre, he couldn't prevent himself from mouthing the lyrics while Barbra Streisand sang "Evergreen." The television cameras drifted away from Streisand—as Clinton knew they must—and discovered the tear-stained face of the new president devouring the words as if they were made of chocolate.

President Clinton's delight in the company of movie stars would have been well understood by President William Howard Taft, who learned the lesson of modern celebrity in the summer of 1911 when he found himself traveling on a train with Mary Pickford and Francis X. Bushman, the silent screen stars who were then the wonder of the age. When he saw how the actress was mobbed by eager crowds at the station, he summoned Bushman into his presence and confessed that he envied him the adoration of the public. "All the people love you," he said, "and I can't have the love of even half the people."

Nearly a century later, the news of Woody Allen's estrangement from Mia Farrow superseded the news of the Republican convention in Houston. Allen commanded the cover of *Time* magazine, and in an interview with the editors of the magazine he made no apology for the destruction of his family or his liaison with Farrow's adopted daughter. "The heart," he said, "knows what it wants. There's no logic to those things. You meet someone and fall in love and that's that."

The blurring of the distinction between love and power has a diminishing effect on the people excluded from the sacred grove of celebrity and for whom the fates have neglected to provide even a supporting role. In order to fuel the engines of fame, the media suck so much love and adulation out of the atmosphere that unknown men must gasp for breath. They feel themselves made small, and they question the worth, even the fact, of their existence. If the bloated persona of the chairman of the Federal Reserve Board takes up so much space in the public mind, who can feel respect for the president of the local bank? Once the audience is accustomed to making obeisance to the images of Nobel Prize laureates, how can it honor the advice of the local physician? At any one time the ecology of the media can bear the weight of only so much celebrity, and as the grotesque personae made for the mass market require ever more energy to sustain, what is left for the weaker species on the dark of the camera?

Once it is possible to believe that the world can be redeemed by the sudden advent of a god from a machine—either in the person of a newly minted celebrity or by one's own transformed self— then it is also possible to believe that if things don't work out quite the way the audience had hoped, maybe the mistake can be corrected by an equally abrupt departure. If the god cannot be made to listen or to feel the pain of the supplicants murmuring in the shadows beyond the circle of magical light, perhaps he can be touched by other means. Unlike the rule of law, which derives its force from its impersonality, the rule of love can be overturned as easily as can a Nielsen rating.

A few days before going to Washington in March 1981 with the notion of shooting President Ronald Reagan, John W. Hinckley wrote a letter to an actress he had never met, saying, "If

you don't love me, I'm going to kill the president." Mr. Hinckley
had seen the actress, Jodie Foster, in *Taxi Driver*, in which the
deranged protagonist attempts to assassinate a U.S. senator because one of the senator's legislative assistants has disdained to
notice, much less requite, his love. Although it is impossible to
know what Mr. Hinckley had in mind while he waited for President Reagan to come out of the Washington Hilton Hotel, it is
probably safe to assume that he had watched a lot of television
and had accepted the symbolism of the national celebrity theater
as a literal rendering of the world. He owned a television set, a
guitar, and a gun. These were his only possessions. Every important event he'd ever seen he'd seen on television. Wandering from
hotel room to hotel room, unnoticed by the management, he
may have come to think of himself, in Justice Holmes's phrase, as
"a puny anonym." Maybe he would have been content with an
appearance on the Johnny Carson show. Maybe he wished to
abrogate his treaty with the United States. Whatever his reasons,
they would have made sense to Rousseau.

They also would have made sense to John Wilkes Booth, the
actor who assassinated President Abraham Lincoln. On several
occasions before Mr. Lincoln's murder Booth talked com-
pulsively about pulling down the Colossus of Rhodes. He was
once quoted as saying, "You have read about the Seven Wonders
of the World? Well, we'll take the Statue of Rhodes, for example.
Suppose that statue was now standing, and I by some means
should overthrow it. . . . My name would descend to posterity
and never be forgotten."

On the Thursday before the Monday that he was shot, President Reagan attended a command performance at Ford's Theater
in Washington, the same theater in which President Lincoln was
shot. The event was televised; Mr. Reagan made a theatrical show
of applauding the star turns performed by a succession of singers,
comedians, and magicians distinguished principally by their celebrity.

The media, of course, portrayed Mr. Hinckley as a near lunatic
who in no way could be said to represent anything fundamental

to the homespun steadiness of the American character or the
wholesomeness of the American experience. Once they had pronounced Mr. Hinckley a uniquely alienated young man, the promoters of correct opinion went on to ask the customary questions
about what might be wrong with the country. Will the violence
never cease? What is the matter with those people out there who
keep showing up with cheap guns and third-rate film scripts?
Nobody could find convincing answers for these questions. *The
New York Times* admitted to a feeling of "raging helplessness."
The late Max Lerner blamed the Secret Service (apparently for
failing to impose martial law throughout the District of Columbia), the laxity of the gun laws, and Mr. Hinckley's parents (for
not employing detectives to follow their son on his appointed
rounds). Other columnists mentioned the rising levels of crime in
the United States, the pervasiveness of the presidential symbol,
and the porousness of a political system that allows the head of
state to walk around in a shopping center without a sullen escort
of lictors.

All these observations having been duly noted on the record,
the authorities took pains to warn against the drawing of over-
wrought generalizations about the illness of American society.
They didn't want anybody to get the wrong impression. Yes, it
was true that the president of the United States had been shot
down in broad daylight almost within sight of the White House,
and yes, it was also true that the secretary of state had yielded to a
seizure of megalomania, but American society wasn't sick, and it
was irresponsible of anybody to say so. The president recovered
bravely from his wound, and within a few days the worried
questions had died away to a distant mutter. The impresarios of
the media circus encouraged everybody to go back to what they
were doing before the program had been so tastelessly interrupted by a commercial for the assassin as celebrity.

What the impresarios neglected to say was that the pagan
worship of rock singers or television anchorpersons, like the
pagan worship of stones and trees, implies the joyous return to
barbarism. Rousseau was talking about power, the power to do as

one pleases, and his premise that every man remains free to declare himself a god encourages the adoration not only of political and theatrical celebrities but also of figures as otherwise unlike one another as Pat Robertson, H. Ross Perot, and John Gotti. To the extent that they present an image of omnipotence and so relieve their followers of the burdens of anxiety and dread, they sustain the rank of minor deity. The sentiment is as primitive as it is antidemocratic. Just as the hope of civilization defines itself as an advance toward impersonality, toward an idea of justice that doesn't depend on the whim of a judge or the failure of the White House, so also democratic government discounts the question, Who is the best ruler? and asks instead, Which ruler can do the least harm?

Like Gotti, H. Ross Perot appeared in the theater of celebrity as a law unto himself, and his admirers—many of them wearing T-shirts emblazoned with the motto Ross for Boss—recognized him as a man who would prefer to conduct the affairs of government as if he were the warden of a prison or the abbot of a monastery. Hearing in his speeches the promise of benevolent despotism and stirred by feelings of nostalgia, they stood willing to vote their fear instead of their courage. If only Perot would keep them safe from the passage of time (as well as from foreigners, bad news, existentialism, crime, and contradiction), why quarrel with his vision of America as a utopian real estate development in Arizona or Southern California—the kind of walled town or private community likely to be named Sunset Estates or Rancho Paradiso? Why not paint all the houses blue and trim all the rosebushes to the regulation height of two feet six inches? The pittance of a few civil rights or liberties surely was a small price to pay for a vigilant sheriff and a decent gardener.

The wish for kings is the fear of freedom, and under the pretext of rescuing people from incalculable peril, the government over the last fifty years has claimed for itself enormously enhanced powers of repression and control. The obsession with security in all its forms and declensions—national, personal, and municipal—has shifted the balance of the American equation.

The Constitution was made for the uses of the individual (an implement on the order of a plow, an ax, or a surveyor's plumb line), and the institutions of American government were meant to support the liberties of the people, not the ambitions of the state. It was the law that had to give way to the citizen's freedom of thought and action, not the citizen's freedom of thought and action that had to give way to the law. The Bill of Rights stresses the distinction in the two final amendments, the Ninth ("The enumeration in the Constitution, of certain rights, shall not be construed to deny or disparage others retained by the people") and the Tenth ("The powers not delegated to the United States by the Constitution, nor prohibited by it to the States, are reserved to the States respectively, or to the people"). Contemporary thought and practice reverses the premise. The government reserves to itself unenumerated powers and seeks to limit the freedoms of the individual to a list of enumerated rights. The increasingly punitive uses and interpretations of the law support the ambitions of the state, not the liberties of the people.

As the cold war faded into the mists of warm and nostalgic memory, the war on drugs provided the rubrics of constant terror and ceaseless threat under which the government could subtract as much as possible from the sum of the nation's civil rights and impose de facto martial law on a citizenry that it chooses to imagine as a dangerous rabble. When the Bush administration cried up the war on drugs in the autumn of 1989, William Bennett, the warrior intellectual appointed to command the federal forces in the field, never missed the chance to demand more police, more jails, more judges, more arrests, more punishments, more defendants serving more millennia of "serious time." His voice was that of an intolerant scold, narrow and shrill and meanspirited—the voice of oligarchy afraid of liberty and mistrustful of freedom.[29]

If democracy is about people doing different things, and a nation-state is about people doing the same thing, then somebody, preferably somebody in uniform, has to reconcile the contradictions. The United States now boasts the largest prison population in the Western world—426 inmates for every 100,000 people in 1990 as opposed to 333 for every 100,000 in South Africa and 268 for every 100,000 in the old Soviet Union—and the cost of its private security forces increased by a factor of 500 percent during the decade in which the Reagan administration congratulated itself on its love of freedom. In line with Bennett's zeal for coercion, the courts in recent years have granted the police increasingly autocratic powers: permission (without probable cause) to stop, detain, and question those travelers passing through the nation's airports in whom the police can see a resemblance to drug dealers; permission (again without probable cause) to search almost anybody's automobile or boat, hire police spies, stop motorists, inspect bank records, and tap phones.

During his first two years in office President Bush continued President Reagan's policy of elevating to the federal courts only those judges who had proved their loyalty to conservative ideological doctrine. He appointed as associate justices of the Supreme Court Clarence Thomas and David Souter, both of them inclined to favor the interests of oligarchy over any nonsense about any individual's claim to an unenumerated right. In June 1991, during the same month that Justice Thurgood Marshall announced his retirement (on the ground that "power, not reason, is the new currency of this court's decision making"), the Supreme Court ruled that the Constitution permits the imposition of mandatory life sentences, without hope of parole, for nonviolent first offenses. The anticrime measure approved by Congress that same year limited the uses of habeas corpus and codified the Supreme Court's decision to permit the use of illegally obtained evidence at trial if the police conducting the search relied on their "good faith" in a warrant that later proved defective. The Congress also added fifty new crimes to the list of those punishable by death, among them the killing of a federal official. This last provision endowed the criminal code with a class distinction. A commoner who murdered a noble did so on pain of death, but a noble who murdered a commoner retained the right to a prison sentence.

The spirit of the age is feudal, and the broad retreat to the suburbs over the last twenty or thirty years correlates to the fear of the future and the wish to make time stand still. The politics of the Nixon, Reagan, and Bush administrations made manifest a San Diego realtor's dream of heaven and defined the great, good American place as an exclusive country club. Expressions of the same sentiment take forms as various as the judgments of the Rehnquist Court, Senator Jesse Helms's suspicions of the National Endowment for the Arts, the ascendance of conservative and neoconservative socioeconomic theory, the sermons of George Will, and the division of the county of Los Angeles into a series of residential enclaves as fiercely defended (by gates and electronic surveillance and regiments of liveried police) as the feudal manors of medieval Europe.

Codified in increasingly repressive interpretations of the law, the instinct to censure, deny, forbid, prohibit, and suppress serves the interests of oligarchy and enlarges the desire of the state to impose on the American people the habits of obedience. Royal prerogative and ideological doctrine supersede democratic assembly and reasoned argument, and the government doesn't lightly relinquish the spoils of power seized under the rubrics of apocalypse. The agents of the state take it upon themselves to examine the citizenry for flaws in its blood, its urine, and its speech. The government in 1989 placed 5,506,720 documents under the seals of secret classification, and even minor federal officials must accept a degree of censorship comparable to the Mafia's code of *omertà*. The agreement prohibits them from writing or saying anything about their government service without official permission.

A similar bias shows up in the increasingly puritanical rules and regulations governing all forms of social freedom and behavior. The cardinal of New York insists on the excommunication of Catholic politicians who approve the practice of abortion, and a married woman in Wisconsin finds herself arraigned on charges of adultery. At least twice a week the papers bring word of a new committee established to impose a proper regimen of ethics on the moral sluggards who operate the nation's government and manage the nation's commerce. The bulletins often appear in conjunction with the news of a more stringent regulation governing the use of alcohol or tobacco, with the report of another television program forced off the air because of its sexual immodesty, with official statements and paid advertisements castigating junk bonds, the cocaine trade, and poor muscle tone. The announcements almost always bear the stamps of sanctimony and intolerance, and the latter-day Puritans make no secret of their wish to blame, to punish, and to cast what they trust will be the first of many stones.

What surprises me is the lack of objection. Like the habit of telling the truth, liberty withers and decays unless it's put to use, and for the last ten years it seems as if a majority of Americans would rather not suffer the embarrassment of making a scene about so small a trifle as a civil right. They learn to speak more softly in the presence of political authority, to bow and smile and fill out the printed forms with scarcely a murmur of dissent. An opinion poll conducted during the week following President Bush's declaration of the war on drugs in September 1989 showed 62 percent of the respondents "willing to give up some freedoms" in order to hold America harmless against the scourge of narcotics. Another 55 percent of the respondents supported mandatory drug testing for all Americans, 82 percent favored enlisting the military in the war on drugs, 52 percent were willing to have their homes searched, and 83 percent favored reporting suspected drug users to the police, even if the suspects happen to be members of their own family. In October 1989 *Newsweek* took note of an inquisition in progress in Clinton, Iowa. The local paper had taken to printing cutout coupons that said, "I've had enough of drugs in my neighborhood! I have reason to believe that _____ is using/dealing drugs." The paper collected the coupons for the town police, who reported the response as "excellent." During the spring of 1990 the Times Mirror Center for the People and the Press conducted a survey of the political attitudes prevailing among a random company of citizens between the ages of eighteen and twenty-nine. To nobody's surprise, the survey discovered a generation that "knows less, cares less, votes less and is less critical of its leaders and institutions than young people in the past." More ominously and to everybody's surprise, the study also found that most of the respondents didn't care whether a fair percentage of the nation's politicians proved to be scoundrels and liars. Such was the nature of their task, and it was thought to be unfair to place on the political authorities the additional and excessive burden of too many impolite questions. "Let them," said one of the poor respondents, "authoritate."

On my own travels around the country I notice that my attempts to engage people in political argument all too often meet an embarrassingly audible silence. If I make a speech about the waning of the democratic spirit or the pleasures of smoking, one or two people take me to task for emotional overstatement, and another asks me for a program of political reform. To almost everybody else in the room I appear as entertainment imported from the intellectual department store in New York, a wandering juggler of words who must be humored in his eccentric opinions.

Although accustomed to the attitudes of polite indifference at the nation's better universities, and knowing that the democratic premise can count on very few advocates among the nation's ruling and possessing classes, I was still surprised in May of last year by the feeling of contempt for politics expressed by the guests at a dinner dance in New York that was meant to raise money for the city's homeless population. The worst of the evening's news was the change of heart in a man whom I had long admired for his idealism and his buoyant optimism. We had known each other at college in the 1950s, and I remembered that after his graduation he had experimented with careers as a novelist, a teacher, and an inventor of children's toys before discovering his talent as a financier. By the time he was forty he had acquired a fortune trading foreign currencies, and during the middle 1980s the business magazines often listed his name among the economic wonders of the age. But he never took part in the revels of conspicuous consumption that delighted so many of his contemporaries on Wall Street, and he used his fortune to expand the perimeter of the common good. He became a trustee of two hospitals and three schools, and he was known among the organizers of committees in New York as a man who could be counted upon to give handsome sums of money to community housing projects as well as to the Metropolitan Museum of Art.

Although I hadn't seen him for several years, I had expected him to retain at least the trace elements of what he had once described, paraphrasing Jefferson, as "the ancient republican hostility" to the rule of the self-serving few. The expectation proved to be misplaced. The once-upon-a-time philanthropist and disciple of e e cummings had resigned himself to the rule of oligarchy. As we stood drinking champagne, he jabbed a forefinger into my chest, making emphatic points about Perot's strength, Perot's decisiveness, Perot's resolve, Perot's grit.

Yes, he said, he had considered all the usual weak-kneed objections, but he was sick of politics, sick of feeling sorry for people who, when you really thought about it, got what they deserved. He had given up most of his charities (except for the ones in which his wife still took an interest because of the annual balls), and these days he spent most of his time in his houses in Connecticut and Palm Beach. If it was up to him, he said, he would reorganize the American government along the lines of a constitutional monarchy. Maybe, he said, we'll come to the point of electing presidents as ritual kings, adored for two or four years by a grateful mob and then offered as sacrifices on "Larry King Live" or set out to sea in an open boat.

The general disillusion with the democratic premise follows from the failure to appreciate its character as an improvisation. Democracy proceeds on the assumption that nobody knows enough, that nothing is final, that the faith in human reason offers neither comfort nor immortality. To the extent that democracy gives its citizens the chance to come to their own conclusions and chase their own dreams, it gives them the chance not only of discovering their multiple glories and triumphs but also of surviving their multiple follies and crimes. Too often we forget the proofs of our courage. If we wish to live in a state of freedom, then we must accustom ourselves to the shadows on the walls and the wind in the trees. The climate of anxiety is the cost of doing business.

Because a democracy protects the freedom of thought, it proceeds by means of additions of opportunities, knowledge, questions, factions, wealth. The additions to what might be called the forward side of the ledger lead to equivalent additions of disorderliness, humiliation, uncertainty, and doubt. If every new good raises the possibility if not the fact of a new evil, the proliferation of knowledge confronts the citizens of a democracy with the constant recognition that the world is not oneself. Most people feel uncomfortable with the discovery, but discomfort is the condition under which the oyster creates a pearl. Freedom of thought brings societies the unwelcome news that they are in trouble, but because all societies, like all individuals, are always in trouble of one kind or another, the news doesn't cause them to perish. They die instead from the fear of thought and from the paralysis of mind that accompany the worship of kings and the wish to make time stand still. Transposed into the realm of biology, the American dialectic corresponds to the process of evolution, which also expresses itself in the transitory nature of its forms and which, like democracy, offers no immutable coalitions.

For two hundred years it has been the particular genius of the American democracy to exist in a state of more or less permanent uncertainty, but we seem to have lost the stomach for the enterprise. All the evidence presented in 1992's presidential campaigns—the paltry speeches, the definition of politics as a synonym for economics, the media spectacle, the apathy of the electorate, the enthusiasm for Perot—testified to the retreat from democracy. "A republic if you can keep it," said Franklin, knowing, as did everybody else who had a hand in drafting the

Constitution, that the principle of liberty always stands at risk and that the practice of self-government is all too easily overturned. Democracy assumes a constant making and remaking, and in line with Jefferson's observation that "a little rebellion, now and then, is a good thing, and as necessary in the political world as storms in the physical," the gentlemen in Philadelphia in the summer of 1787 assumed that the old order—of ideas as well as of men and governments—would be carried offstage every twenty years. The other fellow always has something to say (without being prompted by the police), and maybe what he has to say will shake the earth or shift the angles of perception. Later in the nineteenth century Mark Twain described as "the makers of the earth after God" those people who discovered how to make grass grow where none had grown before, who invented Texas, barbed wire, and electric light.

The authors of the Constitution framed their hope of freedom for people who knew how to read, who subscribed to the Christian faith and numbered among their company no more than four million souls. The present set of circumstances requires the translation of the American promise into new forms of government and a new political language that corresponds to the terms and conditions of the late twentieth century—in Europe and Asia as well as in the United States. The emptiness of last year's presidential campaign followed from the failure on the part of all three candidates to attempt the translation. Allied with the smiling of the courtier spirit and owing their allegiance to the inertia of things-as-they-are, the Republican and Democratic parties embraced the great cause of incumbency. The "new world order" that President Bush proclaimed (and Governor Clinton endorsed) could as easily have been proclaimed by Caesar or Saladin or the Duke of Wellington.

The post–cold war world begins to look like medieval Europe. The frontiers run between markets and spheres of commercial interest, not along the boundaries of sovereign states. If a company is large enough and rich enough (commanding assets worth several billion dollars and employing more people than lived in fifteenth-century Venice), the company, of necessity, conducts its own foreign policy. In part, this is because the nation-state can make good on so few of its promises. What nation can defend its borders against disease, ballistic missiles, the drug trade, or the transmission of subversive images? What nation can protect its air or its water against the acid rain drifting east across Canada or the radioactive cloud blowing west from Chernobyl? What nation can secure its currency against predatory speculations on the world's money markets?

The new technologies sap the authority of the centralized state and shift the locus of decisive action to the more modest concentrations of intellect and will. These smaller organisms can be defined as the transnational corporation (IBM, say, or Mobil Oil), as the merchant city-state (Singapore, Taiwan, Lyons), or as a militant cause (the PLO or the IRA). The systems of modern communications allow the hierarchies of international capitalism to imitate the feudal arrangements under which an Italian noble might swear fealty to a German prince or a Norman duke declare himself the vassal of an English king. The lords and barons of the transnational corporations offer their allegiance less to a government (any government) than to Sony or McDonnell Douglas or Citicorp. It is the company that pays their pensions, insures their lives, bestows on them their symbols of identity.

A similarly antidemocratic bias dictates the structure of the institutions appointed to regulate the conduct of international trade. Whether made manifest as the North American Free Trade Agreement, the General Agreement on Tariffs and Trade, the World Bank, or the International Monetary Fund, the operative principle is the rule of oligarchy—the power of decision in the hands of relatively few people conferring behind closed doors, fixing the prices of silk and wine and linseed oil and wheat. The European Economic Community makes no secret of its resemblance to a medieval guild. The sixteen unelected members of the governing directorate formulate the rates of exchange (for goods as well as currencies) that affect the lives of 340 million people in Europe, and the elected Parliament that sits ceremoniously in

Strasbourg serves, without power to make or unmake the laws, as an ornamental chorus meant to sing the praises of democracy.

The American oligarchy increasingly has less in common with the American people than it does with the equivalent oligarchies in Germany or Mexico or Japan. The possessing classes recline at their ease behind the barbican of a high interest rate, content among computers and fax machines and megatrends and cellular phones. On the other side of the walls, in the desolate slums of the third, fifth, and ninth worlds, the nomadic mass of the heathen poor, known to the French policy journals as "the terminally impoverished," tear at one another for bones.

But at what cost, and for how long, can the kingdom of wealth protect its comfort and preserve its cynicism? With what weapons and against how many enemies? Whether expressed in the language of diplomacy or in the deployment of troops, the rules of power politics fail to take into account the number of people in the world who believe they have more to gain by the risk of war than by the prospect of negotiation. Most of the world is hungry, armed, and not much impressed by the rules of diplomatic procedure set forth with such earnest longing in the editorial pages of *The New York Times*. Of the nations now buying weapons in the international arms markets, the majority must be considered young, both in terms of their existence as states (of the 178 nations represented at the UN, nearly half have come into being within the past thirty years) and in terms of the average age of their populations. In the industrialized West the average age of the inhabitants continues to rise; in the third world the demographics go the other way.

The passions of transcendence seize the young, and as more and more nations suffer the anxieties and enthusiasms of youth, they can be expected to confuse the purposes of government with the freedom of individuals. The doctrines of nationalism hold that certain nations emerge from the chaos of history as objects of divine favor; the states that interpret those doctrines with the fervor of youth presumably will conduct their foreign affairs as if they were affairs of the heart. Since the end of the Second World

War—probably since the end of the First World War—the supposedly civilized nations of the world have been noticeably unsuccessful at transmitting to the next generation the public
virtues of patience and self-restraint. They have distributed instead a more profitable line of private goods, among them visions
of God and definitions of the higher truth, as well as cameras and
transistor radios. Within the arenas of domestic American politics
the romanticism of eager factions has dissolved the common
interest into a multitude of special interests, all of them warring
with one another for the available money and authority.

Over the next ten years I can imagine a comparable spectacle in
the arena of international politics. Together with single-issue
lobbies in Congress, I can conceive of single-issue nations dedicated to the proposition that their own flag, their own folk songs,
and their own way of making fish soup constitutes a foreign
policy. At the same time they will find themselves armed with
weapons capable of inflicting vast oedipal punishments on an
older generation perceived to be obstructive and corrupt. In the
absence of an imperial peace imposed on a recalcitrant world by
parental fiat (a task for which the United States possesses a
notable lack of talent), I find it hard to imagine a political order
balanced by a squadron of gunboats. The more prosperous and
settled a nation, the more readily it tends to think of war as a
regrettable accident; to less fortunate nations, among them Bos-
nia, Serbia, and Herzegovina, the chance of war presents itself as
a possibly bountiful friend.

The hope of democratic government descends from the ancient
Greeks by way of the Italian Renaissance and the Enlightenment,
but no matter how often it has been corrupted and abused (simply by reason of its being such a difficult feat to perform), it
constitutes the only morality currently operative in the world.[30]
Now, as in Athens in the fifth century B.C., democracy represents
the attempt to organize the freedom of mind against the tyranny
of money, force, and superstition. Because democratic institutions do not renew themselves as effortlessly as flowering trees,
they demand the ceaseless tinkering of people willing to accept

responsibility for even their most inglorious acts. We are likely to die as ignorant as we began, advancing from one bewilderment to another. The mistake is to pretend to know too much, to speak, as do the courtiers on the dais, as if we were privy councillors to deity. The courage of the human mind always presents itself as an affront to whatever idols have been set up as the local Godhead. But people who have lost faith in themselves, who no longer possess their own history or trust to their own experiments, no longer can summon the energy to imagine their own future. They subside into a state of holy dread, waiting for signs and portents, seeking to make peace with anybody who will promise them another twenty minutes of life, liberty, and the pursuit of happiness.

The cold war imprisoned the nations of the earth in attitudes of fear. It wasn't only the threat implicit in the weapons, although the weapons were many and terrible; it was also the pattern of thought bent to the service of slogans. Brutal simplifications made it hard to conceive of a world that was anything other than a military campground. But let the peoples of the earth rescue themselves from their paralysis and inhibition, and with their newfound freedom of mind they might find a use for the moral as well as the political imagination. It turns out that the world is a far more beautiful place than it has been represented to them in the story told by the prison guards—far more beautiful and by no means simple. To the extent that the twentieth century has rescued itself from barbarism, it is because the hopes of ordinary people have prevailed over the interests of the state. The state or the transnational corporation defines power as the power inherent in things—in tax revenues, barrels of oil, and miles of road. The people define power as the power inherent in dreams—in laughter, photograph albums, and songs. For the time being at least, in the moment of profound change at the end of the cold war, the advantage lies not with the policies of fear and restraint but with the reaching of the human spirit.

Notes

1. Democracy at Bay

1. Perceived as a deft robbery rather than a failed economic policy, the story of the savings and loan swindle—now expected to cost the American taxpayers roughly five hundred billion dollars—is the story of a silence successfully maintained by the political and financial interests busy with the work of pillage. As long ago as 1985 the prospect of substantial loss was apparent to the banking committees in the Senate and the House, to the Treasury Department, the Federal Deposit Insurance Corporation, the General Accounting Office, the Federal Reserve, and the Office of Management and Budget. If one or more of these agencies of government had acted on behalf of the public interest, the loss might have been limited, in 1985, to ten billion dollars. None of the interested parties said a word. James Baker, then the secretary of the treasury, found no reason to express concern, and numerous politicians continued to receive campaign money from the proprietors of the corrupted banks. The Democrats were as closely acquainted with the fraud as were the Republicans, but nobody wanted to mention the swindle to the American people until after the election of 1988. Too many people— not only the principal investors but also a small army of lawyers, brokers, and accountants—were making too much money in the capital and real estate markets. The delay offered the further advantage of shifting the financial responsibility for what all present knew would prove to be a catastrophe. Had the crimes and misdemeanors been addressed at a cost of only ten billion dollars, somebody might have thought to suggest that the savings and loan industry pay its own debts. But if the loss amounted to five hundred billion dollars, then it could be defined as a patriotic obligation entailed upon the whole of the American democracy.

As needs hardly be said, almost all the fine gentlemen in Washington escaped the financial ruin without censure or personal loss. A few of the more notorious swindlers went to jail, among them Michael Milken and Charles Keating, but elsewhere in the country several thousand investors lost their life savings and quite a few companies went bankrupt. In the stately hearing rooms on the banks of the Potomac the news of any distant unpleasantness was a tale told by the lying, liberal press. The Senate Ethics Committee staged a *tableau vivant* signifying its rebuke of five senators who had been a trifle too careless with the sale of their favors, but Alan Greenspan, who had appeared as a character witness for operators of fourteen of the failed banks, was named chairman of the Federal Reserve, and James Baker became the secretary of state.

2. The rich know how to ward off the corrosive evil of government subsidy and inherited stock portfolios. Similar temptations placed in the way of the poor—in the form of welfare payments, student loans, or food stamps—invariably corrupt their morals and destroy their sense of self-worth. The philosophers of the liberal left, several of whom composed Governor Clinton's thesis of economic deliverance, believe that although money is wicked in the hands of mere individuals, it regains its blessedness in the hands of the state. If left to their own selfish devices, even Harvard professors squander their substance on German automobiles and French wines. But if they distribute the money through the agencies of government, their extravagance deserves the name of virtue.

When the news of recession first seeped into official Washington in November 1990, Nicholas Brady, the secretary of the treasury and himself a rich man, put the matter as plainly as possible in answer to a journalist's question about the state of the deteriorating economy. "I don't think it's the end of the world," he said, "even if we have a recession. We'll pull back out of it again. No big deal."

No big deal for Mr. Brady, who rests comfortably on an expensive fortune, and certainly not the end of the world for Mr. Brady's fellow members of the Links Club and the Essex County Hunt, who welcome the bracing atmosphere of bankruptcy and debt as a sign that soon they will have the chance to buy property at gratifyingly distressed prices.

3. During last year's election campaign both President Bush and Governor Clinton professed their unswerving loyalty to the defense budget. The president made a show of appropriating $1.5 billion to build F-15s for Taiwan and Saudi Arabia, and Governor Clinton was careful to announce his support for the B-2 bomber, the Sea Wolf submarine, and the V-22 Osprey. In effect, each candidate offered more or less the same reassuring bribes to the defense industries in Texas, California, Missouri, and Connecticut.

4. Bill Clinton was a good deal more comfortable than President Bush in the role of the great, good American governess. Playing to the factions of grievance (i.e., to people oppressed by "heightism," "looksism," and "sizeism," as well as by "racism," "sexism," and "ageism"), he cast himself as the friend of the American victim. The promises that he made in the name of a custodial state could easily have been confused with a program of diet and exercise for a generation of lost children. An abbreviated list of his promises reads as follows:

TRAINING AND EDUCATION
Impose a 1.5 percent payroll tax on large employers to finance training and education for low-skilled workers.

Increase federal spending on education and training generally by ten billion dollars a year starting in 1993 and twenty billion dollars a year by 1996.

Create a national service trust fund to give everyone the right to borrow money for college.

Offer guaranteed apprenticeships for half of all students not going to college.

HEALTH CARE
Create a new system of universal health care.
Extend Medicare to cover long-term care.

INFRASTRUCTURE AND TECHNOLOGY
Inject twenty billion dollars a year in transportation, communications, and environment to stimulate growth and to revitalize essential systems.

Create a civilian advanced technology agency.

Establish 170 manufacturing extension centers to help smaller businesses choose equipment and learn cutting-edge techniques.

URBAN DEVELOPMENT

Create a hundred community development banks and a thousand microenterprise programs to help small businesses and revitalize communities.

Establish 75 to 125 urban enterprise zones.

Increase community development block grants.

TAX CUTS

Create a targeted investment tax credit.

Reduce income taxes for some number of the middle class, costing twenty billion dollars over four years.

Raise the earned income tax credit for the working poor.

Create tax incentives and credits for recycling and pollution reduction.

CRIME

Establish a Police Corps to train ten thousand new officers a year for ten years.

Help states create boot camp prisons.

SOCIAL POLICY

Boost poor children by fully funding Head Start and the WIC health program.

Institutionalize low-income housing tax credit.

INTERNATIONAL

Increase contributions to the World Bank.

Increase assistance to Russia.

Pay overdue U.S. dues to the United Nations.

2. *The Courtier Spirit*

5. As the editor of *Harper's Magazine* I write an essay every month about one or another of the topics in the news, and I've noticed over a period of years that whenever I remark on the selfishness and vanity of the American ruling class, I receive, by return mail, at least five letters taking me to task for reckless overstatement. The readers deny the existence of the class in question and remind me, with exclamation marks and indignant adjectives, that I'm a free citizen living in a democracy, not the enslaved subject of a faithless prince. How could I possibly think that so large and exuberant a country was owned and operated by so small and so frightened an oligarchy? Had I never read the Constitution? Did I not know that the United States was governed by no fewer than five hundred thousand elected officials?

Sometimes a reader concedes that what I have to say might be true of a few Washington politicians (possibly also true of a small number of Wall Street financiers and pretentious journalists), but emphatically not true of American society as a whole—not true of most of the country's businesses and legislatures and schools, not true of the honest Middle West, not true of the real America that drives pickup trucks, drinks draft beer, and knows the difference between a firm handshake and a false smile. At least one correspondent invariably suggests that I resign my commission as editor, abandon the foul and pestilent city of New York, and take up residence in Omaha or Fort Myers.

I wish I thought that the letters from the readers of *Harper's Magazine* proved the rule instead of the exceptions. I'm sure that vast tracts of the country remain uncontaminated by the stale air of complacent privilege, and about the courage and exuberant energies of the society at large I have not the slightest doubt. The country possesses so many genies of invention that even the government's swarm of zealous clerks cannot keep track of all the people following the chronologies of electrons, experimenting with the properties of hydrogen, observing the permutations of cells. The nation's research vessels voyage in the reaches of deep space, sending back photographs and radio transmissions from the other side of Mars; its scientists make their bows every year in the Nobel Prize lists; and its children play with computers as carelessly as they play with blocks. Occasionally I have the chance to spend an afternoon in a research laboratory, and although I seldom understand the whole of the supporting lecture, I form an impression of people intensely excited about their journey toward the horizons of the human mind. I sense something of the same adventurous spirit among the freebooting lawyers in both the public and the private services who, over the past thirty years, have shifted the balances of wealth in the United States almost as casually as if they were moving pieces on a chess board. In a wheat field in western Kansas, I talk to an agronomist who thinks of revising the world's fertilizers in ways that will transform the lives of as many as two billion people, and I am reminded of the high-energy physicist who flings together atomic elements in the hope of achieving temperatures of forty million degrees. Or again, in the company of investment bankers, I cannot help being impressed by the rigor of the conceptual imagination that goes into the making of stock swindles and bank frauds, by the almost polyphonic combinations required to merge corporations, and by the capacity for abstraction that can make visible the transposition of money through five currencies and seven tiers of taxation. Within the arenas of major league sports the coaches don't align the batting order or the defensive backfield with the whim of the owner's mistress, and I'm sure that within numerous other industries and professions (even within some university English departments) a great many individuals achieve their places in the world primarily by means of their talent, their intelligence, and their character. But I've met so few of them over the last twenty years that I incline to think of them as anomalies, people who have accomplished their purpose against increasingly heavy odds.

6.   The story of Kissinger's life is the story of the perfect courtier, and Walter Isaacson's biography, published in 1991 under the title *Kissinger*, provides abundant proofs and instances of the gentleman's talent for servility and betrayal. Kissinger was particularly adept at flattering a man to his face and then, behind the man's back (or as soon as he had left the room or hung up the telephone), mocking him as a fool. During his term of service as national security adviser to President Richard Nixon, Kissinger was forever complimenting Nixon on the brilliance of his policy and sending him notes of fulsome praise. By way of example, Isaacson gives the text of a handwritten note from Kissinger in 1971, before another one of Nixon's lying speeches on Vietnam: "No matter what the result, free people everywhere will be forever in your debt. Your serenity during crises, your steadfastness under pressure, have been all that prevented the triumph of mass hysteria. It has been an inspiration to serve. As always, H."

At precisely the same time, while speaking to a number of other people in Washington, from whom he hoped to curry favor, Kissinger was describing Nixon as a pathetically deluded egomaniac, hysterical and ignorant and poorly informed. Kissinger's habitual air of contempt—for his employer, for everybody else in the throne room, for the rabble beyond the White House gates—expressed the vanity of the court eunuch. Staring so intently for so many years into the face of power, he couldn't help remarking on the weakness and corruption of his nominal overlords. Maybe it is easier to pay court to men one despises, and it is understandable that Kissinger, having seen with what little wisdom the world is governed, should have formed an excessive opinion of his own.

7. Translated into the modern American language of self-help and self-promotion, Castiglione's advice becomes one of a thousand texts on the order of *Daywear Standards for the Successful Washington Man*, a newsletter published in McLean, Virginia, and sold in three pamphlets for thirty dollars a year. A few passages from the first issue in the spring of 1991 may be taken as representative:

> *Daywear Standards for the Successful Washington Man* details what to wear, what *not* to wear, how to wear it, and where to buy it for less. *Daywear Standards* is a must for Hill government workers, diplomats, doctors, lawyers, businessmen, bankers, and others who must dress for respect but don't want to spend all their money on clothing. The man who dresses to make a statement and to express his personality gets compliments; the man who dresses to the standard gets respect.
>
> There are identifiable daywear standards for the man who goes to work in the Washington area in a coat and tie. These standards are not only worthy of emulation but are within the financial reach of middle-class men. The standards are not established, however, by middle-class men; rather they are subtly dictated by the top men in the top law firms, banks, and businesses in the urban corridor between suburban Washington and suburban Boston.
>
> The three most important items of clothing (in order of importance) are: shoes, necktie, wristwatch and strap.
>
> **SHOES**
> Store your shoes between wearings in full-shoe cedar trees. Polish at least before third wearing—polish your shoes before they need it.
>
> **NECKTIES**
> We recommend ten to twelve mostly red, regimental-type stripes and reps and foulards by Robert Talbott and Brooks Brothers. Here are the standards: At the big end no narrower than 3 1/8", not wider than 3 1/4"; tip-to-tip 56" to 58"; never ever the bottle/canoe-paddle shape, but rather a natural taper to about 1 1/4" at midpoint in the tie's length.
>
> **WRISTWATCHES AND STRAPS**
> Never wear a new-style Rolex. A Hirsch tan camelskin strap ($30) is important. Far more important than the particular brand is the following:

round (or almost) with sweep second hand. Or round with subsecond hand. Or tank-shape with sweep second hand. Or tank with subsecond hand. White-face background. Twelve Arabic numbers. Black or gold numbers and hands. Gold color case.

ODDS AND ENDS

—The color tan is important. That's the color of the quite-thin Hartmann briefcase—which we recommend if you must carry a briefcase. Tan is the strong preference for the leather on the dark blue silk suspenders. The Daytimer should be pigskin and the strap for the wristwatch tan camel-skin. If you carry a tightly wound umbrella—and it is becoming increasingly apparent that you should—the crook handle, ideally, is maple (tan, again).

—One of the worst menswear ideas of 1991 is the matching suspender and necktie sets. They're selling like wildfire among those whose opinions and behavior are of little consequence.

—Too short and too fat? These suggestions could help: Do not wear sharply contrasting trousers—the medium grays—with your blue blazer. Wear only suits that are plain weave, dark blue or dark charcoal, and single-breasted. Keep your hair short; no facial hair. Wear elevator shoes. Always wear your complete suit or blue blazer—avoid casual clothes.

8. The New York literary salons do not take kindly to even the least and most mild-mannered criticism. This lesson was handsomely illustrated in June 1991, when *The New Republic*, a journal of Washington opinion, published a lengthy article entitled "Rough Trade: The Sad Decline of American Publishing." Written by Jacob Weisberg, a young journalist unknown to the gentry at the Four Seasons, the article brought the familiar articles of indictment: books poorly or carelessly edited, ungrammatical sentences, editors more interested in making deals than revising manuscripts, etc. Although the article was written more in sorrow than in anger, its tone as inoffensive as its content, the New York literary press declared it an act of infamy. The preferred gossip identified Weisberg as a scoundrel, accepting information from tainted sources—"from anonymous tipsters and disgruntled authors"—and various publishers in town denounced his article as "either the most disgraceful" or "the most irresponsible" work of journalism that they had ever seen.

Two weeks later *The New Republic* published an anthology of indignant letters to the editor, among them a letter from Morton Janklow, a self-important literary agent, that said most of what needs to be said about the corrosiveness of the courtier spirit—not only as it afflicts the publishing business but also as it blights so many other facets of the nation's thought. Janklow began his letter by striking a pose of aristocratic condescension: "I have no idea who Mr. Weisberg is, but his is not a name that I or any of my colleagues have come across in our many years of intimate involvement with the publishing industry. . . ."

Notice that the sphere of judgment, like the sphere of judgment at Versailles, coincides with the sphere of Monsieur Janklow's acquaintance. Because Monsieur Janklow doesn't know the scoundrel Weisberg, the scoundrel Weisberg cannot be said to exist, and his opinion is therefore worthless.

9. The chronic careerism in the United States Army encourages the exuberant flowering of the courtier spirit in all its most grotesque forms. Promotion depends on the bringing of good news, and much of the American military failure in Vietnam followed from the eagerness with which so many officers in all ranks told expedient lies about every aspect of the war. Intent on maintaining the illusions of impregnable strength and perfect order, they learned that if it is possible to lick one boot, it is possible to lick the boots of a regiment. The army's annual order of merit is derived from the efficiency reports that rate every officer not only according to his or her performance of duty but also according to a roster of twenty-four character traits that include "appearance," "enthusiasm," "sociability," and "tact." The form is filled out by the officer's immediate superior, and the grades range from one (excellent) to five (abysmal). Generals rate colonels, and colonels rate majors, and so forth through the entire sequence of command. Together with all other relevant documents (letters of censure or commendation), the efficiency reports gradually accumulate in a file at the Pentagon. It is on the basis of his or her file that an officer is judged, and given the toadyism implicit in the data, it is not surprising that an officer as incompetent as William Westmoreland could become commander of the American forces in Vietnam. He had a talent for looking like a general; his uniforms were always faultlessly pressed, and he had the wit never to contradict his superior officer or insist on an unpleasant fact. Several years after the war had been lost, on being asked about the photograph of the Vietnamese girl blazing with the light of napalm, General Westmoreland said he had been told, and always had believed, that she had been burned by an hibachi stove.

10. The talent for self-promotion is by no means unique to Washington. In New York it is common practice for authors to write the jacket copy for their own books, and about four years ago I remember reading an ode to oneself nearly equal in its grandiloquence to the genius of Richard Darman. Composed by Gordon Lish by way of introduction to a new collection of his own short stories, the encomium was extravagant in its expense of adjectives: "There is no other contemporary figure in the nation's literary community whose presence is as widely or as urgently felt. . . . [N]o reader will go away from these pages unshaken by the force of their sentences, nor will any reader not know why it is that Gordon Lish has so powerfully and indelibly entered the literary history of this century."

11. A few days prior to my banishment from *Harper's Magazine*, I had accepted an invitation to dinner at the Council on Foreign Relations in honor of Valéry Giscard d'Estaing. Giscard had departed his post as the president of France, but his views on international affairs were still held in high esteem, and the council made it plain that the invitation to dinner was being made to a very small cadre of New York journalists deemed worthy of Giscard's presence and capable of appreciating his cynicism.

Having accepted the invitation in early August, I thought no more about it until late September, when, four days before the dinner, a secretary at the council telephoned to confirm my attendance. By that time, of course, I was no longer editor of *Harper's Magazine*, and my lack of an appropriate title caused the woman a good deal of embarrassment and alarm. After what seemed like a very long silence, she said that she didn't know how she could present my name on the guest list unless I could align it with the name of an important organization. She was terribly sorry, and she wished that she didn't have to remind me that it was the council's practice to distribute the guest list to all those present at the table, but what, after all, could she do? Never in the years of her service with the council had anybody ever come to dinner without the dignity of an institutional connection.

She was genuinely upset, and I could imagine a court functionary at Versailles making the same sort of awkward apology to a minor cousin of the great Condé who made the mistake of arriving for supper and cards dressed in the wrong wig and wearing the wrong shoes. When I told her that I still retained a distant connection to *The Washington Post*, her relief was as heartfelt as it was audible. Oh, she said, I was sure that we could think of something, and I'm so glad that you can attend the dinner, and I know that President Giscard d'Estaing will be so pleased. I told her how much I always had admired the president and how much I looked forward to hearing what he had to say about the fate of nations and the destiny of mankind.

12. A fair percentage of the country's economic overlords require acts of submission from their dependents and retainers, but during the last two or three years in New York the humiliations appear to have become both more frequent and more grotesque. My impression is probably skewed by my acquaintance with salesmen of magazine advertising. Business has not been good, and the salesmen have been forced to provide prospective clients with a range of goods and services seldom reported on their expense accounts. I remember in particular the unhappiness of an account executive in his early fifties, a pillar of the Presbyterian Church in New Canaan, Connecticut, the father of three children (two of them still at college), a man of considerable reputation in the community, who, on the third Sunday of every month, was obliged to administer an enema to the president of a corporation that bought advertising space in his magazine worth two million dollars a year. He told the story in the bar at the Yale Club, waiting for a train to Stamford and wondering whether he might not be better off in some other line of work. If he lost the account, he would lose his job, and with it his house and possibly his marriage. On the Sunday excursions to the hotel in Secaucus, New Jersey, he was expected to wear a seersucker suit and a bow tie, either yellow or pink.

3. Versailles on the Potomac

13. The habits of mind consistent with the defense and worship of great wealth permeate the higher tiers of Washington political society just as they permeate the higher tiers of the commercial society everywhere else in the country. A plurality of the Senate holds assets well in excess of $1 million, and quite a few of the members—among them Herbert Kohl (D., Wis.); Edward Kennedy (D., Mass.); and Frank Lautenberg (D., N.J.)—can be counted as men of large and substantial fortune. Senator John Warner divides his time between an apartment at the Watergate and a 777-acre estate in Middleburg, Virginia; Senator John Glenn commutes to Ohio in his own plane. Of the twenty newly arrived cabinet officials appointed by President Clinton, most were corporate lawyers (among

them Warren Christopher, the secretary of state; Mickey Kantor, the U.S. trade representative; and Ron Brown, the secretary of commerce), several were multimillionaires, and in 1992 every one of them had earned at least $100,000.

The presumption of entitlement seeps downward through the whole of the government bureaucracy, and it is not surprising that the Congress in 1992 allocated $2.8 billion to the cost of its own privileges and comforts. The comparable sum in 1970 amounted to $343 million, in 1980 to $1.2 billion. No other form of government expenditure has expanded at so grandiose a rate. Over the course of the last twenty years the Congress has increased the spending on itself by 705 percent—more than twice the 280 percent rise in inflation or the 311 percent rise in the defense budget. As the costs have increased, so also has the number of congressional household servants. The ladies and gentlemen on Capitol Hill in the 1950s made do with a staff of 5,373; the two houses of Congress now employ a staff of 38,696. Each member of Congress—with 535 U.S. representatives and 50 senators—receives an annual salary of $129,500, but the pay is augmented by perquisites (pension plan, health insurance, thrift plan, tax deductions, etc.) worth an additional $38,722 a year. The pensions, which are far more generous than those offered in private industry, allow quite a few of the members to retire with as much as $155,000 a year, and they support a good many other members with as much as $2 million over the course of their retirement. Together with the routine luxuries of free parking, subsidized meals, gymnasiums, attending physicians, valets, florists, and hairstylists, the Congress provides its members with the services of 89 video producers (annual salary $44,000), who arrange their publicity, and at least 4 upholsterers (annual salary $35,000), who tend their office furniture.

The 1992 election campaigns excited a good deal of furor in the news media about the wastefulness and incompetence of the Congress, but the members agreed to reduce their collective expenses by only the trifling sum of $1 million.

14. Like the young Monsieur R., Richard Darman, a principal figure at court in both the Reagan and Bush administrations, always took particular care to dress up his opinions in the reigning political fashion. As a maker of White House policy during Reagan's first term, and then as a Treasury Department operative under the tutelage of Secretary James Baker, Darman provided the economic theory that ran up the deficit and

supported the habits of shortsighted and self-indulgent spending policies. Reincarnated as the director of the budget in the Bush administration, Darman described the wreckage of the Reagan prosperity as proof
of the nation's "self-indulgence and collective shortsightedness." In a
speech delivered at the National Press Club in August 1989, Darman
condemned not only "the morally corrupt hustlers" on Wall Street
(whom he had so ably abetted during his years in Washington) but also
the spirit of "Now-Nowism" (of which he had been the loudest
prophet) that accounted for the ruin of the nation's schools. His speech
was gratefully received by the attending members of the press, almost
none of whom possess the faculty of memory. Writing in *The Washington
Post*, the columnist David Broder praised Darman for the "courage"
with which he sounded "a note of alarm."

Again like the young Monsieur R., Darman was always at pains to
study the whims of his patron. When he understood that President
Reagan couldn't bear to read briefing papers, he presented his economic
theories in the form of sentimental anecdotes, and when he discovered
the mainspring of President Bush's sense of humor, he appeared at the
president's birthday party of 1989 dressed in a gorilla suit.

15. The newspapers published the schedule of fees for the dinner, but they
didn't mention Team 100, which consisted of those individuals who
contributed at least a hundred thousand dollars in what is known as soft
money (i.e., money that evades the federal election laws) to the Bush
campaign. The members of the team in the 1988 campaign numbered
among their company William Lloyd Davis (a real estate developer with
an interest in a Denver airport that received thirty-five million dollars in
government subsidy), Joseph Zappala (who became ambassador to
Spain), J. W. Brownell (operator of a business in California's Central
Valley that received, contrary to the ruling of the Interior Department,
an allocation of 326 million gallons of federally subsidized water),
Robert and Anne Bass, Donald Trump, Henry Kravis, Melvin Sembler
(who became ambassador to Australia), Trammell Crow, Edward Addison (president of Southern Company Services, an electric utility from
which the Justice Department relieved the burden of a fifty-million-
dollar criminal tax investigation), J. W. Marriott, Jr., Walter Annenberg,
T. Boone Pickens, and Charles Hostler (who became ambassador to
Bahrain). As published by *Common Cause*, the list continued through
249 names, aggregate campaign contributions of twenty-five million

dollars, and a disbursement of federal favors amounting to well over one hundred billion dollars.

16. Although the established news media do their best to obscure the self-serving aspects of national politics (preferring the general discussion of issues to the specific instances of fraud) the workaday voice of the Washington oligarchy occasionally seeps through the surface of abstraction. At about the same time that Greider's book appeared last spring, Bill Moyers presented a television documentary entitled "Who Owns Our Government?" in which various operatives explained the mechanics of Congress. None of the respondents spoke more directly to the point than Stephen P. Pizzo, a correspondent for the *National Thrift* (formerly *National Mortgage*) *News*, who had coauthored a book about the savings and loan swindle and assumed (wrongly) that the Senate Banking Committee might be interested in what he had learned:

> MR. PIZZO: Let me tell you something about civics. After our book came out, I went into the fact that Congress was—the Senate was actually considering bank deregulation. It was going to be before Senate Banking. And my coauthors and I flew to Washington with copies of our book and had a meeting with the staff members of the Senate Banking Committee and argued against the logic of bank deregulation. I said, you know, "Don't do this, guys. I mean, at least until you understand what you've done to the S and Ls." And finally one of the Cong—staffers looked at me and she said, "Steve, do you have any idea why the senators sit on this committee?" I thought that was sort of a Civics 1A question, and I said, "Sure, to hold hearings on banking-related matters and propose legislation." She didn't let me finish the sentence. She said, "No, they sit on this committee to attract campaign contributions from the banking industry. And let me tell you something, bankers are paying mightily to get bank deregulation through." And she said, "Now, just who do you have in mind that'd be willing to pay against it?"

17. The prominent people in Washington tend to regard the rest of the country as the back lot of a movie studio—a collection of regional or ethnic backdrops against which, as the occasion requires and preferably not too often, they consent to pose for photo opportunities. Because they have no interest in ideas that fail to conform to government specifications, they take little notice of variations on a theme without a quorum. If a subject requires the court's grudging attention, somebody will come to Washington to ask a favor or testify before a congressional committee. President Bush established a measure of the court's distance

from the common citizenry by the degree of his astonishment at a grocers' convention in Orlando, Florida, where he saw, for the first time, an electronic scanner that had been in common use for at least ten years at the nation's supermarket checkout counters. William Webster, a former director of central intelligence, was equally astonished by the Washington subway. About a week after he resigned his office, and with it the use of his chauffeured car, he confided to a friend and former colleague the news of his discovery:

"I'm doing things on my own again for the first time in ages. I went down to the Washington metro the other day."

"You rode the subway?"

"No, I didn't ride it. I watched people buying their tickets."

18. During the long prologue to the Persian Gulf War that extended across the six months between the Iraqi invasion of Kuwait and the American bombing of Baghdad, President Bush's explanations of geopolitical purpose acquired the tone and character of royal pronouncements. In the manner of Louis XIV or George III, Mr. Bush presented himself as the embodiment of the state, and the expression of his private emotions served as statements of public policy. As arranged in more or less chronological succession by James David Barber in *The Washington Monthly*, the president's remarks describe the progress of a grand illusion:

"I want peace."

"I will continue to be patient."

"I will not say exactly what I will do."

"Consider me provoked."

"I'm not all that hopeful."

"I want Congress on board."

"I have not crossed any Rubicon."

"I want 'em all home, as soon as possible."

"I don't feel we are close to a peaceful solution."

"I do not have that much of a feel."

"My gut says he will get out of there."

"I've had it."

4. Rosencrantz and Guildenstern

19. The United States never has had much use for dissenting opinion. Benjamin Franklin earned his living as a printer of government circulars. Tom Paine died bankrupt, so bitterly reviled by the American public that his body was refused burial in consecrated ground. Throughout the nineteenth century the newspapers constituted a "booster press," zealously promoting the natural wonders and business opportunities said to be synonymous with every new settlement on the western frontier, and as long ago as 1896 Henry Adams put the matter plainly in a letter to Sir Robert Cunliffe: "The press is the hired agent of a monied system and set up for no other purpose than to tell lies where its interests are involved."

An exemplary proof of the news media's congenital sycophancy decorated *Time* magazine's last issue of 1992, the one in which it proclaimed President Bill Clinton "Man of the Year." Seven months earlier the magazine's editors didn't think that Clinton was likely to win the election, and they had published a critical appraisal, reinforced by a cover photograph made from a negative print, under the headline, "Why Voters Don't Trust Clinton." The candidate at the time was presenting a poor figure in the public opinion polls, and his campaign was seen and understood as the work of an energetic demagogue willing to tell any audience anything it wanted to hear. On the day after the election, the editors of *Time* realized that the country had been blessed with the advent of divinity, and by December their editorial committee's prose aspired to the tone of worship: "Clinton's campaign, conducted with dignity, with earnest attention to issues and with an impressive display of self-possession under fire, served to rehabilitate and restore the legitimacy of American politics and thus, prospectively, of government itself."

20. In February 1992, at a seminar staged under the auspices of Walter Mondale in Minneapolis, Tom Oliphant, a Washington columnist for *The Boston Globe*, trembled with a courtier's rage as he denounced the prurience of the press reports about Governor Bill Clinton's liaison with Ms. Flowers. Such a tasteless and baseborn rumor was beneath the dignity of "the mainstream media" (i.e., the happy few among whom Oliphant counted himself a precious ornament), and the columnist advised his fellow oracles to "back off, just back off" from so squalid a story. A little later in the spring C-Span convened a symposium of prominent television anchormen, all but one of whom (Bernard Shaw of CNN) seconded Oliphant's motion of indignation and alarm. Tom Brokaw worried that the media might be making it "unbearable" for

would-be candidates to appear in public; Peter Jennings said that the high seriousness of presidential politics was too easily "derailed" by a preoccupation with scandal; Jim Lehrer thought that television news would find itself "in really serious trouble" if it descended into the arenas of gossip.

21. Among journalists long accustomed to writing for the institutional press, the fear of coming to one's own conclusions shows up in the pronouns. As managing editor of *Harper's Magazine* in the early 1970s I once received from a writer employed by *Time* a ten-thousand-word article that until the last paragraph was cast in the omniscient third person. In the final sentence the writer permitted himself the phrase "I think." When he saw the text in galley proof, he became so frightened of his descent into the first-person singular that he changed the phrase to read "millions of people think."

22. Prior to 1960 within what was still called the newspaper game it was generally believed that a reporter and a government clerk were as different from each other—by instinct and temperament as well as by definition—as an elephant and an aardvark. The reporter presumably allied himself with the readers of the paper and the popular suspicion of the scoundrels in office. The clerk allied himself with the privileged few and the convenient truth. A sympathy with one of the audiences supposedly precluded a sympathy for the other. The distinction vanished during the 1960s, and as more and more individuals entered journalism by way of government service, so also the newspapers and television broadcasts increasingly acquired the character of official announcements. Even a partial list of the journalists who began their careers as federal aides-de-camp explains why the story of the news has lost much of its pungency and humor:

Bill Moyers—speech writer and press secretary for President Lyndon Johnson

Diane Sawyer—speech writer for President Richard Nixon

William Safire—speech writer for President Nixon and Vice President Spiro Agnew

David Gergen—communications director for President Ronald Reagan

Tim Russert—press aide to Senator Daniel P. Moynihan

Bob Woodward—Pentagon briefing officer to the Nixon White House

James Fallows—speech writer for President Jimmy Carter

Patrick Buchanan—speech writer for Presidents Richard Nixon and Ronald Reagan

23. The flattering biography of Vice President Daniel Quayle that Woodward published in the spring of 1991 is representative of his approach to the wisdom in office. Like his biography of the late William Casey, the book relies on the accumulation of anecdotes rather than on a line of observation or thought. *All the President's Men*, the account of the Watergate burglaries that Woodward wrote with Carl Bernstein in 1973, depends entirely on unidentified sources, all of whom deployed the authors to their own ends and purposes.

24. Careful politicians keep up a voluminous flow of agreeable notes— notes of praise, acknowledgment, gratitude, regret, and appreciation— sent to people with whom they have even the slightest connection or from whom they have hopes of even the smallest service: notes to mayors and county sheriffs; notes to campaign contributors, dinner companions, newspaper editors, bandleaders; notes to corporation presidents, town supervisors, and foreign heads of state. During last year's campaign the newspapers often marveled at the number of notes written by President Bush and Governor Clinton, and one reporter compared the size and extent of the president's correspondence with the collected works of Balzac or Ann Landers.

Among court journalists the coin of flattery takes several distinct forms: admiring adjectives bestowed on books by one's patrons and friends; letters of fawning explanation to the subjects of biographies that might otherwise be misunderstood; elaborate acknowledgments meant to curry favor with people who might advance one's career. The first form of flattery is so common as to need no illustration. The following instances of the second and third variations—one of them a letter written by the late Theodore White to President Nixon, the other an extravagant act of obeisance on the part of a journalist eager to please—more or less define the toadying parameters of Washington journalism:

Dear Mr. President:

Herewith the first run off the press of a book called THE MAKING
OF THE PRESIDENT—1968, whose hero is Richard M. Nixon.

There will, of course, later be another suitably bound special edition
for the President of the United States. But the words will be the same; and
I want this first day's run in your hands as soon as possible.

The book goes to you with my great thanks for your help. I have had
few somersaults of emotion greater than in the years 1967–1968. My
previous reporting of Richard Nixon must, I know, have hurt. I felt that
way then. If I feel differently [*sic*] now it is not that there is a new Richard
Nixon or a new Teddy White, but that slowly truths force their way on all
of us. The campaign that this book tries to describe was the campaign of a
man of courage and of conscience; and the respect it wrung from me—
which I hope is evident—surprised me week by week as I went along.

I hope I have not abused your confidences. Much of our conversations I
have left out hoping that I can use them later, when the edge of imme-
diacy is off, in the campaign of Richard Nixon in 1972. I so much want to
start the next book with our talk in Indianapolis, as you began to describe
the administration you wanted to create and the style you wanted to give
it; then, run through the conversations at the Pierre Hotel and the White
House as you were shaping the administration; and finally, in 1972 describe a campaign in a country which the President has brought to peace
and in which he has stilled hates.

There's so much difference between being a reporter and being a
citizen. A reporter owes a duty to the "public," and tells it as he sees it
which sometimes hurt [*sic*]. But a citizen owes a duty to the country; and
the President describes the duty. I am both a reporter and a citizen. And
this President can also call on me as a friend.

Sincerely yours,
Teddy White

From the acknowledgments to *Grave New World: The Superpower Crisis of
the 1980s,* by Michael Ledeen, published by Oxford University Press,
New York:

It is always a pleasure to acknowledge one's indebtedness to friends and
colleagues, for knowledge and understanding are best advanced by coop-
eration and dialogue. I have been unusually fortunate to be able to learn
from some of the outstanding men and women of our time, and I wish to
thank them here. I owe a particular debt of gratitude to two men: to
General Alexander M. Haig Jr., for inviting me to work with him at the
Department of State, and for having confidence in my abilities and respect
for my ideas; and to the Honorable James Schlesinger, for taking the time
to read part of this manuscript at an early stage, for pointing out many

errors, for helping me think through some difficult problems, and for explaining several things I had not understood.

I am indebted to Walter Laqueur, who years ago gave me the opportunity to come to Washington, and who has patiently helped me learn the skills of which he is such a great master; to the Honorable David Abshire, currently American ambassador to NATO, who directed the Center for Strategic and International Studies so well and permitted me to work there; to Edward Luttwak, friend and colleague, constant source of creative thought and stimulating wit; to the Honorable Richard Perle, whose strength of character, quality of intellect, and moral tenacity have been so inspiring; to the Honorable Henry Kissinger, who has encouraged me in so many ways; to the Honorable Robert C. McFarlane, who through friendship and the force of his example showed me the meaning of intellectual courage and discipline; to General Vernon Walters, one of the great personages of our time, whose tireless service and remarkable personal qualities have done so much for our country; to the Honorable Jeane Kirkpatrick, whose clarity of thought and political courage are so well blended with her personal warmth and breadth of human understanding; to Norman Podhoretz, whose amazing intuitive understanding of American culture goes hand in hand with his exceptional stylistic and logical rigor; to Midge Decter, who has somehow combined the talents of an extraordinary leader with those of the selfless colleague; to Martin Peretz, who offered me the dream of my life—the chance to write for the *New Republic*; to Rabbi Augusto Segre, whose life and thought represent a unique fulfillment of faith and action, and whose affection and wisdom guided me during a most difficult time; and to Renzo de Felice, who years ago gave me the opportunity to work with him on the study of fascism, who has constantly encouraged my intellectual peregrinations and remains a dear friend. Thank you all.

25. Rather's statement is worth quoting at length. Like Tom Wicker, he well understands the journalist's place as a courtier attending the pleasure of a corporate prince, but also like Wicker, he wishes that he could conceive of journalism as a noble or romantic search for truth. The full text of his statement to MacArthur reads as follows:

> We begin to think in terms less of responsibility and integrity, which get you in trouble . . . , and more in terms of power and money. I do not except myself from this criticism by the way. . . . That increasingly anybody who subscribes to this [idea that] the job is not to curry favor with people you cover . . . finds himself as a kind of lone wolf, [who] probably ought to wear one of those shirts that says "last of the independents," and will be in the minority. In the best halls of American journalism not too long ago those who subscribed to what I've described to you

earlier were clearly in the majority. If you wanted into the club, that's how you got in, and you had to prove it. Now those are like the yellow-banded bower-birds or wolverines or some other endangered species in which their part of the forest gets smaller and smaller, and they're rarer and rarer to see. And probably most important, I do subscribe to the idea that journalism with guts starts with a publisher who has guts. . . . [Nowadays] the publisher [or network equivalent] says, "[L]isten, I've got to have circulation, I've got to have ratings, I've got to have numbers. . . . You know, I've taken a look at X, I've taken a look at the station in—name the place—California and you know [X] just makes people feel good. Why can't we have a broadcast like that?" Or why can't we have a newspaper like that? Max Frankel is an old, dear friend of mine. I not only love him but I respect him as a journalist as I do very few people. . . . But there are days when I see the *Times*, when I see the *Washington Post*, days when I see the *Los Angeles Times* with something on the front page . . . or White House coverage—when I covered the White House you'd get hooted out; you certainly wouldn't be able to drink with the big boys if you caved. . . . Now read the best papers in the country. . . . Suck-up coverage is in.

5. The Wish for Kings

26. During the 1960s I spent a good deal of time traveling around the country in one or another of the press entourages that attend the comings in and goings out of the nation's more prominent citizens, and it always surprised me to discover that most of the other reporters on these journeys, sometimes as many as forty or fifty print and television correspondents, were afraid of airplanes. Because they were so often in the air, frequently in bad weather en route to obscure destinations, they figured that sooner or later the odds were bound to catch up with them and that somebody other than the managing editor would punish them for their presumption. They escaped their habitual feeling of dread in only two circumstances: when traveling aboard Air Force One with the president of the United States or when traveling on a private aircraft in the presence of an individual who owned or controlled assets in excess of five hundred million dollars. I once asked a correspondent for *The Washington Post* why this was so, and he said he hadn't thought much about it, but he enjoyed a similar peace of mind when riding with celebrities in stretch limousines. We had boarded a commercial flight for New York after leaving the season's candidate to the comforts of a weekend in California. Somewhere over Missouri the gentleman from the *Post* ordered his fourth scotch and said that not even God would dare strike down the president of the United States, the chief executive officer of Mobil Oil, or Barbra Streisand.

27. Remarking on the mythological aspects of the campaign in *The New York Times*, Maureen Dowd relied on the authority of the late Joseph Campbell, the scholar made famous on television by Bill Moyers as a preacher of the New Age faith in pagan superstition. She cited a passage from his book *The Hero with a Thousand Faces*, published by the Princeton University Press in 1949: "A hero ventures forth from the world of common day into a region of supernatural wonder; fabulous forces are there encountered and a decisive victory is won; the hero comes back from his mysterious adventure with the power to bestow boons on his fellow man."

28. About eighteen months after the reception for Michael Jackson I came across another of Hitler's remarks that further amplified his image as a heavy metal rock star:

> Don't waste your time over "intellectual" meetings in groups drawn together by mutual interests. Anything you may achieve with such hope today by means of reasonable explanation may be erased tomorrow by an opposite explanation. But what you tell the people in the mass, in a receptive state of fanatic devotion, will remain words received under an hypnotic influence, ineradicable, and impervious to every reasonable explanation.
>
> A new age of magic interpretation of the world is coming, of interpretation in terms of the will and not of the intelligence. There is no such thing as truth, either in the moral or in the scientific sense.
>
> I am restoring to force its original dignity, that of the source of all greatness and the creatrix of order.

29. The same angry tone of voice controlled the speakers' podium at the Republican National Convention in Houston in August 1992—the voices not only of William Bennett and Pat Robertson but also of Patrick Buchanan and Senator Phil Gramm, all of them proclaiming a holy war against any infidel Americans who continue to insist on the freedom to think their own wicked thoughts. To large numbers of citizens the harangue was both frightening and hideous to behold, and the exhibition of intolerance severely damaged President Bush's chance of reelection.

30. Between 1918 and 1939, in the generation between the two world wars, experiments with parliamentary democracy were attempted by the peoples of Italy, Turkey, Portugal, Spain, Bulgaria, Greece, Romania, Yugoslavia, Hungary, Albania, Latvia, Lithuania, Austria, and Germany. In all instances the attempt either failed or was abandoned.